For my husband, whoever you are.

Mr Good Enough

LORI GOTTLIEB

The Case for
Choosing a Real Man
Over Holding Out
for Mr Perfect

Collins

Published in 2010 by Collins

HarperCollinsPublishers
77–85 Fulham Palace Road,
London, W6 8JB

www.harpercollins.co.uk

13 12 11 10
6 5 4 3 2 1

First published in 2010 by Dutton, Penguin Group (USA) Inc.

ISBN 978-0-00-736279-0

Printed and bound in Great Britain
by Clays Ltd, St Ives plc

Contents

PART FOUR: WHAT REALLY MATTERS

PART FIVE: PUTTING IT ALL TOGETHER

Mr Good Enough

The events and facts presented in this book are true and based upon my real-life experiences and research. Names and personal details of some of my friends and others who appear in the book have been changed or, in a few instances, composites created either at the individual's request or out of my concern for their privacy.

You know you're in love when you can't fall asleep because reality is finally better than your dreams.

—*Widely attributed to Dr. Seuss*

Prologue

The Husband Store

A NEW STORE HAS OPENED. A HUSBAND STORE!
THERE'S A SIGN AT THE ENTRANCE:

YOU MAY VISIT THE HUSBAND STORE ONLY ONCE.
THERE ARE SIX FLOORS, AND THE VALUE OF THE PRODUCTS
INCREASE ON EACH SUCCESSIVE FLOOR. THE SHOPPER CAN
CHOOSE ANY ITEM FROM A PARTICULAR FLOOR, OR GO UP
TO SHOP ON THE NEXT FLOOR, BUT SHE CANNOT GO BACK
DOWN EXCEPT TO EXIT THE BUILDING.

So, a woman goes into the store. On the first floor the sign on the door reads:

FLOOR 1—MEN WHO HAVE GOOD JOBS.

"That's nice," she thinks, "but I want more." So she continues upward, where the sign reads:

Floor 2—Men Who Have Good Jobs and Love Kids.

She's intrigued, but continues to the third floor, where the sign reads:

Floor 3—Men Who Have Good Jobs, Love Kids, and Are Extremely Handsome.

"Wow," she thinks, but feels compelled to keep going.

Floor 4—Men Who Have Good Jobs, Love Kids, Are Extremely Handsome, and Help Equally with the Housework.

"It can't get better than this!" she exclaims. But then a voice inside her asks, "Or can it?" She goes up and reads the sign.

Floor 5—Men Who Have Good Jobs, Love Kids, Are Extremely Handsome, Help Equally with the Housework, and Have a Great Sense of Humor.

Having found what she's looking for, she's tempted to stay, but something propels her to the sixth floor, where the sign reads:

Floor 6—You are visitor 42,215,602 to this floor. There are no men on this floor. This floor only exists to prove that women are impossible to please. Thank you for shopping at the Husband Store.

PLEASE NOTE:

To avoid gender bias charges, the store's owner opened a Wife Store right across the street.

The first floor has wives who Love Sex.

The second floor has wives who Love Sex and Are Kind.

The third floor has wives who Love Sex, Are Kind, and Like Sports.

The fourth, fifth, and sixth floors have never been visited.

—My version of an old joke about choosing a husband

Okay, here they are. The qualities, off the top my head and in no particular order, that would be on my shopping list if I visited a Husband Store.

- Intelligent
- Kind
- Extremely funny
- Curious
- Loves kids
- Financially stable
- Emotionally stable
- Sexy
- Romantic
- Passionate
- Compassionate
- Irreverent
- Intuitive
- Generous
- Same religion but not too religious
- Optimistic but not naive
- Ambitious but not a workaholic
- Talented but humble

- Warm but not clingy
- Grounded but not boring
- Soulful but not new-agey
- Vulnerable but not weak
- Quirky but not weird
- Free-spirited but responsible
- Charismatic but genuine
- Strong but sensitive
- Athletic but not a sports nut
- Open-minded but has conviction
- Decisive but not bossy
- Mature but not old
- Creative but not an artist
- Supportive of my dreams and goals
- Has a sense of wonderment about the world
- Is close to my age (shares my cultural references)
- Good listener and communicator
- Flexible and can compromise
- Sophisticated—well-educated, well-traveled, has been around
- Over 5'10" but under 6'0"
- Has a full head of hair (wavy and dark would be nice—no blonds)
- Has shared political views
- Has shared values
- Is not into sci-fi or comic books
- Has good taste/sense of aesthetics
- Health-conscious and physically fit
- Cares about the community at large
- Cares about animals
- Competent

- Handy around the house
- Cooks
- Likes the outdoors (hiking, biking, Rollerblading)
- Likes my friends (and I like his)
- Not moody
- Trustworthy
- Is a team player
- Is literary and enjoys wordplay
- Is math- or science-oriented
- Likes discussing (but not arguing about) politics and world events
- Stylish
- Stimulating
- Not a slob—respectful of our living space
- Is madly in love with me

Actually, this isn't my current list. This is what I started off with when I sat down to write this book. I'd never made a "list" before, but a married friend put me up to it. I told her I didn't have a list, and she insisted I did, even if it only existed in my head.

"I can't quantify what I'm looking for," I said. "I always just fell in love."

But she was right: It took me all of three minutes to give a detailed description of my ideal guy. Even if I'd never written a list, I clearly kept a mental file. Then she took it a step further: Hone down the list to make it more realistic.

I gave it a try. I crossed off some easy items—he doesn't have to know how to cook (besides, he could always learn); if he's 5'7" instead of 5'10", I could live with that. But even as I eliminated some qualities, I found it hard to get rid of most entirely. Maybe I could compromise on "funny," but where do you draw the line between a guy whose banter makes your heart race and one whose sense of humor merely makes you smile? On a sliding scale, how much passion would he need to be considered "passionate"?

There were so many variables. In the past, I dated a freelance artist, only to say that next time I wanted someone financially stable. Then I dated a doctor, but we didn't connect creatively. Finding a financially stable artist or a doctor who wrote novels in his spare time wasn't impossible—but pretty rare. And combine that with all the other characteristics I wanted, not to mention "chemistry," and suddenly the mystery of why I was still single was solved.

Maybe the man I was looking for on paper simply didn't exist. And maybe, as my friend suggested, some of these qualities weren't that important when it came to a happy marriage anyway.

Yikes. What if she was right? Had I overlooked men who might have turned out to be great husbands because I was drawn to an instant spark and a checklist instead of a solid life partner?

Of course, I wasn't completely clueless. By the time I hit 30, I knew that nobody was perfect (including me) and that whoever I married would be a flawed human being like the rest of us. I wasn't expecting perfection so much as intense connection. I also knew that none of that heady first-blush excitement guaranteed everlasting love, but I felt that without this initial launching pad, romance would never get off the ground. As far as I was concerned, there was no point in going on a second date if there wasn't a strong attraction on the first.

So, at least in the beginning of a relationship, I expected to be dazzled (even if that meant being so distracted by my object of affection that I nearly lost my job and risked my very livelihood). I expected to "just know" that he was The One (even if it often happened that a year later, I'd "just know" that I wanted to break up). I expected to feel some sort of divine connection (even if that meant being in a constant state of nausea and having an obsessive need to check my voice mail every thirty minutes). This was what "falling in love" felt like, right?

Meanwhile, my unconscious husband-shopping list grew even longer. Like a lot of women, the older I got, the more things I wanted in a guy, because while life experience taught me what I didn't want in a relationship, it also gave me a better sense of what I did want. So the thinking would go: *The last guy wasn't X, so next time I want X . . . plus all the things I had on my list before.* Basically, my Husband Store went from a six-story building to the world's tallest skyscraper. And I didn't think I was alone.

Could this be one reason that in 1975, almost 90 percent of women in the United States were married by age 30 but in 2004, only a little more than half were? Or why the percentages of never-married women in every age group studied by the U.S. Census Bureau (from 25 to 44) more than doubled between 1970 and 2006?

I wanted to find out.

A Different Kind of Love Story

This book is a love story. It's not mine, exactly, but it could be yours.

It all started with a dinner I had with my editor at the *Atlantic*. I was 39 years old, a journalist and single mother with a toddler, and I was grumbling about a date I'd had the night before with a lisping 45-year-old lawyer who chewed with his mouth open and talked nonstop for three hours about his ex-wife but failed to ask a single question about me. I didn't know if I had it in me to go on another date. Ever. I was so tired of having to talk to strangers over plates of pasta when all I wanted was to hang out in sweatpants with my husband on a Saturday night, like my married friends did.

How had this become my life?

Just two years earlier, I'd written "The XY Files" for the *Atlantic*, where I told the story of my decision, at age 37, to have a baby on my own. Obviously, this wasn't my childhood dream, but neither was marrying someone who wasn't The One—and so far I didn't think I'd found him. I wanted to have a baby while I still could, so instead of signing up with another online dating site, I registered with an online sperm donor site. Soon I found myself pregnant and still hopeful that I'd meet Mr. Right. My plan was to have a baby first, find "true love" later. At the time, I felt empowered and even wrote in the pages of the magazine that what I was doing seemed somewhat romantic.

Well . . . hahahahahahaha!

Now, at dinner with my editor, I couldn't stop laughing. Of course, I was ecstatically in love with my child, but let's face it: Things weren't so romantic over in the Gottlieb household. Like my married friends with small children, I was sleep-deprived, cranky, and overwhelmed, but unlike them, I was doing it all alone. Sure, sometimes they complained about their husbands and, at first, I felt proud of my decision not to end up like them—in what seemed like less-than-ideal marriages, with less-than-ideal spouses. But it didn't take long before I realized that none of them would trade places with me for a second. In fact, despite their complaints, they actually were really happy—and in many cases, happier than they'd ever been. All those things that seemed so important when they were dating now had little relevance to their lives. Instead, the idea of choosing to run a household together—as unglamorous and challenging and mundane as that was—seemed to be the ultimate act of "true love." Why hadn't I looked at marriage that way five years ago?

"If I knew then what I know now," I told my editor, "I would have approached dating differently." But how could I have known?

As a single 42-year-old friend put it, for many women it's a

Catch-22. "If I'd settled at thirty-nine," she said, "I always would have had the fantasy that something better exists out there. Now I know better. Either way, I was screwed."

I remember being surprised that my friend, a smart and attractive producer, was basically saying she should have settled. But she explained that I had it all wrong. She didn't mean resigning herself to a life of quiet misery with a man she cared little about. She meant opening herself up to a fulfilling life with a great guy who might not have possessed every quality on her checklist. In her thirties, she told me, she used to consider "settling" to mean anything less than her ideal guy, but now, in her forties, she'd come to realize that she'd been confusing "settling" with "compromising."

I'd come to the same conclusion, and I started asking myself some important questions. What's the difference between settling and compromising? When it comes to marriage, what can we live with, and what can we live without? How long does it make sense to hold out for someone better—who we may never find, and who may not exist or be available to us even if he did—when we could be happy with the person right in front of us?

I brought up these questions with my editor that night, and neither of us had the answers. For the next two hours, he talked about his marriage and I talked about the dating world, and when the check came, he thought I should explore these issues in an article.

Over the following weeks, as I spoke with friends and acquaintances about their relationships, something surprised me. Whether or not these people went into marriage head-over-heels in love, there seemed to be little difference in how happy they were now. Both kinds of marriages seemed to be working or not working equally well or poorly. Meanwhile, the women I spoke to who were single—and unhappy about their single state—were still nixing guys who were "obsessed with sports" or "too short," because they figured that if they married the short guy who didn't read novels, they'd be unsatisfied in that marriage. Yet the women who had done just that weren't.

When "Marry Him: The Case for Settling for Mr. Good Enough" appeared in the Valentine's Day issue of the *Atlantic*, I pored over e-mails from complete strangers—men and women, married and single, ranging in age from 18 to 78. The notes were incredibly personal, and most people admitted that they'd struggled with these same questions in their own lives. Some had resolved them happily and felt grateful to be with a more realistic Mr. Right. Others regretted letting a great guy go for what now seemed like trivial reasons. Still others said that marrying for "fireworks" left them feeling like they were settling once the pilot light went out because once they could see each other clearly, they realized they weren't that compatible after all. Some—including priests, rabbis, matchmakers, and marriage therapists—felt that adjusting our expectations in a healthy way would help members of their congregations, clients, friends, or family members find real romantic fulfillment.

But where did that leave me? Out in the dating world, I was doing exactly what I'd suggested in the *Atlantic* article. I was trying to be more open-minded and realistic, and focus on what was going to be important in a long-term marriage instead of a short-term romance, but somehow that didn't seem to be working. I was still drawn to guys who were my "type," and when I dated guys who weren't, I just wasn't feeling "it." I wasn't looking for instant butterflies anymore, but there had to be some "it" there, right? And if so, how much "it" was enough?

What If I Want a Different 8?

Then I got an e-mail from a single woman who wrote that she wasn't looking for the perfect 10 in a mate—an 8 would be great.

She was even dating an 8. But there was just one problem, she said: "What if I want a *different* 8?"

That, I realized, was exactly my problem—and so many other women's, too. She agreed that we should be looking for Mr. Good Enough (who exists) instead of Prince Charming (who doesn't), but she didn't know how to make it work in practice. Neither did I. In fact, when readers wrote in saying that they'd decided to get engaged because of my article, I worried that five years later, I'd get a slew of e-mails saying that they were getting divorced because of my article, since nobody knew what being more realistic actually *meant*. How much compromise is too much compromise? How do you know if you're being too picky or if you're really not right for each other? If being with Mr. Good Enough means sharing both passion and connection, but also having more reasonable expectations, how do you balance those things?

In order to find out, I decided that I'd have to become a dating guinea pig. I'd go out there and get some answers—then apply them to my life in the real world.

I started by talking to cutting-edge marriage researchers, behavioral economists, sociologists, psychologists, anthropologists, neurobiologists, couples therapists, spiritual leaders, matchmakers, divorce lawyers, dating coaches, and even mothers. I also listened to stories from single and married people who had helpful experiences to share. I didn't expect anyone to have *the* answer, of course, but I was hoping that with some guidance and insight, I'd come closer to finding the right guy. Maybe I'd help others do that, too.

What follows isn't an advice book or dating manual. There are no worksheets to fill out or "rules" to follow. Instead, it's an honest look at why our dating lives might not be going as planned, and what our own roles in that might be. Then it's up to the reader to decide what kinds of choices she wants to make in the future.

I'll warn you that you might not like what some of these experts have to say. At first, I didn't either, and I spent a lot of time kicking and screaming in denial of the facts. But eventually I realized that knowledge was power, and this journey changed me and my dating life profoundly. It could change yours, too.

Because in the end, I discovered that finding a guy to get real with is the true love story.

PART ONE

How Did We Get Here?

WOMEN WAITING FOR THE IDEAL MAN

© Sage Stossel

The Dating Trenches

One night, my friend Julia called to say that she had just broken up with her boyfriend, Greg.

"I just wasn't inspired by him," she said.

When Julia met Greg two years earlier, they were both 28 and he was her coworker at a nonprofit. She thought he was cute, sweet, and very smart. He was kind of unstylish—he wore nerdy high-waisted corduroys all the time—but she liked how "real" he was, how "unpretentious" and "nonmaterialistic." She also felt at ease with him in a way she hadn't with previous boyfriends. Julia had never dated anyone as supportive as Greg. Whatever her goals were, he helped her out. Whenever someone wronged her, he had her back. Whenever she felt insecure, he made her feel beautiful. You'd think this would have made her love him all the more, and it did—at first. But now, as Greg started talking about marriage, it began to have the opposite effect.

"Greg made me feel like I was the most wonderful woman in

the world," she said. "So then I started thinking, 'If I'm so wonderful, maybe I should be with someone *better*.'"

By "better" she meant, in part, "someone more charismatic." Greg could be shy and somewhat insecure in social situations, while Julia was confident and outgoing. Julia was quick with the one-liners, while Greg had a more subtle sense of humor. Greg came from a more modest background than Julia did, so he didn't always share the more sophisticated references that came up with Julia's friends in conversation.

Meanwhile, thanks to Greg's encouragement, Julia had risen up the ladder at work—and eventually earned more money than he did. Not a lot more, but it made Julia uncomfortable.

"I want to work," Julia said. "But I don't know. It's not how I imagined my marriage would be."

When I asked how she imagined it, she let out an embarrassed sigh.

"Honestly?" she said. "I guess I want my husband to be more of a go-getter."

I pointed out that Greg was sweeter than anyone she'd dated, especially her last boyfriend, the ambitious lawyer who often "forgot" to call her when he said he would. Greg was loving and reliable. He was passionate about his work. They had great sex. They shared similar interests, especially because they worked in the same field. They had a lot of fun together.

"But he wasn't inspiring enough," Julia repeated. "He's just this, you know, really nice, regular kind of guy. I started feeling like, 'This is it? *This* is the guy I've waited all my life for?' I'm worried that long-term, I'm going to outgrow him. I'm going to want more."

"More what?" I asked.

The phone line went silent for what seemed like a long time.

"More like I imagined," Julia said. "He just wasn't husband material."

And with that, another great guy bit the dust. Or did he? What were people looking for in a husband nowadays anyway?

ANYTHING BUT BORING

Not long after my conversation with Julia, I got together with five twenty-something single women at a bar in Los Angeles and asked why it's so hard to find "husband material." Their consensus: We'd like a guy, but we don't need a guy. So why should we lower our standards?

"I'd rather be alone than settle," said Olivia, a 27-year-old Web designer. "I've had annoying roommates in my early twenties, but I can't imagine having to eat all my dinners and sleep in the same bed with a male roommate who happens to be the husband I settled for."

The others nodded.

"I don't know about you," Olivia continued, half-joking, "but I would need to love someone very deeply in order to brush my teeth two feet away from where he's taking a dump every morning."

I suggested that, all kidding aside, bathroom doors can be closed, but opportunities to meet good men aren't always open, and I asked the group how they defined settling. Did it mean picking a guy who's truly annoying, or compromising on some desired qualities but getting other, more important ones? And what would those important ones be?

"Even if he's nice and smart and attractive, I can't be with someone boring," said Nora, a radio producer.

"Exactly," said Claire, a graduate student. "There are guys who are smart but then you're shocked to learn that for all that intelligence, they're just not that interesting. They have to be smart in an interesting way. They have to be *curious*."

"Curious, but not earnest," said Nina, a marketing executive. "They have to be a little edgy."

"But not *too* edgy," said Nora. "They have to be normal. But just not boring."

I asked the women for examples of what they meant by boring.

"They have to have a sense of humor," said Nina. "They can't just be sitting there laughing at something funny I might say. Boring guys aren't funny, but they think *you're* funny."

"Or the opposite," said Claire. "They think that if a woman laughs at *their* jokes, *she* has a sense of humor. Only a boring person believes that."

"Or a narcissist!" said Lauren, a fund-raiser for political causes.

"Well, narcissists are boring!" said Olivia, and the group broke into laughter.

I told these women—all reasonably attractive but not drop-dead gorgeous; all interesting but not off-the-charts fascinating—that at a certain point, they might get lonely going on all these dates looking for The Perfect One instead of building a nice life with Some One.

"I'm already lonely, but loneliness is better than boredom," said Lauren. She's finds her stable fund-raising job boring at times but it's often fulfilling, too, so she won't leave it for her true passion, painting, because it seems too risky.

"So you'll compromise in your choice of a job but not your choice of a partner?" I asked. "You're willing to spend eight hours a day in a good enough career instead of leaving it for your true love, being an artist?"

Lauren thought about this for a minute.

"Well, that's different," she said. "I'm practical about my career. But to be practical about love? You can't be practical about a feeling. That seems so . . . unromantic."

Just then, a cute-ish guy who seemed to be about thirty walked by and checked out the women. They ignored him. I asked why.

"Too short," said Olivia, who is 5'2".

"And what's up with those glasses?" added Claire, who wears chunky glasses herself.

I wondered if they'd be open to dating a short guy with last year's style of glasses if he had many of the other qualities they wanted: smart, funny, slightly edgy, kind, successful—and, of course, not boring. How much do first appearances matter?

"I've tried that," Nora said, "but I can't make myself become attracted to someone. You have to feel it from the beginning. If you aren't physically attracted when you meet them, you're always forcing it and it never works."

At first I was surprised by how readily the twenty-somethings dismissed this cute guy without even considering starting up a conversation to learn more about him. I mean, this wasn't college, where the playing field was pretty evenly matched in terms of available romantic prospects. This was the adult world, where people were pairing off and getting married, where the pool of single men was getting smaller, where there wasn't a built-in mechanism for meeting like-minded people the way there'd been in the past.

But then I remembered myself in my twenties, when the possibilities still seemed tantalizingly endless—even if they weren't.

DESPERATE BUT PICKY

Ah, the difference a decade makes. A few nights later, five single women in their late thirties to early forties met me at the same bar, where I asked the same question: Why is it so hard to find a good guy? I filled them in on the conversation I had with the younger women about boredom and loneliness.

"Check back with them in ten years," Stephanie, an attractive 39-year-old pediatrician, said. "If they're holding out for Prince

Charming, they'll be bored *and* lonely. The job won't seem as exciting anymore, drinks with the girls will get old, and on holidays, they'll be hanging out with their married friends and their kids, or their nieces and nephews, which will only make them depressed that they don't have a family themselves."

I admitted that I related to those younger women, who wanted to be in a relationship but had a very specific idea of what that guy would have to be like. And as I got older, I explained, my dating life slowly became this lethal paradox: *desperate but picky*. They knew exactly what I meant.

"That's so true!" said Liz, a 37-year-old screenwriter. "I want to shake younger women and say, you know, the guy who laughs too loud in public may not love the way you chew raw carrots at dinner parties, but it's not a deal-breaker for him."

These women could easily list their former deal-breakers—the reasons they didn't pursue relationships when they were younger. Here's what they said:

- "He was very loving but he wasn't romantic enough. On Valentine's Day he made a mix tape of my favorite music and gave me an hour-long massage, but all day at work, whenever I saw the flower guy going up the hall delivering flowers to my colleagues, I kept thinking, where are *my* flowers? I wanted a guy who sent flowers."
- "He brought me flowers, but cheesy ones that just spoke to bad taste—and the sense that I wasn't worth something more thoughtful."
- "He wasn't exciting enough. I felt like we were already married, which was nice in a way, but this was supposed to be the courting period."
- "He had long nose hairs and they grossed me out, but I

didn't have the courage to ask him to trim them, so I stopped seeing him."

- "He cried. The first time, I wasn't thrilled, but okay. The second time, I bailed. I felt he was too weak for me."
- "He was too predictable. Then I started dating guys who always kept me on edge and I never knew what to expect. It was terrible. Now I'd give anything for predictable."
- "I was embarrassed by his voice. Sometimes when he'd answer the phone at my place, people would think he was me, because I have kind of a low voice. But otherwise, he was very masculine. And a great guy."
- "He was too optimistic. He was so cheery all the time, even early in the morning when the alarm went off, and I found that grating. He always found a silver lining—'The stove broke, let's go out to dinner!'—but I'd be upset that I had to buy a new stove. I didn't want to 'look on the bright side' all the time. Then I dated a guy who was more cynical and after a while, it depressed me. So I tried to get the optimistic guy back, but he told me I was too pessimistic!"
- "He was completely bald except for one of those rings of hair around his head and a little tuft poking up in the front. It was such a turnoff, but I tried to get over it because I really, really liked him. My friends said, 'He has a nice face, he has a nice body, and besides, most guys lose their hair eventually.' But he was only thirty-five. I'd always been attracted to guys who had the kind of hair you could run your fingers through. Now I'm lucky if the guys I meet have any hair at all."
- "He thought it was funny to make up strange words, like 'fabulosa.' He did this a lot—and in public, too. Once he

said to someone at a party, 'Being a doctor isn't just one fabulosa after another' and I was so embarrassed. I broke up with him the next day."

- "He loved me too much. I felt like he was too much of a puppy dog, always looking at me with those adoring eyes. I wanted more of a manly man."

- "He wasn't refined enough. He couldn't order off a wine list. He'd never seen *Casablanca*. I wondered, how can you be thirty-two years old and not have seen that?"

- "I just wasn't feeling it—and now I think, what was I supposed to be feeling? Because, actually, I liked being with him more than any of the guys I felt strong chemistry with before or since."

Listening to these women, I thought about the reasons I'd passed up guys when I was younger, often sight unseen. One of the most memorable is Tom, a client of my lesbian hairdresser. She'd told me he was a handsome, charming, brilliant chemist and wanted to set us up on a blind date.

"He's the *only* guy who does it for me," she said, which sounded like quite an endorsement. Add the fact that I have a science background, and this guy seemed incredibly hot. But I said no, back when I was 29, because when my hairdresser said that Tom had red hair, I didn't think I'd be attracted to him. I just knew that red hair wasn't going to work for me. (Apparently, my bar for men was higher than that of a lesbian.)

There was also the cute, smart, funny lawyer I went on several dates with until I lost interest because he overused the word "awesome." I remember telling a friend, "Everything is 'awesome' with him. It's not 'great' or 'wonderful' or 'interesting' or even 'cool.' It's always 'awesome.'" I tried to get past it, but it irritated me every time he said it. (Somehow, the fact that I said "like" and "you know" all the time didn't seem to irritate *him*.)

In my early thirties there was the adorable software developer I met at a party who gave me his work number and told me to call there anytime because, he said, "That's where I *always* am." I didn't want to be with a workaholic, so I never called. It didn't occur to me that maybe he was at work all the time because he was starting his own firm, or that if he had a girlfriend, he might have more of a reason to leave at night. Nor did I bother to find out, because I always assumed there would be another setup, another guy at a party, or another on-line prospect. And even when the available guys and the opportunities to meet them seemed scarcer as I edged into my mid-thirties, I only got into serious relationships with men who met my rather strict and, in hindsight, superficial criteria. I had the attitude of, "I didn't wait this long searching for The One, only to end up settling." But would I really have been settling with the red-headed chemist, the lawyer who liked the word "awesome," or the software guy who happened to work until midnight as he launched his business?

I'll never know.

Like me, the women I met with at the bar were embarrassed by the way they'd dismissed men in the past, evaluating every guy as either too-something or not-something-enough. These guys didn't fit our image of the person we thought we'd end up with, leaving us to end up with nobody.

I asked the group if these types of things would still be deal-breakers for them now.

"If I met a guy now who hadn't seen *Casablanca*," said Kathy, a 38-year-old consultant, "I wouldn't rule him out, but I would still be aware of it in the back of my mind. I can't say I'd dismiss it completely because it speaks to a larger issue of cultural void. Overall, though, my deal-breakers have changed."

What would be their deal-breakers now? Someone with an addiction, someone who had a bad temper, someone who's unkind, someone who doesn't have a job, someone who's not warm or doesn't have a generous spirit, someone who's inflexible, someone who's irresponsible, someone who's dishonest, someone who wouldn't be a great father, someone who's old enough to be their own father. The rest, these women feel, is negotiable, but it's a realization that might have come too late: In their experience, the men who will date them now often come with these more serious deal-breakers, whereas the guys who would date them ten years ago didn't.

"In a way, I'm still looking for the same kind of guys I was when I was twenty-five, except that I also want them to be family-oriented and be good providers, which I wasn't thinking about back then," said Beth, a 37-year-old pharmaceutical rep. "Those are the guys I used to break up with."

Amy, a 43-year-old interior designer, agreed. She said that she always had boyfriends until she was 39, when, she explained, "I suddenly stopped getting asked out by anyone younger than fifty."

So, I asked, why can't they go back to those guys they'd passed up, who now sound pretty appealing?

In unison, they said, "They're all married!"

WHO CARES IF HE'S SEEN *CASABLANCA*?

I had to wonder: Who were the women that married those guys? A week later, I met with some of them. On the surface, they seemed a lot like the women who'd dumped their husbands. They were around the same age, and similar in terms of looks and education. In fact, I could imagine these married women having become their single counterparts if it hadn't been for one distinguishing quality: the ability to redefine romance. Nancy, who is married to the "predictable" guy, explained it like this:

"I think the difference between women who get married and women who don't is that women who don't get married never give up the idea that they're going to marry Brad Pitt, and it never occurs to them that they might not get married at all. They may say, 'I'm never going to meet anyone,' but that's just like saying, 'Oh, I'm fat' when you don't believe you are. It's something women just say, in a self-deprecating way. When you're young you're always meeting guys, so deep down you believe that The One will suddenly show up. It doesn't occur to you that maybe it's okay if The One doesn't look like Brad Pitt and earn a gazillion dollars and make your knees go weak every time you're together. Well, it occurred to me, but not until I was thirty-five."

That's when she met Mr. Predictable.

"So many women say they'd rather be alone than settle, but then they're alone and miserable—and still holding out for the same unrealistic standards," Nancy said. "They assume their soul mate will appear and it will have been worth the wait. Then they're blindsided and shocked when that doesn't happen. And it's too late."

Too late, she meant, for the life she has with the predictable guy.

"It *is* predictable," Nancy admitted. "But it's a lot better than always wondering what was going on with the more exciting guys. That wasn't love. What I have now is love. I have an amazing husband and two wonderful kids. I couldn't ask for a better family. And my husband *is* exciting, just in less obvious ways."

Sara, who's 42 and married to the ring-of-hair guy (who, at 43, is now completely bald, except he still has that tuft sticking out in front), told me that she feels lucky to have been at a place in her life at age 34 when she finally stopped getting hung up on things like how much hair a guy had.

"A year or two earlier, I wouldn't even have considered meeting a bald guy," she told me.

She's glad she changed her mind, she said, because if she hadn't, she would have missed out on falling in love with her husband—and probably ended up with no husband at all.

"I don't know one available guy out there who's as desirable as my husband *and* would also date me at this age," she said. "If I were single today, my own husband probably wouldn't date me either. I wouldn't be on his radar. Why would a forty-three-year-old guy who's kind and successful and funny date a forty-two-year-old woman when he could easily attract an equally interesting thirty-five-year-old who's prettier and young enough to have kids with instead?"

I told Sara that a lot of women would be offended by that kind of thinking, but she just shrugged her shoulders.

"Let me put it this way," she said. "It's a good thing I met my husband when I did. Because if I'd passed him by, he'd be married, and I'd still be sitting around wondering where the few good men were."

A FEW GOOD MEN

That's exactly what I was wondering: Where were a few good men? When I sent out a mass e-mail looking for single men, ages 25 to 40, to interview for this book, a typical reply went like this: "I don't know any single men, but do you need any single women? I know a lot of those."

Two weeks later, I got a quorum—but only after I expanded my definition of "single" to include men who weren't married but were in committed relationships. These guys, for their part, seemed as baffled as the women when I went back to the same bar and asked the familiar question: Why are women saying they can't find a good guy?

David, a funny 29-year-old professor, thinks the problem is that good guys are out there, but women don't recognize them as the good guys.

"A woman broke up with me because she didn't like the clothes I wore," he explained, "but she's madly in love with a guy who dresses well but doesn't call her."

His 32-year-old colleague Dan laughed—he'd been there before. "Women never want what's available," he said. "If they can't find the perfect guy at thirty, they move on to find something better. But they don't learn from this. Even if they're still alone five years later, they get pickier. Then they're almost forty and they haven't found the perfect guy, so they start to regret having broken up with us, but now we're not interested in them anymore."

Kurt, who's 38 and engaged, said that's exactly what happened with his exes. "And those perfect guys, if they do exist, want to date maybe the top one percent of thirty-year-old women. But every thirty-year-old woman I know thinks she's in that top one percent. All women want a ten, but are *they* all tens?"

His question reminded me of something my married friend Julie once said: "The culture tells us to approach dating like shopping—but in shopping, no one points out the shopper's own flaws."

Steve, who's 35 and dating a lawyer, feels the same way. "I think the reason some women have an inflated view of themselves is that in high school, they really did have the power, so they grow up thinking it will always be that way. And even in their twenties, they still do, to some extent, because they're so in demand. A guy will spend all of his money courting her, investing in the relationship, and then one day she'll suddenly say, 'You know, you're a great guy, but I'm just not feeling like this is what I want.'

"In their thirties," he continued, "it's the opposite. The girl gives the guy free sex, thinking she's investing in the relationship that will lead to marriage, but then the guy, who is now the one in demand, suddenly says, 'You know, I think you're great, but you're not who I want to marry.' And the women are shocked, because guys used to worship them, but the balance of power has changed. And I can't say I don't feel slightly vindicated that those same women who rejected me five years ago now complain that they can't find anyone."

The Married Men

Eric, a 38-year-old married writer friend of mine, is still friendly with the three girlfriends who broke up with him before he met his wife. He said he's going to write a book one day about the way women analyze men.

"I've got two working titles," he explained. "The first is *My Wife Isn't Perfect (But I Don't Consider That Settling)* and the second is *I Have No Idea Why She Broke Up with Me (But I'm Married and She's Still Single)*."

Women, he said, might call ten of their friends and discuss, point by point, how a guy measures up on a whole host of attributes. Then, in the areas he falls short (he's too messy, he's not sensitive enough, he's not making enough money), they think about whether they can "fix him" or "train him" to make him into what they want. Men, he believes, know that what you see is what you get—and accept it.

"When we decide to marry someone, we don't think we're going to fix our wives and we don't try to change them," he said. "We don't get out the spreadsheet and break it down on a microscopic level the way women do. We either want to be with her, or we don't."

Another married friend, Henry, who's 36, said that while some men are afraid of commitment, most aren't. They want to get married as much as women do. Often, he said, it's just a case of the guy not being into that woman, but also not wanting to give up the perks of the relationship.

"He knows he's not going to marry her," Henry said, "so he says, 'I'm not looking for anything serious right now' or 'I'm not sure I want to have kids' or 'I'm focused on my career right now,' which he thinks is telling her that if she wants this relationship to lead to marriage, she should look elsewhere. But women think the guy is confused and she can change him, when really the guy has made up his mind.

"Meanwhile," Henry continued, "women can't make up *their* minds. Every perceived flaw is dissected for months or years until a verdict comes down on whether they'll marry him. Men know early on when they've met the person they want to marry. It's a very visceral feeling. That's why women are always flabbergasted when their 'commitment-phobe' boyfriend goes off and gets married a year later."

For all their talk about romantic love, Henry said, women tend to analyze the situation too much. "They're hypocritical," he explained. "They say they want true love but you'd better be this tall and make this much money—and not have bad moods or be a real person, either."

He's probably right. Two months after my friend Julia broke up with her "uninspiring" boyfriend Greg, she started dating Adam, a sexy, ambitious surgeon. Adam was all the things that Greg, her nonprofit boyfriend, wasn't. But the low-key, supportive nonprofit guy was all the things her new beau wasn't. She was starting to miss Greg.

"I just don't know which things I can live with," she sighed, as she was about to fly to Hawaii for a romantic weekend with the surgeon.

But does it have to be this way? Isn't there a middle ground between cold, hard analysis and intense passion?

What Sixty-Somethings Say

When I asked half a dozen of my mother's friends who had married in their twenties about this middle ground, they said the problem they've seen in their kids' generation is that the middle ground doesn't exist.

"I hear constantly from my daughter's friends that they want men to have the same emotions they do, but men and women express emotion differently," said Susan, who has two daughters in their thirties. "Young women expect men to be soft and caring and rich and gorgeous—they want everything."

Connie shook her head. "You can wait for Prince Charming," she said, "but even Prince Charming will have holes in his socks. You can marry the most perfect person in the world and you'll still have problems to work through. But once young women see those holes, they're no longer interested."

"Our expectations were different," said Melinda. "We expected to have disagreements. You didn't go in thinking, 'I'll get married and if it doesn't work out, we'll get divorced.' There's a sense of being a team. You were committed to working it out. Today's girls always think they'll find something better."

Of the group, none of the moms believed in the concept of your soul mate being the only person on the planet you were meant to be with. To them, a soul mate meant someone you have a deep connection with, someone who accepts you for who you are and vice versa, someone who is there for you at the end of the day.

"I think going through difficult times together makes you feel like soul mates," said Kathryn. "Working through an illness, a financial issue, a parent's death."

"People don't expect to work in relationships today," June added. "There have been phases of our marriage when both of us needed things at the same time, and that could be very challenging. But I think a lot of women nowadays expect that they'll always get every single one of their needs met and if they don't, something's wrong. Nothing's wrong—that's just the nature of two people being in a relationship."

I asked them what women should give up if they want to find a good mate.

"I don't know that you'd have to give up anything—don't start off with the negative!" Diane said. "Women today start off with that mind-set—they have a long list of what they want and think they have to cross things off of it. Why not just look for someone you enjoy being with and see where it goes? Start off from a place of optimism instead of what the guy might be lacking."

Kathryn agreed. "I have a very dear friend who has single girls," she said. "I wanted one of them to meet a young attorney who's smart and funny and donates time to kids. She Googled him, found a photo, and said he wasn't good-looking enough. She wouldn't even meet him. Girls today are stopping relationships from happening before they even have an opportunity to develop. There's a romanticized expectation of being swept off your feet from the get-go and sustaining that level of excitement, but the way love happens is over time."

That's how it happened for Connie. "I didn't even like my husband when I met him," she said. "I was working in fashion and he was schlubby. He was sort of an oddball. He asked me out and I didn't want to go out with him. But he was persistent and as I got to know him, he not only turned out to be a wonderful guy, but he turned out to be the love of my life."

The more I spoke to people about relationships—younger single women, older single women, married women, single men, married men, and women from my mother's generation—the more I found myself asking the same questions: How did the search for love get so confusing, and was this modern way of dating making women happy?

2

The Romantic Comedy
That Predicted My Future

I was 20 years old when I first saw the movie *Broadcast News*, but little did I know that it would predict my future. Holly Hunter plays Jane, a single network news producer whose best friend is her talented and witty colleague Aaron, played by Albert Brooks. They talk on the phone late at night, finish each other's sentences, laugh at the same things, and understand each other the way nobody else does. Aaron, who is smart, funny, and kind, is in love with Jane, but Jane falls for Tom, the handsome but shallow newscaster played by William Hurt. Tom, who's all about style over substance, stands for everything Jane rails against. Jane is drawn to him anyway. In the end, she realizes that she can't compromise her values enough to be with Tom—nor can she compromise enough to be with Aaron. She loves Aaron deeply, but she doesn't feel any fireworks.

We've all been there, haven't we?

Jane's dilemma—the choice between fireworks and friendship—

may seem age-old, but it's not. The internal struggle might be, but the freedom for women to choose not just one or the other, but *neither*, is relatively new. Instead of picking Aaron or Tom, Jane decides to wait for Mr. Right, who, incidentally, never shows up. At the end of the movie, when we see these characters *seven years later*, Jane vaguely mentions that she's dating a guy, but so what? What are the odds that this relationship will work out, given that she's probably been in several relationships in the past seven years that seemed promising but didn't pan out? Besides, who's to say that this guy is better-suited for her than Aaron, her emotional and intellectual soul mate? Meanwhile, we learn that Aaron is married with a son, and Tom is engaged.

It's a sad ending, but when I was 20, I didn't question whether Jane had made the right decision. That Jane ended up unmarried and childless, well, I chalked that up to—get this—the filmmaker's misogyny! I'm not kidding. I'm completely embarrassed by this now, but I actually had conversations with female friends about how Hollywood wasn't ready to show a strong woman standing her ground without somehow punishing her for it. It never occurred to us that this was simply *a likely outcome* to Jane's choice. In fact, many of us went through our twenties and thirties making that very same choice—Prince Charming or nobody!—and ending up single.

What my friends and I called "misogyny" turned out to be "reality."

It wasn't until I watched the DVD in my late thirties that I realized I'd become Jane, passing up the Aarons of the world only to appreciate too late that what I want most in a partner *is* an Aaron. But like Aaron in the film, those guys my friends and I passed up earlier had gotten married.

At 20, I remember thinking that the saddest moment in the film was when Aaron confesses to Jane, "And I'm in love with you.

How do you like that? I buried the lead." My heart broke for Aaron.

Two decades later, the saddest moment for me was when a heartbroken Aaron predicts the consequences of Jane's rejecting him for the charming but shallow Tom: "Six years from now, I'll be back here with my wife and two kids. And I'll see you, and one of my kids will say, 'Daddy, who is that?' And I'll say, 'It's not nice to point at single fat women.'" Now my heart broke for Jane. I knew how truthful Aaron's cutting remark could be.

A Better-Looking Billy Crystal

A couple of years after *Broadcast News* came out, *When Harry Met Sally* hit theaters. This time, best friends do fall in love. There was something incredibly romantic about the idea of, *Hey, wait a minute, take a second look at the guy who's your buddy*. But still, back in my twenties, I wasn't interested in the Billy Crystals of my world. Again, stupidly, my friends and I considered this message insulting. Why should someone like Meg Ryan *lower her standards*? In real life, we asked, would someone as beautiful as Sally go for someone like Harry? Probably not. He'd have a crush on her, and she'd say she just wants to be friends.

But in our "real-life" scenario, we didn't think through what might happen next: She'd reject him and date more attractive men, while he'd go off and marry someone else. Maybe she'd find someone, but maybe she wouldn't. Or maybe she would, but not someone she connects with as strongly as Harry, or not in time to have the children she wants.

I had no sense of this when I was 22 years old and watched Sally sob to Harry, after she learns that her ex-boyfriend is getting married, "I'm going to be forty!" Harry reminds her that she's only

32 years old and that 40 is eight years away, but Sally cries: "But it's there, it's just sitting there like a big dead end. It's not the same for men. Charlie Chaplin had babies when he was seventy-three."

At the time, the idea of being 40, much less 32, seemed eons away to me. I took it for granted that I'd be married by then. I never thought my life would be like Jane's at the end of *Broadcast News*; I thought my life would be more like Sally's, a wonderfully romantic story of best friends who fall in love, except it would happen at age 30, and I'd be married to a man I considered to be not just my best friend, but also incredibly sexy—a better-looking Billy Crystal, a smoother Albert Brooks. Quite an assumption, given that I look nothing like Meg Ryan and, on a good day, have maybe half the charm of Holly Hunter. But like many young women, I identified with Meg and Holly. Delusional as it sounds, when I was dating in my twenties, I thought my romantic prospects should be on par with theirs.

And so did many of my friends. Sure, we would have denied it, but we would have been lying. We said we didn't believe in the fairy tale, but when push came to shove, we wouldn't settle for less than the fairy tale, either. We said we wanted true love, but we sought out romance and confused it with love. We knew that movies were fiction, but on some unconscious level, we watched them as if they were documentaries.

As Allison, a single 38-year-old in Minneapolis wrote to me, "At twenty-seven, when I got into an argument with my boyfriend— who I loved—I was looking for the romantic comedy response. My mistake." They broke up, and she regrets that decision. Now with no romantic prospects on deck, she was planning to get inseminated to become a mom on her own.

BRIDEZILLA

It's not just movies, of course. There's an entire industry devoted to fairy-tale weddings (which, incidentally, became a source of conflict in the hugely popular *Sex and the City* movie), and even the newspaper announcements themselves, with their over-the-top "we looked across the room and our eyes met instantly" stories, fuel the fantasy of what love is supposed to look like when we find it. But just as in the movies, these newspaper accounts—the so-called sports pages for women—never tell you what happens in the actual marriage.

Elisa Albert, whose own wedding was featured in *The New York Times*, knows this all too well. As she put it: "My *Times* wedding announcement read, as so many do, like a smug sigh of relief." What followed, though, was a train wreck of a relationship. She was separated within a year, and divorced shortly thereafter.

In her essay in *The Modern Jewish Girl's Guide to Guilt*, Albert describes her whirlwind romance leading up to the *Times* announcement, the fabulous and moving wedding ceremony, and the post-wedding reality that set in as she and her husband realized they were—and always had been—incompatible when it came to marriage. Just as it might be helpful if movies made sequels showing the couples' marriages, Albert wishes that wedding columns would print "divorce announcements" as follow-ups to all the enviable romantic courtship stories. At least then, she believes, single people would have a better idea of what love is and isn't.

She has a point. I went through my twenties and thirties saying that I wanted true love, but how could I even know what that was? Married people rarely talk about the reality of their marriages with their single friends, and the only "love" stories most of us see on-screen are the kind where once a couple finally kisses after working out their conflict, it's like a collective orgasm for the audience. After that, our interest in them deflates. The story's over. We're left to assume that these couples go on to happily ever after, but if the couple had so much trouble simply getting together, what makes us think they'll have more success in holding a marriage together?

You're probably wondering why any of this matters in a book about finding the right guy. You're probably wondering why I think anyone with half a brain is going to be influenced in their dating lives by movies or TV shows or romance novels or wedding announcements or the covers of *People* magazine. If you'd asked me years ago whether I thought this stuff influenced me, I would have rolled my eyes. I mean, we all know that even leading men don't meet the leading man ideal in real life. (Remember Hugh Grant cheating on Elizabeth Hurley with a prostitute? How about Brad Pitt leaving Jennifer Aniston for his costar?) But then why do many of us overlook men who don't fit a fantasy man ideal but who would make wonderful life partners?

I thought about what the late psychologists Willard and Marguerite Beecher wrote about what they called "the infantile attitude toward marriage" in their book *Beyond Success and Failure: Ways to Self-Reliance and Maturity*: "We can only guess at the extent of it when we realize the number of love stories that are ground out and consumed each month for books, periodicals, TV, radio, movies, and the like. People would not buy such stuff if they did not believe in its probability. We find no such sale for fairy stories, which are no more fantastic."

The Non-problem Problem

These days, in the movies or in real life, there's not a lot of external conflict to overcome in order for two people to get together. It's less about class or religion or geography or valid value differences than it is about the inner conflict of not knowing whether this person is The One.

In other words, nowadays you don't fall in love with Romeo and say that the relationship is doomed because he's a Montague. Instead, you start dating Romeo and overlook the fact that he's a Montague, but the second he spends too much time playing video games, or he forgets the name of your best friend from high school, you wonder if you should try to find someone more mature or attentive. Instead of falling for a guy and discovering a seemingly insurmountable practical obstacle (like, there will be a civil war if you get together), we fall for a guy and then create our own seemingly insurmountable obstacles as to why we can't be with him (isn't funny enough, has a tendency to get stressed out during tax season). It used to be that lovers knew they wanted to be together but couldn't. Now it's that lovers can be together but aren't sure they want to. And then we complain that we can't find a suitable spouse.

I was starting to realize that despite everything I believed on an intellectual level—despite the strong, sensible person I thought I was—deep down, I had a classic Cinderella complex. I expected that, as the famous song goes, someday my prince would come and "thrill me for ever more." It never occurred to me to trade those impractical glass slippers for shoes I could actually wear.

A SOLE SOUL MATE

When I look back on the way I dated in my twenties and early thirties, it's not surprising that I thought it was perfectly reasonable to stay single while holding out for my ideal man. After all, everyone else seemed to be doing that—in real life and every time I clicked the remote control. During my peak dating years, prime-time TV was packed with series featuring sexy, successful single women looking for love, surrounded by surrogate families of wise-cracking, lovelorn singles like themselves. Two notable exceptions were *Everybody Loves Raymond*, a show about a marriage that, ironically, seemed to be of little interest to young single women aspiring to marriage, and *Mad About You*, a hip, smart comedy about a young couple adjusting to married life, which did appeal to young single women until a baby was added to the show, at which point viewers stopped watching and the show went off the air. Was this perhaps too much reality for single women dreaming about happily ever after?

On the single gal shows—*Ally McBeal, Caroline in the City, Friends, Sex and the City, Grey's Anatomy*—viewers would tune in to watch a woman date a guy, only to talk endlessly with her girlfriends about why he's not right for her, and why maybe she should look for someone better. There was always the assumption that she'd end up with her "true love" in the end—that there was a single soul mate and therefore a clear right choice when it came to a partner. These characters worried about making a mistake because there seemed to be only one chance at getting right, so they'd better be darn sure this guy was *it*. Nobody seemed to be saying there might be lots of "right" guys. In real life, of course, each partner has his pleasures and his drawbacks, but we rarely see real life played out onscreen.

"REALITY" SHOWS

The closest we get to "real life" are so-called reality shows like *The Bachelor*. It's telling that the audience was horrified when Brad, one season's bachelor, whittled his choices down to two women, picked DeAnna, then changed his mind before he was supposed to propose to her.

The audience was incensed: What was wrong with DeAnna,

they wanted to know. She was charming, family-oriented, smart, and attractive. Who did Brad think he was, letting her go?

But Brad just wasn't feeling it. If a woman turns down a perfectly acceptable partner because she just isn't feeling it, we support her and tell her to go find "true love." We say that she made an empowered decision. But if a man turns down a perfectly acceptable partner because he's just not feeling it, he's a villain. Brad was whipped on everything from talk shows to blogs because viewers wanted him to take this woman and grow into that big love if he didn't feel it right from the start. They didn't want him to hold out for something better.

DeAnna, of course, got her own shot on *The Bachelorette*, but when she was down to her final two candidates, she choose the wacky snowboarder who wasn't sure he was ready to get married and have babies over the single dad who doted on her and who already lived the domestic life she claimed to want so badly. Audiences supported her decision to pick romance over practicality. For a woman, viewers seemed to think, romance was more important. Never mind that DeAnna later broke off her engagement.

The messages about love that we take away from the media are as contradictory as they are counterproductive. If the typical love story goes like this—Boy meets Girl. Boy and Girl hate each other. Boy and Girl exchange witty banter. Boy and Girl grudgingly realize they love each other. Boy and Girl live happily ever after (although we never see this part)—what message does that send? Should we look for the person who annoys us initially or who attracts us initially? And if love comes when we least expect it, does that mean if we actively seek love, it's not true love? That we shouldn't even try because true love will find us only when we aren't looking? Should we go by the message "You can't hurry love" or "Get out there and be proactive"?

Of course, as confused as I was, I knew that I wasn't still single just because I'd seen too many romantic comedies or watched too much reality TV. Earlier generations of women grew up on similar themes, but my generation and those after me have another set of conflicting messages to make sense of, too: What does it mean to be empowered and also want happily ever after? In other words, if feminism taught us that we don't really need the White Knight, how do we reconcile that with the fact that many of us are women who want a husband and a family?

If the fairy tale is to "have it all," what does "having it all" even mean?

How Feminism Fucked Up My Love Life

I know this is an unpopular thing to say, but feminism has completely fucked up my love life. To be fair, it's not feminism, exactly—after all, "feminism" never published a dating manual—but what I considered to be "the feminist way of doing things" certainly didn't help. It's not that I would give back the gains of feminism for anything. Believe me, I wouldn't. It's just that I wish I hadn't tried to apply what I believed to be "feminist ideals" to dating.

Growing up, my friends and I thought feminism was fabulous. To us, feminism meant we had "freedom" and "choice" in all aspects of our lives. We could pursue professional careers, take time to "find ourselves" before getting married, decide not to get married at all, and have our sexual needs met whenever we felt like it. The fact that we didn't need a man to have a fulfilling life felt empowering. After all, who wanted to do what our moms did—find a man, marry him, and have kids—all before most of us had gotten our first promotion?

But then, in our late twenties and early thirties, as more of us moved from relationship to relationship, or went long periods with no meaningful relationship at all, we didn't feel quite so empowered. The truth was, every one of my single friends wanted to be married, but none of us would admit how badly we craved it for fear of sounding weak or needy or, God forbid, antifeminist. We were the generation of women who were supposed to be independent and self-sufficient, but we didn't have a clue how to navigate this modern terrain without sacrificing some core desires.

We didn't want yet another Sunday brunch with the girls. We wanted a lifetime with The Guy.

Meanwhile, we were praised for our ambition out in the world, but at the same time told that our ambition would distract us from finding a husband. That never made sense to me. I don't think that women are so caught up in their careers that they "forget" to focus on their personal lives. After all, 90 percent of conversations most women I know of dating age have, even those trying to make partner in a law firm or slogging through a medical residency, involve men: who the cute new doctor is at the hospital, whether to move in with a boyfriend, what it means that the guy stopped calling after five dates. In fact, working in environments where we're likely to meet interesting men may actually be a dating advantage. Our long hours and high-minded aspirations weren't the problem, but none of us could figure out what was.

It wasn't until I found myself still single in my late thirties that something hit me. Maybe the problem was this misconception: We thought that "having it all" equaled "happily ever after."

Except that a lot of us weren't so happy.

Instead, I started to see a pattern that went like this: We grew up believing that we could "have it all." "Having it all" meant that we shouldn't compromise in any area of life, including dating. Not compromising meant "having high standards." The higher our standards, the more "empowered" we were.

But were we?

Here's what *actually* happened: Empowerment somehow became synonymous with having impossible standards and disregarding the fact that in real life, you can't get everything you want, when you want it, on your terms only. Which is exactly how many of us empowered ourselves out of a good mate.

I Had It All—at 23

According to the most recent Census Bureau report, one-third of men and one-fourth of women between 30 and 34 have never been married. These numbers are four times higher than they were in 1970. At first, this might look like a positive trend—people are more mature at the age of marriage now. But many single women I talked to feel differently. It may seem liberating to look for love when it's expected that we'll date a lot of people (and have a lot of choices) before we find The One, but dating all these people ends up being exhausting and painful, not to mention confusing. The cultural pressure to marry later (but not *too* late!) often hurts us more than it helps us.

Jessica, a 29-year-old communications director for a museum, told me about the night, six years ago, when her college boyfriend, Dave, proposed to her. They were both almost 23 and living in Chicago. He was in medical school. She was applying for her first job. They'd been together for four years, and she was very much in love with Dave, but Jessica turned him down for one reason and one reason only: She thought she was too young to get married.

"I thought, what kind of independent woman gets married before she even has her first job? So I told him I had to grow on my own, and I worried that if we got married so young, I wouldn't be able to do that. I also thought I shouldn't marry the first serious boyfriend I ever had. I thought I should have other experiences with men."

After their breakup, Dave was heartbroken and asked that they have no contact, and Jessica started doing everything she felt she needed to do to "grow as a person." She moved to a new city, met new people, focused on her work, and went on lots of dates. But she couldn't stop thinking about Dave.

Over the next two years, she often considered calling him up and telling him what a huge mistake she'd made, but her friends, who were also living the so-called empowered single girl life, would talk her out of it.

"Every time I considered calling him," she said, "my friends made me doubt myself. 'What, you're going to settle down at twenty-four? What about your life?' I started to wonder, is this life so wonderful? I liked my work, I liked my friends, and I hated dating. I had a couple of boyfriends that I got excited about at first, but I didn't ultimately feel the way about them that I had about Dave. I didn't have that comfort level. They didn't 'get me' the way he did. Either I wasn't into them or they weren't into me, and I kept thinking, what am I looking for when I already found the guy I want to spend my life with?"

Secretly, Jessica would Google Dave at night, but she didn't find much information, other than that he was still in medical school.

"I'd sit there on the computer at night, like a junkie, and I'd be thinking, this is pathetic," she said. "This isn't the exciting life I was supposed to be having as an empowered single woman in the big city! Dating other people and having more life experience didn't enrich my life in any substantial way. I loved my work, but I could have gotten a similar job in Chicago. Instead of ordering takeout for myself or going out to dinner with a group of single friends, I wanted to make Dave dinner when he was on call." But she hid all these feelings because she was embarrassed by them.

Finally, three years after Dave's proposal, Jessica found his number through the medical school switchboard and got up the nerve to call him. Her heart was pounding when she heard his voice.

"The second he answered," she said, "it felt like home again. I almost cried." But then, as she told him why she called, Dave went silent. Now it was Jessica's turn to have her heart broken. Dave had spent more than two years trying to get over Jessica, and finally, about eight months before, he'd met someone new. They were dating exclusively. She was a year older than Dave—a 27-year-old resident at the hospital—and was looking to meet the man she would marry.

Dave is now married to this woman and both are pediatricians. Jessica learned through a mutual college friend that they recently had a son.

Jessica's voice cracked as she spoke. "I gave him up because it was drilled into me that first you establish your own life, then you share it with someone else. That first you go out and pursue your dreams. Well, here I am, still dreaming I'll meet someone as great as Dave."

I could relate to Jessica's story. I also grew up believing that my early twenties were a time to experiment with different careers and different men and then suddenly, according my time table, The Guy would arrive on my doorstep. I didn't even consider looking for a spouse in any serious way in my early or mid-twenties—when I was, in fact, most desirable in the dating pool. The goal was to go out and become "self-actualized" before marriage. I didn't imagine that one day I'd be self-actualized but regretful.

Nor did Jessica. "I thought the message was, 'You can have it all—but not at twenty-three,'" she said. "But now that I'm twenty-nine and I'm *supposed* to have it all, I don't. I had it at twenty-three!

The problem is that people judge you if you marry too early, but then if you end up single at thirty or thirty-five, they judge you for not being married."

She was right: There's a stigma for not waiting long enough, and there's a stigma for waiting too long. People may have called me "brave" for having a baby on my own when my biological clock was ticking, but it was always said in the way you might call a cancer patient "brave." I knew all too well that many people considered me a mildly tragic figure, if not a cautionary tale. For some, I was their biggest nightmare. They may not want to be tied to any old-fashioned rules, but they also want a traditional family. The women I spoke to in their late twenties and thirties seemed baffled by the way the feminist messages they grew up with don't necessarily reflect what they might want personally. What they're *supposed* to want and what they *actually* want seem at odds.

And that's how a lot of us get screwed.

No-Strings-Attached Dating

Brooke is a 26-year-old in Boston who's getting a graduate degree in women's studies. I told her that I'm all for empowerment—sexual or otherwise—but I was surprised after a lot of young women told me that if you don't get physically intimate with a guy by the third or fourth date, he'll think you're not interested and move on. Since when, I wanted to know, does not being physically intimate with someone you've known a total of, say, *eight hours*, indicate lack of interest?

More important, I wanted to know what's in it for women, who often get emotionally attached to the men they sleep with, or who for the most part find casual sex unfulfilling. What's so empowering about a sexual free-for-all?

Brooke sighed like I was an old fuddy-duddy. "It gives us the same choices men have," she explained matter-of-factly.

"Okay," I said. "But is casual sex what you want?"

"No," she admitted. "But I'd want any woman who had that desire to have the freedom to pursue it."

Meanwhile, Brooke has been living with her boyfriend for two years and confessed that she's been wondering whether to move out when she turns 27 next month. "I'm ready for a serious relationship," she said.

I wondered what she meant by a serious relationship. Wasn't living together pretty serious?

"Everyone's living together," she replied. "It's no big deal." Indeed, thanks to the "freedom" we now have, half of women 25 to 29 have lived with a guy. What do marriage-minded women get out of spending their most desirable years with a boyfriend instead of a husband? I wondered why Brooke moved into her boyfriend's apartment in the first place if she wanted marriage instead of cohabitation.

She thought for a minute. "I guess a part of me wanted living together to mean something it doesn't," she confessed. "Most people who move in together don't talk about what it means for the future. I mean, vaguely, but it's not like they're engaged. They just move in because they're in love."

Love with no future plans: Hooray for freedom! But has this kind of "freedom" made us happier?

D-a-t-e Is a Four-Letter Word

Take our approach to romance. Today's singles talk about romance like it's the Holy Grail, but do we even have romance anymore? What happened to courtship? The very word sounds quaint to the single women I spoke to, who are used to hookups and group dates and friends with benefits. I don't even know if "dating" would be the right word for what happens today. Somehow d-a-t-e has become a four-letter word ("It's not a date; it's just coffee"), and I have no idea what "dating" means in an era when people say, "We're not in a relationship, we're just dating," while spending time and sleeping together. Sometimes there isn't even an actual "date" involved in a date. You'll be invited to join a guy and his friends at a party (and to bring attractive girlfriends!), you'll be called from a cell phone at 9 p.m. and asked to "hang out" and watch a video at his place, or you'll be asked to meet him for coffee for twenty minutes after his basketball game (which means he shows up reeking of sweat and letting you buy your own latte).

And women are supposed to be cool with all this. There seems to be lack of respect in the dating world but, these women say, we're supposed to deny any expectations of chivalrous behavior, traditional gender roles, and marriage within a reasonable time frame because that level of detachment or independence supposedly makes us empowered.

Some women say they actually appreciate these non-date dates, and I have to admit, I used to be in that camp. Then an older married friend set me straight.

"Why should I waste time having a two-hour dinner on a first date when I know within thirty seconds of meeting for a quick coffee whether a guy is my type?" I asked her.

"Because you don't know within thirty seconds whether he might be a person who would make you happy in a marriage," she said.

And that's just it. I was so busy trying to "have it all" that I lost sight of what might make me happy in a marriage. Marriage used to be thought of as comfortable and stable, and those were good things. But since women don't need marriage for economic security and even to have children anymore, the primary purpose of marriage, many singles say today, is to make us happy—immediately and always. We don't wait to see if connection develops by spending real time with a person. If a relationship takes too much effort, we decide it's no long-er making us happy, and we bail. The One doesn't get grumpy. The One doesn't misunderstand us. The One doesn't want some alone time after work when we want to give him the rundown of our day.

In my mother's generation, you were "happy" in your mar-riage because you had a family together, you had companionship, you had a teammate, you had stability and security. Now women say they also need all-consuming passion, stimulation, excitement, and fifty other things our mothers never had on their checklists. And yet, according to data on marital satisfaction compiled by David Popenoe at the National Marriage Project at Rutgers Uni-versity, women in those early marriages were happier.

But because I had a twisted notion of what being a "feminist" meant, my priorities were all mixed up.

What *Should* a Woman Want?

Caroline, a 33-year-old fashion buyer, told me that she considers herself a feminist but still wants "a guy to be a guy."

As she put it, "I don't need a guy to take care of me, but I wouldn't be with someone who couldn't. I want to have a career when I have kids, but I want to have the option not to work if I change my mind." Interestingly, when I asked what qualities she's looking for in a relationship, she talked about romance and passion and chemistry, but none of the practical things that would give her the option not to work.

Then there are women like many of my college classmates who, when they were dating, got offended if they were disqualified as relationship material by a guy who wanted to marry a woman who would stay home with the kids. They felt that these modern-seeming guys who also wanted a more traditional family structure reduced the number of eligible men even more—and yet, much to their surprise, most of these same women ended up becoming very happy moms who work part time or not at all. They weren't as progressive as they once believed themselves to be, and were glad that they weren't expected to bring in half of the family income.

In a 2006 *New York Times* column, John Tierney wrote that whereas the age-old question used to be, "What does a woman want?" modern feminists ask instead, "What *should* a woman want?" He went on to cite a study by two University of Virginia sociologists, Bradford Wilcox and Steven Nock, who looked at the question of what makes a woman happy in her marriage nowadays. It turns out that stay-at-home wives were more satisfied with their husbands and their marriages than working wives—and that even among working wives, those who were happiest had husbands who brought in two-thirds of the income.

"Women today expect more help around the home and more emotional engagement from their husbands," Wilcox told Tierney. "But they still want their husbands to be providers who give them financial security and freedom."

And no wonder: The traditional workplace often turns out to be unfulfilling for women after they've been at it for fifteen or twenty years. With its inflexible hours, office politics, fifty-hour weeks to stay "on track" for promotions, and later, younger bosses making irrational demands, the whole setup isn't just a drag, it's incompatible with the kind of family life many women want.

As the study's other sociologist, Steven Nock, told Tierney, "A woman wants equity. That's not necessarily the same as equality."

WHY MEN CAN'T FIGURE US OUT

Many guys I spoke to say this affects the way people date.

"I have a daughter, and I'm glad she's growing up in an era when women can run for president," said Eric, who is 38 and has been married for seven years. "But when I was dating, most women wanted to be able to run for president but didn't really want the actual job. They just wanted the *opportunity* to have it. Because now when we men say, 'Great, go for it,' our wives tell us they want to work part time or work fewer hours. Our wives want us to do half the child care and half the laundry, but they don't want to earn half the income. So while I'm all for feminism, I do find it thoroughly confusing."

My friend Paul, who is a 30-year-old lawyer, told me that while he'd only be interested in dating a smart woman, he's less interested in how professionally successful she is or what she does for a living.

"Some of my single women friends can't understand why guys don't find them unbelievable catches because they made partner in their law firms at thirty, or make a certain amount of money in a business they started," he explained. "But honestly, the point of being successful for a woman is for personal fulfillment and so that she can support herself. It's not so that she can attract a man, because men know that we can't count on women to provide the lion's share of the income, so we're more interested in what kind of partner this person is going to be. Do we like being around her? Is she interesting? Will she be a good parent?"

Paul said he was reluctant to talk about this because he worried it would make him sound sexist. Then again, he added, "I wouldn't pursue a woman just because she was very successful, but I know many women who can find a man attractive based on success or wealth, and still call themselves feminists."

Paul's colleague Brandon, who is single and 33, told me that the women in his law firm think guys have it made because they don't have a biological clock to contend with. That's true, he said, but at the same time, when he and his friends are ready to get married, women hold them to impossibly high standards.

"You can't just be a woman's equal—you have to be slightly

more successful than she is," he said. "That rules out most of their colleagues, and many men in general. Then if you *are* more successful—you're more senior in the firm than they are—you also have to be tall enough, and funny enough, to be worthy of even a *first date*."

Paul, who is 5'7" and starting to lose his hair, told me that when he was dating a shoe store sales clerk (they met when he was trying on loafers), his women friends complained that male lawyers don't want to date their equals.

Paul says that's not true. "I was dating her for two reasons: One, I genuinely liked her. And two, she would actually date me! Women say that their equals won't date them, but *they're* the ones who won't date their equals. They think they're so empowered or whatever but they just seem standoffish. And I don't think they're that happy."

EMPOWERED OR ALONE?

Paul might be right. I grew up interpreting feminism to be about this idea of empowerment: We aren't just supposed to be strong and independent—we're also supposed to be *happy* about it. We're supposed to focus on our own lives, and when a partner comes along, that's gravy, not the main course. We can't be happy in a relationship until we learn to be happy alone.

For many years, I went along with these notions, but deep down, I didn't want to learn to be happy alone. No matter how full my life (career and good friends; later, delightful child, career and good friends) I always wanted to go through life with a partner. And while I wasn't someone who tore out pictures of bridal dresses or dreamed of my wedding day in great detail, I took it for granted that it would happen. It never occurred to me that my life wouldn't include the husband and the kids and the Little Tikes slide in the backyard. So I certainly wasn't trying to be a "trailblazer" by having a kid on my own. I simply wanted to be a mother before it was too late.

But the mere fact that, at 40, I outed myself in the *Atlantic* article by saying that I craved a conventional family with a good enough guy put me in the category, in some people's minds, of the kind of woman who wanted it too badly. According to some readers, I was nothing short of an affront to the entire women's movement. Here's what some said:

"Could you be any more desperate?"

"How sad that your son is not enough for you."

"I am totally appalled by your need for a man."

"You are positively tragic."

"Get some self-esteem!"

"You have taken codependency to a whole new low."

"I feel sorry for you that you had such an all-encompassing desire to reproduce. Now I feel sorry for you that have such an all-encompassing desire to be married."

"Don't you think you owe it to yourself to be a little more comfortable with yourself before you look for a mate?"

"Maybe if you change your outlook, and aren't so needy, you might meet the right person."

"If my daughter grows up to want a man half as much as you do, I will know that I've done something wrong in raising her."

Somehow, post–Jane Austen, it's become shameful for a woman to admit how lonely she is and how strongly she wants to be part of a traditional family. What kind of educated, sophisticated modern woman with an active social life has time to be lonely?

You're lonely? Get a life! Get a promotion! Get a hobby! Get a haircut! You go, girl!

I remember seeing a group of women on a morning TV news show discussing the fact that they'd rather be alone than with Mr. Good Enough. Would they? Really? They'd rather be 40 years old and going to bars with a group of female friends who are all looking past them for Mr. Right to walk in the door? None of the women on the show was movie-star attractive, a fact that didn't seem to shake their belief that they'd land Prince Charming. One even said she'd rather be alone because you never know when you might find true love—maybe you'd find it in the nursing home. *The nursing home!* Would she really like to be single until she's 80? And even then, doesn't she realize she'd have even more competition for the one single man (who probably has Alzheimer's) in the entire retirement community than she has now?

My 29-year-old colleague Haley told me that while she'd like to go through life with a partner, she doesn't want to have to change for anyone. But is that empowerment or inflexibility? Isn't change integral to compromise and being in a mature relationship? Has "girl power" made us self-absorbed, poor partners?

It's probably no accident that once women adopted this "I don't need a man" attitude, many of us were left without men. In a 2007 *Time* magazine article entitled "Who Needs a Husband?" (um, me), *Sex and the City*'s Sarah Jessica Parker is quoted as saying that because women don't have to rely on men for financial support anymore, "my friends are looking for a relationship as fulfilling, challenging, and fun as the one they have with their girlfriends."

What an idiotic idea! No matter how much I enjoy my female

friendships, I don't want my marriage to be like the relationship I have with my girlfriends. I doubt very many of us would. Factor in your girlfriends' emotional requirements and quirks and mood swings and imagine how "fulfilling, challenging, and fun" it would be to live with them 24/7 for the rest of your life. Your girlfriend may listen ad nauseam to the minutiae of your day, but is she really the person you want to raise kids and run a household with?

In that same *Time* article, one woman, a 32-year-old media producer, explains that she ended a seven-year relationship with her investment banker boyfriend because although she "totally adored him," she felt like life with him would be "too limiting." She wasn't happy, she explained, because she didn't think she could "retain her spirit." Yet she "adored him" enough to stay with him for seven years. What's going to happen to this woman ten years from now when she looks back on this decision?

She might want to listen to what a 49-year-old single woman said in the article: "There was a point where I had men coming out of my ears. I don't think I was so nice to some of them. Every now and then I wonder if God is punishing me. Sometimes I look back and say, 'I wish I had made a different decision there.'"

Another woman is quoted as saying that she can easily get her sexual needs taken care of without marriage. So what? In a *Time/CNN* poll cited in the article, 4 percent of women said what they wanted most from marriage was sex, while 75 percent said it was companionship. Can she get *that* need easily taken care of outside of marriage—on a daily basis, and for the rest of her life?

TEA FOR ONE

Whether we admit it or not, being single is often lonely, especially by the time we reach our mid-thirties and many of our friends are busy with families of their own. It's not that women don't feel complete without a man. It's that if no man is an island, most women aren't, either. How lonely it was, before I had my son, to wake up in an empty house every morning, eat breakfast alone, read the paper alone, do the dishes alone.

How tedious it was to do the post-date play-by-play each week, reassuring my friend that there's nothing wrong with her, that the guy was lame, only to have her parrot back that same bland reassurance the next week, after my own dating escapade. How disappointing it was to waste my short time on this planet in a string of temporary encounters when I could be building a lifetime of shared experience with one committed person. How much longer could I spend my time analyzing phone or e-mail messages, wasting hours talking about a guy who would be out of the picture three days, three weeks, or three months later, only to be replaced by another, and another, and another?

How bleak it felt to move to a new apartment alone, to shop for groceries for only myself, to have nobody to talk to in those intimate moments before bed except for girlfriends on the phone, chatting about—what else?—men! It was so boring. If we ruled out guys because they were "too boring," nothing could be as boring as the endless merry-go-round of single life.

Having a child in the house changes the specifics—you're never alone and, in fact, you desperately crave some solitude—but the longing for an adult partner remains. When I decided to have a child, it had nothing to do with staving off loneliness. It had to do with hoping to find The One without the time pressure of a biological clock. If I was aware enough to know that a child would be no cure-all for a lack of male companionship, I truly believed, in an astoundingly naive way, that I could simply do things backward: child first, soul mate later. But as hard as it was to meet The One before I became a parent, I hadn't anticipated that once you have a baby alone, not only do you age about ten years in the first ten months, but if you don't have time to shower, eat, urinate in a timely manner, or even leave the house except for work, where you spend every waking moment that your child is at day care, there's very little chance that a man—much less The One—is going to knock on your door and join *that* party.

And then there's the question of where you even meet single men once you're a parent. They're certainly not at toddler birthday parties or Gymboree, and the few I'd see at the grocery store weren't exactly looking to pick up a mom singing "Apples and Bananas" to entertain the toddler sitting in the basket. (If the genders were reversed, of course, female shoppers would be *all over* that single dad.)

The loneliness I experienced after having a child wasn't diminished; it was different and perhaps even compounded. It's both single-person loneliness, and the loneliness of not sharing the little moments of my son's life with the one person who cares about him as profoundly as I do.

But saying this aloud makes people uncomfortable. I remember getting an e-mail from a never-married single mom like me who told me that when she shared her loneliness on a single-mom listserve, people told her to stop feeling sorry for herself and to "get a life." One woman even suggested that if she was so unhappy being a single mom, she should put her child in foster care.

"I got flamed for saying I get lonely sometimes," this single mom told me. "But nobody flamed this other woman for telling me to put my kid in foster care!"

What's so hard to accept about loneliness and desire for connection? Is there really something wrong with our self-esteem or our values if we want someone to share the literal and metaphorical driving with? We're so worried about not "settling," but then we find ourselves unhappily "unsettled"—living in our single-person apartments, eating takeout for dinner in front of the TV, and hoping for a guy to show up so we can "settle down."

When I asked several women what "feminism" meant, I got a lot of responses that boiled down to having the same opportunities as men. But the more we talked, the more we came up against the fact that our needs are different and that we might not, in fact, *want* the same things. And when it comes to dating, we *don't* have the same opportunities as men, especially as we get older.

This might seem obvious, but somehow I thought that I could just have a baby on my own, put my dating life on hold for a year or two, and then get right back in the game. I thought that's what "equality" and "having it all" meant.

Then, when I was ready to date again, I went to a Thursday night speed dating event. I was now over 40 and everything had changed.

Let me tell you about that Thursday night.

4

Speed Dating Disaster

I'd heard about speed dating for years, but this was my first attempt at actually sitting down with complete strangers for five minutes each before rating them on a scorecard. It may sound like an odd way of meeting mates, but what the format lacks in substance, I figured it would make up for in volume and efficiency. You basically go on ten mini blind dates in the span of an hour. If, when the evening is over, you check "yes" next to a guy's name—and he checks "yes" next to yours—you're given each other's contact information to continue the conversation later.

The event I chose that Thursday night was for singles 40 to 50 years old. At 41, I could have signed up for the 30-to-40 group—the speed dating company said there's a one-year grace period—but I figured I'd stick with guys my own age.

As I got dressed for the event, I was kind of excited. After all, I'd get to meet ten new single men, which was a lot more than the zero single men I was meeting during a typical day of working from home. I thought it would be fun to "get out there" again, even if I didn't find a romantic connection. How bad could it be?

A Plane Brought Me Here

At 7 p.m., I arrived at a trendy restaurant near the beach where, in a private corner, two-top tables were arranged in rows. Nine other women—seven of them appearing to be no older than 42—were already there. Six had a male counterpart seated across from them. That was the first surprise: There were only six available men for ten available women.

I checked out the six men. Surprise #2: All but one looked older than 50, and one guy looked so old that he bore a striking resemblance to my best friend's father. (So much for the one-year grace period.) So there we were: eight early-fortyish women, two late-fortyish women, one mid-fortyish man, and five men over 50. We were instructed to get to know the person seated across from us until we heard the bell, then the men would move one chair over to the next table.

Seats were assigned. The bell dinged and it was time to begin.

My Guy #1 was Sam. He was bald and wrinkled and wearing a plaid sportcoat with patches on the elbows. We had just five minutes to chat, but after the first minute, I wondered how I was going to make it through the next four. It started off innocently enough. "Are you from Los Angeles?" he asked. I smiled and said that, yes, I'm a local, and then I asked where he was from. New York.

"Oh," I said, trying to make the best of the fact that I was sitting across from someone who looked like a grandpa in Vegas. "So, what brought you to the West Coast?"

"A plane," he replied, barely containing his grin, like he was the first person ever to make this joke. I smiled weakly. There was a long pause.

"Actually, it's a very long story," he continued, despite the fact that this was "speed" dating. A simple "I liked the weather" or "I moved out here for college" or "There was a job opportunity" would have sufficed. Instead, he told me about how he doesn't get along with his family, so he moved as far away from them as he could; how he couldn't finish his Ph.D. because his dissertation advisor had a heart attack; how he tried to transfer schools but he didn't get in; how he moved in with this woman he thought he would marry, but then she left him for another guy; how he ended up working for a temp agency, and how that didn't work out because . . . ding. Thankfully, the bell rang and it was time for him to move to the next table.

Guy #2 was Paul. Paul was another grandpa (thinning gray hair, turkey chin). When I asked what kind of work he does, he told me he was "in transition." I asked what he was transitioning from—and to. He said he used to work as a teacher, which he loved, but he hated the politics so now he was playing a lot of golf. He'd really like to move from his cramped one-bedroom rental, but since he wasn't working, he couldn't afford a two-bedroom. He wanted to change careers, but it's hard when you're 55 because employers only want to hire "youngsters" these days. He was in the middle of a tirade about the principal at his school when I heard the blessed ding. The next guy sat down.

Guy #3 was Sandy. He was cute and the youngest guy there—mid-forties, maybe. "Everyone asks me what Sandy is short for," he said the second we made eye contact, even though I'd asked no such thing. "It's short for Sanford. You know, like Sandy Koufax. The baseball player? His name was Sanford, too. Sanford Koufax."

He smiled proudly. Sandy was a speed dating veteran. He said he'd been doing it for years. He told a lot of jokes that sounded like he'd been telling them for years. He had terrible grammar, and each time he made a mistake, he asked me what the correct word was—"you know, you being a writer and all." He was a sweet guy, in a little-boy kind of way, but we were like oil and water, and after five minutes of his shtick, I was eager for the ding.

Guy #4 was Roger. He was handsome in an older man way, like Bill Clinton. After some small talk, Roger told me that he'd moved to Los Angeles in 1973. "Remember the gas shortage and waiting in all those long gas lines?" he asked. *I was six*, I wanted to say, but instead I smiled gamely and asked what he did for a living. He owned an employment agency, but business was bad. He asked what I do, and I told him I'm a writer.

Roger leaned across the table. "Do you need a job?"

I thought he was kidding, so I said, "Not at the moment, but I'll let you know if that changes. Maybe you can help me."

He didn't get the joke. "You shouldn't wait until you're between jobs to find something. You should look while the iron's hot."

"Thanks," I said, humoring him. "I'll keep that in mind."

"Writers have it so easy," he continued. "What do you do all day, hang out in your pajamas?"

"Um, not really," I said.

"Oprah?"

"Excuse me?" I asked.

"Do you watch Oprah every day? All the writers I work with—they don't *do* anything."

The bell dinged. Roger slipped me his card. "Really, I can help," he said as he moved over to the next table.

I didn't know whether to laugh or cry.

His Daughter Is 34

There was no Guy #5 this round because, due to the dismal male-female ratio, at any one time four of the women were seated alone.

The event coordinator sat across from me to help pass the time. He was cute, thirtyish, and funny. I told him that this was my first speed dating event—wasn't the age range supposed to be 40 to 50?

"I know," he said empathetically, "we use the honor system, but this happens every time. The guys in their forties won't come to this event because, you know, they want to meet women in their thirties. We've thought about enforcing the age limit, but if we tell men in their forties that they can't go to the younger event, we'll lose all our clients." The cute coordinator moved on to keep another partnerless fortyish woman company.

I was alone for round six, too. I started talking to the woman next to me, who was also waiting this round out. She was a tall, blond dentist in a sexy suede dress. She was funny and smart and outgoing. Turned out that we jog at the same park and had just finished reading the same book. After chatting for five minutes, I could imagine becoming friends with her. For the first time all night, I was bummed when the ding sounded.

Finally I got my Guy #5. His name was Kevin. He had a water filtration business. I happened to be in the market for water filters, so I asked if his system filters out fluoride.

"The dentist over there asked me the same question!" he said, amazed by the coincidence. "How weird is that?"

I didn't think it was weird that a dentist would ask about fluoride and so would a woman with a young child, but he repeated this at least three times. After a series of how-weird-is-thats, he answered my question with, "I'm not sure. Is fluoride a compound?" I wondered how he could own a water filtration business and not know something so basic. Fluoridated water shouldn't be an obscure topic to someone who filters water for a living. Most of the national water supply is fluoridated.

Meanwhile, he learned that I'm a journalist and did the hard sell on pitching me an article about his company. I deflected several times—I told him I don't write about business; I attempted to change the subject entirely by asking what he does for fun—but he didn't take the hint and spent the remaining three minutes badgering me about writing an article about his company. Desperate, I was about to tell him that I'm not a journalist after all—*I was kidding! Ha, ha!—actually, I'm an accountant. My job has nothing to do with writing or water or writing about water.* . . . But I didn't have a chance to say it, because, fortunately, I heard the ding.

Guy #6 sat down. His name was Robert. He was a widower. He was smart. He was sweet. He was a lawyer. He probably was extremely handsome thirty years ago. He'd never been to a speed dating event before. He said—"in the interest of full disclosure"—that he's actually sixty, but there are no speed dating events for people his age. I hadn't thought about that—what do people do when they're single past 50 or 55? What if I'm still single? How will I meet men then?

Earlier, during my breaks, I'd looked around and noticed that the two older women—the ones who looked close to 50—were hanging on Robert's every word. Robert wasn't making a lot of eye contact with them. He seemed to be going through the motions. But these women were flirting. They were way into him. They were so . . . eager. And they didn't have a shot. *That could be me in ten years*, I thought. Then I realized—*that is me*. I'm at the same event, meeting the same men as these women. This is my life now, too.

In the few minutes that I chatted with Robert, I found him to be interesting and kind. He admitted that coming here tonight wasn't his idea, but his daughter, who is 34, put him up to it. I thought: *His daughter is 34!* I asked if his daughter had ever tried a speed dating event. "No, she's married," he laughed. "In fact, I just became a grandfather again!"

"Again?" I said, my voice cracking as I tried not to burst into tears at the table. "She has two kids?"

"No, my son has one, too," Robert replied. "He's got a two-year-old." I was speechless. This man's *kids* were married with kids. My son was his grandson's age. I stared at the table and Robert broke the silence with, "So, what about you? Have you ever been married?" *No*, I thought. *And at this rate, I never will be.* I recovered enough to say, "Not yet," and then, in what seemed like an eternity later, the ding sounded.

Since I'd already met all six men, I sat alone for the last two rounds and filled out my scorecard. I checked "no" by every box.

THE POSTMORTEM

That was it—the event was over. The cute event coordinator had us give ourselves a round of applause (*Congratulations! You suffered through this night successfully!*) and asked us to turn in our scorecards. As the younger women collected their purses, the coordinator noticed our shell-shocked expressions. "Try it again another time," he said to us. "Maybe it will be different?" he added unconvincingly.

On the way out, I passed the bar area of the restaurant. Stylish, smiling young men and women were talking and milling about. Nobody seemed to be over 30.

Driving home, I added up the costs of the blown evening. Event tab: 25 bucks. Babysitter tab: 40 bucks. Parking: 8 bucks. Time spent showering, shaving legs, blow-drying hair, applying makeup, and coordinating outfit: 1.5 hours. Round-trip travel time in rush-hour traffic: 1 hour. Lost evening that could have been spent with my beloved son: priceless.

I didn't blame the event sponsor for the fiasco. Instead, I blamed myself. On some level, I realized that it was simply the consequence of my having made bad dating decisions when I was younger. I knew that people met through speed dating all the time. I even knew someone who went to a 25-to-35 event when she was 29 and met her husband, who was 32, there. She'd been to three events, and at each one, she told me, there were an equal number of men and women. Some of the guys were duds, but most were relatively enjoyable to talk to. They didn't have a lot of baggage or sob stories. If they lived in crappy apartments, they had promising careers. They didn't remind her of her friends' fathers. Later, I asked a 40-year-old single friend about her speed dating experience. Was mine unusual?

"Not at all," she told me. "Sounds pretty typical for a forties to fifties event." She said that when she was 38 and 39, she'd gone to a couple of 30-to-40 events, and while the guys were far more appealing—she'd marked "yes" next to several—they were only interested in the women in their early thirties.

I'd always heard that dating gets harder the older you get, but I'd never really taken it seriously before. I didn't consider that *one* decision—say, passing up a good guy because "something was missing"—could change the course of my life forever. Back in my twenties and early thirties, I hadn't yet spoken to women in their forties and fifties who were wracked with regret at having broken up with a wonderfully nice guy for silly reasons, and who now live, as a 48-year-old designer who used to always have boyfriends put it, "a manless existence that consists of an all-female social life."

I thought about my 30-year-old friend Julia who had broken up with Greg, the nonprofit guy, and was now dating Adam, the charming surgeon, but couldn't decide between the two. I wanted to call her up and say that she should get her priorities straight and figure out which compromises she's willing to make, because if she passes up both of these guys now, *they* won't be at the 40- to 50-year-old speed dating event in ten years. But she might be.

Instead, I called up Rachel Greenwald, a dating expert who specializes in coaching single women over 35, to see what advice she might have for me.

I mean, I was 41, but I wasn't dead. I needed to hear something hopeful.

PART TWO

From Fantasy to Reality

Illusions commend themselves to us because they save us pain and allow us to enjoy pleasure instead. We must therefore accept it without complaint when they sometimes collide with a bit of reality against which they are dashed to pieces.

—Sigmund Freud

Older, and Wanting to Be Wiser

Rachel Greenwald is what you might call a sensible optimist. She uses a lot of exclamation marks in e-mail messages, and I could hear them in her enthusiastic voice when I called her up in Denver. She wants people to find love—it's her passion. But if she can sound absurdly hard-core in her bestselling first book, *Find a Husband After 35: Using What I Learned at Harvard Business School*—"Except for something illegal or immoral, would you do *anything* to find a husband?"—it's only because she knows the reality: The dating world changes once you're out of your twenties.

Of course, a few years ago *Newsweek* reported that their article from the 1980s had been wrong—it wasn't true that women over 40 had a better chance of being killed by a terrorist than getting married. Instead, their chance for marriage was as high as 40 percent. That was supposed to be reassuring, but think about it: *Less than half of women over 40 will ever marry.* Besides, some of these women won't get married in time to have children, and they're more likely to marry someone who's divorced with kids and has the difficulties of another family to deal with.

Greenwald told me that the first thing I need to remember is that I'm not dating in a vacuum. "You might be great, but there are so many great women out there just like you at the same time that there are fewer available men. There's a reverse power curve you have to take into account as you get older."

She cited a Census figure in her book—28 million single women over 35 versus 18 million men. When I looked deeper into the Census figures for singles 30 to 44 years old, I found that there were 107 single men for every 100 single women, but for 45- to 65-year-olds, there are only 72 single men for every 100 single women. If those numbers sound daunting enough, Greenwald said that out in the world, there are even fewer prospects for women my age. Why? Because many men want to (and can) marry younger women, and because men big on commitment and starting a family usually aren't the ones who are still available after 35. So women in their mid-thirties probably will end up dating more guys with more complicated pasts and more issues—just like *they'll* have by then.

"I could take two fantastic women at age twenty-five," Greenwald said. "These women are exactly the same in terms of appeal. Now, put them through two different experiences over the next ten years—one gets married and one stays single—then line them up side-by-side at age thirty-five and you've got two totally different women. The one who had a happy ten-year marriage thinks the world is good and the woman who was out in the singles world for ten years is cynical and pessimistic—and that's what it's like for men, too. By the time you put one guy through a successful marriage and another through the mill of dating and failed relationships, they're different kinds of guys. That's what's different about dating older people. They tend to be more jaded. They're not as hopeful and appealing as younger single people tend to be."

I told Greenwald that I didn't consider these factors when I was ten years younger and waiting for just the right guy to pop into my life. It seemed reasonable to think that the longer I searched, the better the guy I'd end up with. But it's faulty logic, she said: The longer you wait, the less likely you are to find someone better than you've already met.

The Checklist of a 25-Year-Old

It's not that the available older men are all "losers"—as many dating women might complain. It's just that they don't look anything like the person you've imagined being with since you were a teenager. If you'd met this person when he was 27, you'd have known him when he was much closer to your mental image of the man you thought you'd marry. But that same guy at 45—even if he looks middle-aged and has an ex-wife and two kids and has experienced disappointment in life—can still be great spouse. The key, Greenwald said, is to realize that "realistic" isn't a dirty word.

"The goal is to marry someone you truly love, who is going to treat you really well and make you happy," Greenwald told me, "but nothing I just said has anything to do with a guy's age, what his hairline is—all the things on a checklist of a twenty-five-year-old. If you're forty years old and you restrict your mental image of Mr. Right, you're going to be disappointed."

Greenwald said that for a lot of women, their search criteria go like this: "'I'm forty and I want to have a baby, and I'm only interested in someone five foot ten and above, and under age forty-five because I'm really active and I look young. I'm Jewish, so he has to be Jewish. I'd prefer someone who has no kids, but if he has kids, I'd prefer that they're older or don't live with him,' and they go on and on and on!"

I was glad that Greenwald and I were on the phone because I

could feel my cheeks turning bright red: *guilty as charged.* I mean, what's wrong with wanting those things? Would she tell an older single guy, *Hey, you know all those women you weren't attracted to or interested in back in your twenties? Well, guess what—they're still available and some are divorced and you should be more open-minded?*

"Not at all!" Greenwald insisted. "I'm not saying that you should end up with an ugly, boring guy, but some women search so narrowly they can't even find a guy to go on a date with! I'm not at all saying I want women to settle. You definitely have to have real chemistry with someone, but how can you tell if you'll have chemistry if you won't even give a guy a chance if he's the wrong age or height? Maybe he's so compassionate and hilarious and has other qualities that don't meet the eye."

A big problem, Greenwald explained, is that we have the same standards at 35 that we did at 25, but the things we wanted at 25 aren't as important to our lives at age 35. We should be looking at things like patience and stability instead of instant butterflies.

In fact, we should be looking for that *at 25*, so we don't marry the guy at 25 and realize at 35 that he doesn't have qualities that are essential in a good marriage.

"I'd give the same advice to a twenty-five-year-old that I'm giving you," she said. "But the twenty-five-year-olds don't want to listen."

SELFLESSNESS AND HUMILITY

The advice Greenwald gives is simple: Knock off anything as a deal-breaker that's "objective" (age, height, where he went to college, what type of job he has, how much hair he has, whether he has kids or an ex-wife) and focus on what's "subjective" (maturity, kindness, sense of humor, sensitivity, ability to commit).

I told her that was easy for her to say—after all, she got married seventeen years ago, when she was 28. How would she feel now, if she were still single in her forties, and someone told her not to pay attention to these objective criteria?

Greenwald laughed at this, but only because she'd been there. She said she almost didn't meet her husband because she'd also been too hung up on objective criteria. Back in business school, she'd spoken to her husband on the phone in a professional context and enjoyed those conversations, but once she looked up his photo in a directory (and wasn't impressed), she ruled him out as a romantic prospect. It was only on meeting him at a party and getting to know him that she started to find him cute—and more.

"When I was looking and single," she said, "I wanted everything! I wanted tall, good-looking, smart, funny. I was so specific, I even wanted curly hair." And while she got some (but not all) of what she wanted, she's quick to point out that none of that has to do with her happiness in her marriage.

"When I was dating, two qualities that never occurred to me as important but that turned out to be critical in our marriage were selflessness and humility," she explained. "A ton of times on a daily basis in marriage, you have to decide whether to maximize your happiness or the other person's, and my husband has proved so often to maximize my happiness. In courtship, we mistake romance for selflessness, but it's not at all the same thing. Romantic gestures like sending flowers aren't the same thing as waking up in the middle of the night and taking care of the baby so I can sleep."

"Also," she continued, "humility is key—the ability to say it doesn't really matter who's right or wrong, and it's okay to have different opinions about things. So I ask people, where on your list do you rank selflessness and humility when you're rejecting a guy based on his age or height?"

In fact, John Gottman, a well-known marriage researcher at the University of Washington and author of the bestseller *The Seven Principles for Making Marriage Work*, has shown that he can predict marital success with 91 percent accuracy by looking at basic qualities like compromise, tolerance, and communication style.

Greenwald isn't discounting the desires many of us have. She's saying, instead, that while we'd like "everything" in a guy, we should reexamine our standards—*and early on*—if we want to find the right partner before it becomes increasingly harder to find him.

When she meets women over 35 and takes their romantic histories, she told me, it's often some variation on *I was in this failed relationship for three years, another for five years.* Or, *I kept getting back with my ex-boyfriend, instead of making myself available to meet someone more appropriate.* Or, *I knew after six months or a year that it wasn't going anywhere, but I stayed anyway, hoping things would change.* What should have changed was the way these women picked their partners.

According to Greenwald, they squandered their peak dating years.

"The men they've been attracted to have generally offered the exact *opposite* of what they actually wanted in the long run—stability, responsibility, compassion, groundedness, maturity, the desire for kids," she said. "You have to remember that you don't have time to waste on a guy just because you're so infatuated with him."

Uh-oh. *Guilty as charged—again.* I thought about the boyfriend who fawned all over me most of the time, but then would suddenly withdraw after offering some lame version of "I got scared." I stayed with him anyway—for two and a half years. There were also a couple of wonderfully exciting and seemingly romantic guys who turned out to be more in love with themselves than with me. When I was younger, I kept thinking that I could let things unfold organically and not bother initiating conversations about our futures, but Greenwald said it's just as important to be proactive early on, before you get into a real time crunch.

"Women who want to get married and have families need to

think about what really matters—*and make their dating choices consistent with their words*—before they end up single in their mid-thirties," she told me. "I'm not trying to be alarmist. It's just a shame to see people come to me with these realizations when it's so much harder than it might have been had they had a different perspective ten years earlier. Say you're thirty-three, and you've been dating for eleven years since college and you want to start a family. Well, I can still set you up with a great forty-year-old who wants to start a family. But at thirty-five, it's more of a challenge. A half shelf-life for a woman is about thirty-five. The real shelf life is forty. Once you're forty and dating online, no guy who wants to have kids is willing to even meet you. Divorced guys who already have kids will meet a forty-year-old, but many of them have had vasectomies."

If Greenwald had told me this when I was 30, I would have thought she was exaggerating—or, at the very least, that I would be the exception to the way things generally went for older women. Even now, I often thought, *I'm still cute*, or *I'm young at heart*, or *I don't look my age*. But everything she was telling me had turned out to be true. Of all my friends, single or married, few knew any single guys my age at all, and of the one or two that they did know, neither was willing to date a woman over 40.

So I had a choice: I could either rail at the plight of the single female looking for love, or I could use this information to my advantage. As Greenwald told me, there was some *good* news: I had a chance to make a fresh start and get it right this time by dating guys with qualities that might actually make me happy in the long run.

The long run seemed to be Greenwald's focus. Over the past decade, she'd had a hand in several hundred marriages. And while many of these women initially resisted casting a wider net and focusing on subjective criteria, none of their marriages, to her knowledge, has ended in divorce.

So maybe she was on to something.

Happy with Mr. Normal

When happily married women told me what they thought was important as you get older, similar themes emerged: What matters is finding the perfect *partner*—not the perfect *person*. It's not about lowering your standards—it's about maturing and having reasonable expectations. There's a difference between what makes for a good boyfriend and what makes for a good husband. Over the years, stability and dependability outrank fireworks and witty banter.

My college friend Amanda, who is 39 and has been married for twelve years, told me that she remembers the pressure that came from society in general—and her social circle specifically—in terms of the kind of guy she should be dating.

"I remember in graduate school, this female professor, who was single and miserable, heard that I was dating Barry, and commented to a mutual friend that I could 'do better.' I remember thinking that she had no clue, and that no one could hope for a smarter, nicer, more promising person. History has proven me right. Barry may not always dress the way I like, or do Mr. Fix-It jobs around the house instead of watching football, but he'll do anything for me. He makes me chicken soup from scratch when I get the flu, and he makes it without any salt to watch out for my blood pressure. In the end, that's love and that's a great marriage."

Amanda said the biggest misconceptions she had when she was single were that consistency equals boring and that compromise is a negative word. She hopes her daughter has her priorities straight when she starts dating one day. "I couldn't have married Barry—or anyone else, for that matter—if I'd nitpicked over the things I see single women rejecting guys over now," she said.

Elise, who has been married for eight years and has two children, described her relationship with her husband this way: "When I turned thirty-five, I had just been dumped by this guy who had the qualities I thought I wanted, and I was devastated. A few months later, I met my now-husband, who possessed only a few of those qualities. The sparks didn't fly immediately. Instead, he has other qualities I really wanted: complete integrity, total honesty, willingness to do the right thing even if it was difficult, stability and, most important, love and understanding of me. The reason I hadn't met Mr. Right yet was because I was wrong about the qualities Mr. Right should have!"

Suzanne would agree. A 30-year-old marketing executive who lives in Austin, she told me that she married the guy who seemed like Mr. Right the first time, but is now married to the *real* Mr. Right. She laughs when she thinks about the mistakes she made in picking her first husband—and almost the second.

"For me," she explained, "zeroing in on the nonnegotiables while being able to forgo the whipped cream was the real key." After passing up a third date with an interesting guy because he wore sandals and had a cat, she told me, "I became 'enlightened,' which basically means that I was willing to overlook the stupid stuff. And now here I am, with the guy I want to grow old with."

Of course, almost everyone out there dating knows that what Greenwald called the subjective traits are important. It's just that we often place the *same value* on the objective traits and the subjective ones, and it's hard to find a real live human being who has equal measures of both. If a guy has more subjective traits than objective traits, we rule him out. But if he has the objective traits, it's harder to rule him out because objective traits are easier to measure, and we assume the harder-to-see-on-the-surface subjective ones are there, but just aren't as apparent. Obviously, this isn't always true.

Lynn, who is 42 and divorced, certainly looks at things differently now. "I had the handsome, square-jawed husband," she explained. "And when he cheated on me for the third time, and we got a divorce, I started to learn that the superficial does not matter in the long run. What matters is finding a person of substance. Unfortunately, some of us don't realize that until we're in the been-there, done-that category."

Lynn told me about two great guys in her office who have had a really hard time dating. One of them, Brad, is stocky and balding but, she said, "when you get to know him, you find he is witty, honorable, hilarious, intelligent, and downright adorable." A lot of women didn't look past the bald head and less-than-perfect body, and it wasn't until last month, when Brad turned 38, that he got married.

"A man doesn't have to look like a Ken doll to be a keeper," she said. "My friend Brad sure is, and the girl who has kept him is a lucky woman."

Lynn has another colleague, Mitch, who is 30 years old and is one of the nicest men Lynn has ever known. He's shy, Lynn said, but when you get to know him, he's a lot of fun to spend time with.

"He doesn't have a super-trendy hairstyle," she said. "He's not a bad-looking guy—he's just an average-looking guy. He has so many great qualities, but it seems to me that women in his age group don't even look at him. It makes me sad. From my perspective, at forty-two, I know that there are many younger guys out there who really want to find love, who want a commitment, who want to be married, who want kids. And they're often overlooked by women ages twenty-five to thirty-five who want to have it all."

SOMEONE TO KNOCK SOME SENSE INTO ME

I knew that Rachel Greenwald was right—I needed to approach dating differently. But even if I tried looking for those more subjective qualities, I still had a problem: I wasn't meeting any men.

I thought I should call a matchmaker.

For me, this seemed like a radical step. It never occurred to me to hire a matchmaker when I was younger because I always believed I'd meet a man on my own. He'd be sitting next to me on an airplane, waiting in line behind me at the dry cleaner, working in the same office, attending the same party, hanging out at the same coffeehouse.

It seemed ridiculous now, when I thought about the odds of this happening. After all, we don't subject other important aspects of our lives to pure chance. When you want to get a job, you don't just hang out in the lobbies of office buildings, hoping an employer will strike up a conversation with you. When you want to buy a house, you don't walk aimlessly from neighborhood to neighborhood on your own, hoping to spot a house that happens to be for sale, matches your personal taste, and contains the appropriate number of bedrooms and bathrooms. That's too random. If that's your only method of house hunting, you might end up homeless. So you hire a real estate broker to show you potential homes that meet your needs. By the same token, why not hire a matchmaker to show you potential partners?

The idea of looking across the room and locking eyes with a stranger still seemed more appealing, but in what room, exactly, would I find this charming stranger: in my office, which consisted of me and only me? In my living room or kitchen, where I went when I wasn't in my office? At a bar, which wasn't exactly a mecca of quality men?

Single women I spoke to complained of the same problem: Where in the heck would a modern busy woman magically "run into" The One? During the week, many single women have a schedule like this: Wake up, commute to work, work all day, stop at the gym or your all-female book club, microwave your dinner, watch a little TV, reply to e-mails, and go to bed. And the weekends? Have lunch with girlfriends, run all the errands you didn't have time for during the week, pay bills, open mail, work out, and spend another Saturday night at a party or trendy bar hoping to lock eyes with that handsome stranger across the room. I'm not saying it can't happen. I've actually dated a couple of those handsome strangers, but I never ended up marrying them. So I didn't want to leave things up to Fate or Destiny anymore.

I wanted a matchmaker's help, but I didn't want her to dismiss my objective criteria completely—I just wanted someone to add some perspective and common sense to my search in the way Greenwald was suggesting. I wanted someone who could say, "You know, he may not seem like your type, but trust me on this one." I wanted her to remind me of what's important, and help me break my pattern of ruling out good guys for all the wrong reasons.

So I got on the phone and called up Wendy, a local match-maker I knew about, and we arranged to meet for coffee. A week later, over steaming cups of latte, I gave her the rundown of my dating casualties: the musician I lived with in my twenties (cute, smart, and creative, but the theory that opposite personalities attract didn't seem to work for us after we moved in together); the lawyer who came next (cute, smart, funny, and successful, but he became so possessive that even my most open-minded friends thought he was creepy); the brilliant entrepreneur (cute, funny, and successful but maddeningly unreliable and egotistical); the TV writer who wasn't ready for a prime-time relationship (cute, smart, funny, and creative but not interested in committing to me); the charming investment banker who picked me up at a party where, I later learned, he was supposed to be someone else's date (that should have been a red flag, right?); the journalist who lived far away (cute, smart, funny, creative, and the nicest guy on the planet, but we could never agree on where to live and the kind of family life we wanted); the political consultant I shared a lot of interests with, and who seemed to be great most of the time, except when he was being dishonest or went off his antidepressant and anti-anxiety medications (cute, smart, and talented, with a Jekyll and Hyde personality); the sexy film-maker from Match.com (smart, funny, and successful, but not good dad material).

All of these guys were initially attractive on paper, I told her, but clearly, I had a pattern of making the wrong choices. Did she think she could help?

Wendy thought she could. In fact, she already had someone in mind.

6

$3,500 for Love

I'm not proud of this, but I almost rejected the first guy Wendy sent me. Mind you, I hadn't even met the guy. I hadn't seen his picture yet. And, in fact, from what Wendy had told me, he sounded a lot like the kind of person I was looking for. He was four years older than me (unlike those speed dating guys in their fifties). He'd been married before (and wanted to be married again). He was a father (and loved kids). He was highly educated (but down to earth). He collected first-edition books (and read them). He was financially stable (and liked his work).

Even so, when I heard that (1) a year earlier, he'd been distraught about his divorce (lately I'd gone out with a string of guys who spent the whole time recapping the collapse of their marriages); (2) he had four kids ("If we got together, there would be five kids in our family," I told Wendy. "That's not a family, that's a litter!"); (3) he was an avid sports fan (a turn-off to me); and (4) he grew up in a place that I associated with beer-can-smashing guys with thick accents, while my "type" was sophisticated intellectuals—I wanted to see who else she had for me.

She listened to my concerns, but asked me to reconsider. A few days went by as we went back and forth on e-mail. She assured me that this guy was far from "the belching, rough-talkin' Bronx-born sports nut," but was instead "Ivy league–educated and corporate-lawyer refined." In response to my questions about his hairline, stature, and wit, she replied that he had "height, hair, and humor."

Wendy didn't mince words. "We simply cannot nitpick people to death (he can be from Manhattan, but not the Bronx; he can have two kids but not four; he can like sports but not too much)." She wrote that my overly analytic mind "runs the risk of precision-thinking yourself out of a human connection!"

I trusted Wendy. She wasn't the pushy, used-car-salesman breed of matchmaker, out to take my money and send me a match that took the least amount of time and effort on her part to find. She wasn't an impersonal corporate entity that signs up anyone who comes along instead of hand-picking men from the community. Nor was she the stereotypical and much-lampooned middle-aged woman in a muumuu who reads your aura and claims to have a "sixth sense" about people.

She was a sharp, hip, happily married thirty-something mom who'd had remarkable success setting up friends, and had become, by accident, a local matchmaker. She didn't advertise. She only took clients referred by people she knew. She had facilitated six marriages in the last few years, with another couple recently engaged. And she thought this guy and I would really like each other.

Finally, I agreed to meet her match.

"Accentuate the positive," she wrote, and sent me his name so I could expect his call.

That's when I realized how far off the deep end I'd gone: I was disappointed by *his name*. I know this sounds nuts, but it was a name you'd give to the nerdy sidekick in a movie, a name that would get a kid teased on the playground. It was like that scene in *When Harry Met Sally* when Sally insists that she had great sex with a guy named Sheldon, and Harry replies, "Sheldon? No, I'm sorry. You didn't have great sex with Sheldon. A Sheldon can do your taxes. If you need a root canal, he's your man. But between the sheets is not Sheldon's strong suit."

So much for being open-minded. Not only had I microanalyzed this guy's background, but I'd judged something as irrelevant as his name! And it gets worse: I took that nerdy name, typed it into Google, found a photo online, and thought, "Hmm, his face looks heavy."

Let's review here: The guy, whom I'll now call "Sheldon," sounded interesting: smart, funny, accomplished, kind, loves kids, wants a serious relationship—and I was spending time analyzing his name and whether he might lose twenty pounds. Thankfully, I came to my senses and said nothing to Wendy. By bedtime, I realized he was the most interesting potential date I'd been set up with in a long time, and I felt genuinely excited to meet him. I eagerly awaited his call, which came the next day, when I was out. He left a nice message. I called him back and left a message. Then it was the weekend and I didn't hear from him again.

On Tuesday, Wendy had some bad news. Sheldon had called her Monday night. Apparently, in my six days of ambivalence about meeting him, he'd gone on a few dates with someone else (not through the matchmaker), and by the weekend things had intensified and now they were physically involved. He wanted to know where his budding relationship might go before he called someone new. Sheldon was no longer available.

Great.

When I told female friends this story, they couldn't understand it. "Wait, he *just* met this woman," one friend said. "Why can't he meet you, too?"

"That's an idiotic dating strategy," said another. "He's known her a week. How does he know he wouldn't like you better?"

I tried to feel reassured by my friends' comments, but instead they made me respect Sheldon more: the thought of "better" didn't seem to occur to him. He had no so-called dating strategy. He was an ethical guy who didn't sleep with one woman and go on a blind date with another. Sheldon's approach was so much saner. The woman dating Sheldon probably didn't overanalyze things to death like me, either. I doubted she was obsessing over whether he's too into sports or needs to lose a few pounds or is slightly nerdy or has too many kids.

Women like me, those who are perpetually single, often do. Relationships are like a game of musical chairs—if you wait too long to take a seat, all the chairs will be taken.

And that's pretty much what happened. Wendy tried to find me someone new, but a 41-year-old single mom isn't an easy match. Weeks went by as she explored the possibility of setting me up with a smart, funny, attractive district attorney who was divorced with no kids, but the more she talked to him, the more she realized that he wouldn't be flexible enough with dating around a child's schedule; he simply had no idea what raising a child involved.

She asked if I would be open to other religions, and although I have a strong preference for someone Jewish, I found myself saying okay. But the more she talked to another potential match, the more she felt that religion would be an issue for *him*. She looked around for someone else, but there was nobody she knew in her small network in the forties-divorced-with-kids category who happened to be available and interested. She would have to go out and search.

When I think about that incident now, I'd like to believe that some of my initial nitpicking with Sheldon had to do with the fact that I'd paid $500 for two dates and, at $250 per date, with the financial stakes so high, it was reasonable to want to get the best two matches possible. But what did "best" mean? Wendy had no way of predicting chemistry between Sheldon and me, and he was, objectively, a match with good potential.

If I'm really honest, I think my reluctance to meet Sheldon actually had more to do with something I hadn't yet admitted to myself: I still hadn't come to terms with the realities of being single and never married at my age. I wasn't ready, on some visceral level, to let go of the idea of being somebody's first and only spouse, of being somebody's The One and having the exclusivity of our own family unit.

I wanted a more conventional setup that didn't involve thorny custody schedules, negotiations over where to spend the holidays, and issues with an ex-wife. But what age-appropriate single guy with no kids and no ex-wife was going to be interested in taking on a woman who was too old to have kids with him and whose time and energy was devoted mainly to her young child? It seemed that my most promising options were going to be divorced men with kids, and I was going to have to not just accept that, but embrace it.

When I overlooked perfectly nice guys in my twenties and early thirties, I never sat down and thought about how complicated a calculus middle-aged dating becomes, if you factor in a much smaller pool of available men, a much smaller pool of available men who interest you, a much smaller pool of available men who are interested in dating someone your age, and the logistical baggage we all carry forward the older we get. Now I began to see all of this. But it wasn't until I let another woman sit in the Sheldon seat and was left standing alone that it finally sunk in how limited my options really were.

Even the local matchmaker couldn't find me another date.

Do as I Say, Not as I Do

While Wendy searched for a new prospect, I'd need to find a way to meet more men. But how? If going to a local matchmaker offered the advice and perspective you can't get from online dating, the greatest disadvantage, it seemed, was how few people she might have in her personal network. On the other hand, smaller seemed better—if you know that's the deal upfront. Had I truly understood that it was Sheldon or bust, I'd have met him (reservations and all) and seen how the date went. Instead, I was still stuck in the online dating mentality—that if you don't like something about one guy, there's a seemingly infinite supply of new dating candidates lined up. I figured a matchmaking company would be a happy medium— more prospects than a private matchmaker, and more guidance than the wild Web.

I got out the phone book and did some searching. After ruling out agencies that seemed to focus on setting up wealthy men with beautiful women (one was actually called Beautiful Women— Successful Men, succinctly summing up our primal longings), as well as those that seemed big and impersonal with offices across the country, I picked Make Me A Match, run by two sisters. I went to their Web site, filled out a short form—name, phone number, gender, how I'd heard of them—and waited for someone to contact me.

A few hours later, I got a call from one of the sisters, Kathy Moore. She started with a brief sales pitch: 550 weddings, personal service, the experience to know what works. She sounded sharp and professional. Then she turned the conversation to me.

"Tell me about yourself," she said.

I explained that I was a journalist, 41 years old, never married, a single parent . . .

"What did you do, go to a sperm bank?" she interrupted.

I paused. It seemed a little forward to ask of someone she'd been speaking to for three minutes. "Um, yes," I said.

"Good for you!" Moore replied. "*I* should have done that."

Huh?

Turned out this matchmaker was a single 45-year-old who wished she'd had kids when she was still fertile. I wondered how that could be: How could she find husbands for hundreds of people but not be able to find one herself?

"You don't have to be sick to be a good doctor," she said, but I didn't buy that explanation. It wasn't even an accurate analogy: Moore wasn't a healthy doctor curing sick patients. She was more like a sick doctor who couldn't cure herself of the same disease she specialized in treating: single-itis. It made no sense. When I pointed this out, she added, "Well, also, I don't date my clients."

Okay, I thought, fair enough. But why not go online, or hire another matchmaker to find her someone?

She seemed to have an answer for everything. "People know who I am," she said, meaning, I guess, what she does for a living. "It's intimidating for guys to date me."

The whole situation seemed a bit kooky: Should I ask a lonely heart to find me a man when she couldn't find one herself? At the same time, I was discovering that we aren't the best people to find ourselves a mate; that sometimes we need outside perspective to counter the fantasies we have about who we should be with.

I asked about the kind of men who came to her. What kind of men sign up with a matchmaker? Moore acknowledged that she had far more female than male clients, but still she felt she could find me someone: If she doesn't have a man for a female client, she told me, she asks other matchmakers for assistance. She also scours online dating sites, and if anyone seems interesting, she'll meet with him in person to see if he might be a good fit. I liked that idea:

someone to screen all those online candidates so I didn't have to go on an endless array of coffee dates myself.

The next step was for me to go in to Make Me A Match, so that Kathy and her sister could get to know me and see which men might be a good fit. It seemed worth a try, until she dropped the bomb. I asked about cost, and she deflected, saying that we could talk details in the meeting. I insisted on knowing upfront and, after she hedged for another couple of minutes, finally she relented: For six dates in the span of one year, the fee was $3,500. I grabbed my calculator and did the math: $583 per date! Their Web site made it seem like they catered to normal people, not just the super-wealthy. $583 is a *very* expensive date. And she wanted me to pay for six of them!

"I know, it's sticker shock," Moore said. "But you get what you pay for. You can expect to be here for at least three hours when we first meet you. Then every time we send you on a date, we get detailed feedback. We might get it right on the first date, but it might take some work to refine it. You're paying for the personal service." I told her I was interested, but I just couldn't afford it.

"How about three dates for a thousand dollars?" I asked. I didn't know the protocol—could you haggle with matchmakers?

"It takes too much work to do anything for a thousand dollars," she said. "It's not worth it for us." I could tell that she wanted to move on. Her phone had been ringing repeatedly in the background and I imagined that there was no shortage of female customers more than willing to pay the full fee.

"You know what I suggest for people like you," she said, in a way that gave me the impression she'd spoken to "people like me" before. "Go on JDate." She was referring to the online dating site for Jewish singles.

I told her that I'd already been on JDate, that I'd met my last boyfriend online, but that I wanted a matchmaker's help in picking appropriate men. My last boyfriend was smart and sexy and funny, but when it came to being a husband and father, he was completely wrong. I didn't trust myself to pick men off the Internet anymore. I needed guidance.

"Well, here's what you do," Moore said. "Save your pennies. I don't want to feel like I'm taking the last of your life savings, but save up. Don't take a trip, or give up that pair of shoes, and put away money for your love life. Make your love life your priority."

She didn't seem to understand that it wasn't about choosing between a vacation (which I hadn't taken since having a child) or a pair of Manolos (which I've never owned) and my so-called love life. It was about the reality of what regular people can afford. When I clarified this, she replied with, "We only take financially stable clients." Her definition of financially stable seemed to be different from mine.

I hung up more frustrated than ever. I suspected that if I were a guy, she would lower the fee or waive it entirely, simply to have more eligible men in her database. I didn't add much value to her business. It reminded me of the dowry system, in which you need to have a lot of money to marry off your daughter. Could this be the modern American dowry: a woman over 35 needs a lot of money to marry off *herself*?

And here's the sad thing: Although I declined to sign up with Make Me A Match, I didn't rule it out entirely. Instead, I thought about ways of "saving my pennies." I'm sure Kathy Moore knew that's what would happen. She may not think of herself as preying on vulnerable singles willing to go to impossible lengths to find a good man, but I'm guessing that a number of women who show up for that initial three-hour meeting and are then shocked by the cost don't leave until they've written a check and signed a contract. I'm also guessing that women like me, who say no on the phone, come back to her eventually—borrowing money from parents or maxing out credit cards—because she leaves them with an impossible question: *At what cost, love?*

After a week or a month or another year of empty dates or, if they're lucky, a failed relationship, they might come to the conclusion that what Kathy Moore is selling isn't exorbitant, but priceless: hope that they won't end up alone.

LESSONS FROM A MATCHMAKING TEACHER

Lisa Clampitt co-owns the the Matchmaking Institute in New York, the only place in the country that trains and certifies matchmakers. I called her up and asked why these services are so expensive. What, after all, do matchmakers know about what makes for a good romantic connection that the singles seeking their help don't?

Clampitt, it turns out, hadn't always been a matchmaker—she'd been a social worker in child protection services at Bellevue Hospital. She enjoyed working with people, but after thirteen years of dealing with trauma and illness, she got burned out. Meanwhile, she'd been having some success setting up friends and, one day, she was inspired by something she read in the newspaper about matchmakers. She'd never considered being a professional matchmaker before—in fact, she didn't even know they existed in this day and age—but she loved the idea and thought it would allow her to do "the fun elements of social work."

To become a "certified matchmaker," she explained, here's what you do: You buy a home study kit from Clampitt's Web site, which, she said, has everything you need to know about the matchmaking industry, including how to prescreen a client, interview a client, do coaching, set up a business, and do legal contracts. Then you take

an online test. If you pass, you come to a one-day certification train-
ing or do six consultation sessions over the phone. After that, you
submit a business plan, and *voila*, you're certified.

For this, I asked, clients pay $3,500? What does some stranger
who took a one-day seminar know about who I might click with?

Clampitt said that matchmaking isn't rocket science.

"Hollywood makes it seem like the hard part is finding the guy,"
she said. "But the relationship is the hard part. Just this morning, my
husband and I had a thing about when he was leaving for work."

Single women, she thinks, make the search harder and more
angst-ridden than it needs to be. She believes that while beauty
matters, women waste far too much time on appearance, when their
biggest obstacle is actually not being realistic enough when they're
younger—and then ending up being even *more* unrealistic later on.

"A lot of women come to me when they're suddenly realizing
they need to do something differently because they're thirty-seven
and still single," she explained. "So they tell me what they want, and
they think because they pay for a matchmaker, they're going to get
the men they request in their interview. But that's not reality."

He's a Good Deal, I'll Take It

Clampitt, who's in her forties, knows this firsthand. She wouldn't
have met her own husband if she hadn't been realistic. "I think my
husband is adorable, but was I like, 'Oh my god, I'm sweating'? No.
He was super-friendly, relationship-oriented, has a Ph.D. and is a
professor. I don't care about money as much as I care about intelligence. So I thought, he's a good deal, I'll take it."

A "deal" is a term Clampitt uses a lot, which may seem like an
odd way of describing your spouse. But in her view, choosing to
spend your life with someone involves deciding which package—
which deal—works best for you given what you want out of life.

"Everybody has their pros and cons," she said, a lesson she learned from her two very different marriages.

Marriage number one was classic: She and her first husband met through friends when they were in their twenties. They both went through grad school, and she thought he was handsome and loyal, a smart guy working in finance. But he didn't have a "life force." He wasn't "feisty."

After two years of marriage, she left him.

Was this the right decision—divorcing the great guy for some intangible life force that she may or may not find in someone else? It's an impossible question.

"I think if I were more mature, I probably could have made it work," she said. "It wasn't my priority to have a family then, but now I think he would have been a wonderful father, and his extended family was fabulous. I didn't know how to respect him—instead I said he was boring. But what's better than someone who will be a really loyal partner? How wonderful to have a really good dad to your kids. You can make having fun a priority in the relationship. But I didn't even try! I was so focused on what might be out there that's better. That's what happens when you're young and don't have life experience."

That's also what happens, she said, to the women she meets in their late thirties, who pass up guys without giving them a fair chance.

Clampitt may seem to have gotten the happy ending—at 39, she met and married a guy who *was* feisty and *did* have a life force—but it was a double-edged sword involving compromises she wouldn't have needed to make in her first marriage. One was giving up having a biological child. She and her husband tried to have kids for years using expensive fertility treatments, to no avail—something that likely wouldn't have been an issue ten years earlier. They're planning to adopt a son. Financially, too, her situation is different in this marriage—a guy in finance makes a lot more money than a professor. And then there's the fact that her husband *is* feisty—which is great most of the time, but at others, it feels more like a case of be-careful-what-you-wish-for.

"My husband's a troublemaker," she said, "and I love that about him. But I need to figure out how to communicate with him when he's being a wild man—when we're trying to plan something together or when he forgets to pay the bills and I have to say, 'Come on, get with it.' That never would have happened in my first marriage."

Her point, she said, wasn't to complain about her husband, but to say that there's no perfect guy out there. "There are a lot of guys you can make it work with, and if you don't realize that, you may end up spending your entire life worrying about whether you're settling. A lot of people second-guess and assess a hundred different things. I'm surrounded by rich guys all the time, and I could go around thinking, *I could have this!* My husband could be thinking this, too, about other women. You both have to think that you got a good deal. Long-term compatibility is about respect and common values and building something, not about judgment of imperfections."

THE TAP WATER INCIDENT

As a matchmaker, Clampitt sees that kind of judgment all the time. Take the tap water incident.

"I introduced this woman to the nicest guy, and they went out and he didn't order bottled water. He said tap was fine," Clampitt explained. "This woman reports back to me after the date and says, 'He ordered tap water. He took the subway to meet me. He didn't even take a cab at night. He's cheap.' In fact, he was tall and handsome and wealthy, so I said, 'He may not care about bottled water or cabs, but if they're important to you, maybe he'd understand that. You'd figure out a budget together. These are things you can discuss if you ended up liking each other. At least go out with him again.' But it rubbed her the wrong way. She wasn't into it."

I said that I'd be happy to meet Mr. Tap Water, but Clampitt had already set him up with somebody else and they were excited about each other. The woman who thought he was cheap, she pointed out, was still available.

Clampitt matches people like this: "Number one," she said, "I look at whether the two people have common relationship goals. Number two, I look at values. Things like independence, family, religion, loyalty. Number three, what are the key qualities this person needs? You get no more than five. Things like, he has to be very intelligent. Number four, I look at shared interests. Interests are great because it's bonding and stimulating and fun to share those, but the other things are more important for the long-term. I put shared interests last for that reason."

I told Clampitt that I'd almost always put shared interests first. Not ultimately, of course, but that I'd become attracted to men initially *because* of our shared interests.

"And how has that worked out for you?" Clampitt asked wryly.

I tried to imagine what it would be like to marry a guy who was smart, funny, loyal, mature, and family-oriented—but who had completely different interests from mine.

What if he was into, say, video games and classic cars and I'm into literature and hiking? What if we had no shared interests at all? Then again, many of my closest friends have completely different hobbies or don't like the same movies and books and we never run out of things to talk about.

"Two smart, funny people who come from similar backgrounds and want similar things often discover that they have some shared interests," Clampitt said. "And if you share an interest in being married and raising your family together, I don't think the video games or hiking would be an issue."

Suddenly I realized that I'd overlooked the two most important—and basic—interests a prospective spouse would need to share with me: family life and raising children. I knew those were important, but my interest list had been full of the superficial things you'd find on a Facebook page.

I asked Clampitt what kind of guy she'd pick for me. What was, you know, realistic? She said she'd pick someone who's "maybe not the most gorgeous guy." Someone who's shorter, older, and with kids.

"You're more of a challenge for matchmakers," she said. "But you're matchable."

How's that for a dose of realism? Clampitt could hear my disappointment in the gaping silence through the phone line.

"Look," she said, "I'll say the same thing to you that I say to younger women who don't want to hear this. I say, 'If you keep doing what you're doing, what's going to change? You don't want to be thirty and the next day you're forty-five and thinking, what have I done with my days?' Because, as you know, it gets harder."

I did know. But I still had trouble with "shorter, older, with kids, and not gorgeous." Not because I think I'm so fabulous (after all, I'm also shorter, older, with a kid, not gorgeous) but because it's hard, as a woman, not to have drilled into you the notion that no matter how objectively ordinary you may be, somehow you "deserve" to be with the crème de la crème of male companionship. Read any article on dating on a woman-oriented Web site and in women's magazines, or check out advice books marketed to single women, and you'll read things like "You deserve to be with a man who pays." "You deserve a man who always puts you first."

"You deserve to be with a man who rubs your feet at night." And of course the man in question will also be tall, dark, and handsome.

Do men get this kind of advice? *You deserve to be with a super-model? You deserve to get blow jobs every day? You deserve to be with a woman who will fly around the country and go to football games with you?* Not as much.

But for women, it seems that "desire" has become the new "deserve." Which is why even though there's nothing wrong with "shorter, older, and with kids," I thought I deserved something better.

THE FUSSY FACTOR

"She's crippled, as far as I'm concerned," said Julie Ferman, the founder of Cupid's Coach, one of the most popular Los Angeles–based matchmaking companies, about a potential client who had come to see her that morning. "I won't take on anyone who will be too picky."

I was asking Ferman to give me the lowdown on women like me who have trouble dating guys that aren't our type.

"No matter what I said, this woman would find something negative," Ferman continued. "I'd bring up gentlemen for her to study, and she'd say he's not right because of this or that. She was, shall we say, unreasonable."

Ferman, who has been both married and matchmaking for two decades, is the antithesis of the Los Angeles stereotype. She's old-school and unfailingly gracious, a middle-aged woman from the Midwest who uses words like "gentlemen" instead of "guys" and euphemisms like "unreasonable" for "unrealistic." She says, with a straight face, "We're here to help people not miss out because of the *fussy factor.*"

Like Lisa Clampitt of the Matchmaking Institute, Ferman is the first to admit that her husband wasn't initially her idea of Mr. Right. Not that she wasn't looking for him. Nearing 30, and established in her career in the hotel business in St. Louis, she'd had her share of blind dates and was, frankly, burned out.

Finally, she signed up with a dating service, Great Expectations, and met the man who became her husband and the father of her two sons. Gil was her matchmaker, and he became her match. If this sounds like a fairy tale, Ferman is quick to give a reality check.

"I made some compromises," she told me. "He was fourteen years older than me and Jewish. I was raised Catholic. He had a scruffy beard that I hated and he wore cheesy-looking clothes. My mother always said, 'You'll know you've found someone when you respect each other and you're really comfortable with him.' I never listened to her. Then I met Gil and I didn't have the hots for him at all, but I got a really wonderful sense of him from being his client."

So much so, that while Gil showed her prospective matches, she wondered why he wasn't asking her out. One day, she laid it out there: She asked him why she didn't see him in the client book. He said, "I don't want to ask out my members." So Ferman said, "What if a member asked you out?" That led to drinks and a long, entertaining conversation at a nearby bar.

But their second date didn't go as well. "It was flat," Ferman said. "I thought, no, he's not The One." Still, she went on a third date, which was "comfortable, but no sparks." It might have ended there, but then Ferman went out of town for a week, and she and Gil talked on the phone each night and became friends. It was then that Ferman started to feel the butterflies. Ferman says that at that point, she had five important criteria on her list of what she wanted in a marriage: someone family-oriented who wants kids, someone who respects her and whom she respects, someone who has her back, someone Catholic, someone who shared her interest in personal growth.

She compromised on issues four and five. "I was willing to be flexible about religion, so our kids grew up Jewish," she said. And if Gil wasn't willing to travel around the country to see various gurus speak, Ferman was willing to suspend her travel and explore her interest locally—through yoga and meditation—with a more manageable schedule.

But what about physical attraction? After all, Ferman hadn't painted a very appealing portrait of Gil, with his bad beard and cheesy clothes. Ferman says she took immediate physical chemistry off her list when she realized that, given a certain level of attraction, she could find someone very attractive over time.

"That difficult woman that I met this morning," Ferman said, "she rarely falls in love over time." (It occurred to me that Ferman would probably find me "difficult," too, for the same reason.) Ferman says she had another client who was 5'10" and would not date short men, bald men, or men who weren't Protestant. She rejected most of the men Ferman tried to match her with until Ferman ran out of acceptable prospects. Then the woman moved to Washington, D.C., and fell in love with a man at work who was 5'8", bald, and not Protestant. She married him. He wasn't what she was looking for on paper, but he was what she was looking for in real life.

Wanted: 30-Year-Old Single Women

When you sign up for Ferman's services—which start at $2,900 for three introductions in three months and can go up to $15,000—she'll get to know you (resume, personal interview, photos), then she'll pull her top five candidates for you. She's quick to emphasize the "for you" part: She bases this assessment on who you are, who you're hoping to meet, who's available at any given moment in time, and—

here's the key—*who she thinks you have a shot at*. She allows clients to search her database for potential matches as well, but only she can arrange a date.

"You may look through the database and think Neil is great, he's your It guy," she said, referring to a popular male prospect. "But I know who he's going for, and it's not you. So I don't put you two together."

Neil, who is 42, is going for younger women, but Ferman doesn't have many female clients in their early thirties. And when she does, it's usually a mother signing up her daughter, like the 33-year-old physician who keeps saying no to the people Ferman wants her to meet.

"She says she's too busy, or this guy isn't tall enough. The thirty-year-olds want to find someone, but they're still picky-picky-picky because they think it will just somehow happen. She says she wants to get married. She wants to have children. Well, she doesn't realize that if she wants to have children, she'd better get with the program!"

Most women come to Ferman when they're nearing 40; the majority of her clients tend to be in their forties and fifties. Women in their forties are especially tough because they have histories by then—either lots of ex-boyfriends or few long-term relationships, and she has to wonder why. Are they always looking for what's wrong with people instead of looking for what's right? These are the women Ferman wishes had come to her when they were 29.

Ferman tells women of all ages to pay attention to the men who are already attracted to them, instead of walking into a room and hoping to find the most attractive man. "The men who are responding to you—those are the ones you want to nurture," she said. "And those are often the ones women will dismiss."

She told me about another client who is 38 years old, and wants someone tall, successful, and who has hair. Everyone Ferman pre-

sented came up lacking. "I said, 'Okay, you can have tall and successful, but give me a break on the hair thing.'" Likewise, if
educational level is a client's top criterion, that's fine, as long as she
won't nix a guy because of the way he dresses. This often meets with
resistance.

"Sometimes they have to get to the point of exasperation or sor-
row before they'll be even slightly flexible," she said. "A woman called
this morning who was forty-seven years old, and she was as picky
and fussy as that woman who came in today who was thirty-seven.
The window of opportunity is going to change drastically for this
woman at fifty, just like it will for that thirty-seven-year-old at forty.
To these ladies I say, 'Are you willing to look at that again?' and if they
say yes, they have a much better chance of finding the man they'll
want to marry. If they always say no, I can't really help them."

While some matchmakers talk about romance, Ferman doesn't
even like to use the word. To her, romance is about the evolving
relationship, as it has been in her own marriage. The most exciting
aspect of her marriage has been learning how someone can surprise
you. A guy may not seem exciting on the surface, but he might offer
something more exciting over the long-term: interesting ways of
looking at the world; the ability to make you laugh after a long day
at work; a sweet way of challenging you to become the best version
of yourself; being a wonderful dad. The man of your dreams? Absolutely. He just doesn't look the way he did in your daydreams.

"Women come into my office and say, 'I'm not going to settle,'"
Ferman says. "And I say, 'I'm not asking you to settle. I'm asking you
to broaden your fantasies.'"

A PERSONAL TRAINER FOR LOVE

Over the next few days, I kept thinking about Ferman's and
Clampitt's husbands. They sounded like guys I wouldn't consider if

a matchmaker presented me with similar prospects, but they make both women very happy. So when these matchmakers ask their clients to consider the guy who is too-this or not-that-enough, they're actually saying something quite simple: You can have rigid expectations and try to find someone who meets them, or you can let go of preconceived notions and find someone you'll fall in love with.

After the Sheldon incident, I felt like I needed more than a matchmaker. I needed to enlist the services of Evan Marc Katz, a well-known dating coach who likens himself to "a personal trainer for love." My learning curve was going to be a lot steeper than I expected, and not only could he give me the guy's perspective on how to do things right, but if anyone could set me straight, I knew it would be Evan.

7

The *What* Versus the *Why*

When Evan walked into my house for our first dating coaching session on a warm fall day, my son's babysitter's eyebrows shot up. Evan is, basically, a dude. He wore shorts and a T-shirt over his tanned body, and his thick, wavy hair looked slightly damp, as if he'd just stepped out of the shower. At 35, he could easily pass for ten years younger. I'm sure the babysitter was wondering how I landed such a hot prospect. But Evan was two months away from his own wedding.

Which is exactly why I wanted his help: He, too, had learned how to be happily realistic. He was about to marry a lovely woman who was unlike anyone he'd ever dated. His fiancée was cute but not gorgeous. She was 39 years old and looked her age. She wasn't impressively accomplished. She didn't disarm people with a rapier wit. She wouldn't stand out in any way at a dinner party. She was, objectively, rather average. And Evan was madly in love.

This was fascinating to me. I'd known Evan as an acquaintance for several years, and while he was reputed to be a very successful, wise, and no-nonsense dating coach, I'd often been amused by his choice of profession. He struck me as a player, always involved with a different woman whenever I saw him. CNN even labeled him a "serial dater." Then, not long before I called him, I ran into him at a lecture, and the woman he introduced me to wasn't just another girlfriend, but his fiancée.

Even Evan, the consummate bachelor, was getting married.

On the phone a week before our meeting, Evan admitted that if he'd come across his fiancée online, he never would have e-mailed her, and if she'd e-mailed him, he would have sent a nice "no thanks" in response. She wasn't his type. She was too old, not an intellectual, not his religion.

"But the people that I was most attracted to in the past weren't good long-term compatible fits for me," Evan explained. "I realized that if I kept going for that one type, I'd never find the right person. The definition of insanity is doing the same thing over and over and expecting different results."

Then he met his fiancée at a party. He wasn't interested in a serious relationship with her, but they started hanging out, and the more time they spent together, the more Evan liked being with her. She was warm, kind, supportive, and flexible. She didn't put up with his bullshit, but she also didn't expect him to be some mythical Prince Charming. She wasn't, as Evan put it, "always on my case, telling me all the ways I needed to change." She wasn't demanding and entitled like the girlfriend Evan pined over after she dumped him, even though she had treated him "like crap" when they were dating. Evan and his fiancée were able to compromise and work out their differences. They shared future goals. They had a lot of fun together. They "got" each other. If he was naturally funnier than she was, she was naturally more organized and less intense in day-to-day life than he was. They complemented each other.

Still, Evan said that neither of them was what the other had imagined as The One.

"I'm an opinionated Jewish guy who complains a lot about the little things in life," he said. "I spend way too much time working. But that also means I have a strong work ethic. I'm family-oriented and want to be a great dad. I'm loyal and fun to be around, when I'm not complaining. I'm introspective and try to be a good person. So my fiancée could go around feeling bad that I'm not optimistic enough, or athletic, or don't have the kind of job that allows me to travel at the drop of a hat even though she loves to travel. Her ideal might have been a tall, less neurotic Catholic guy, but we both realized that our ideals weren't what actually made us happy."

I told Evan that I was also trying not to get tripped up by ideals, but I didn't know what to compromise on. Physical appearance? Sense of humor? Sense of aesthetics? All of the above? How would I know if I was being too picky or not picky enough?

"You have to do the percentages," Evan said. "I just got off the phone with a client, and she asked me the same question. This woman is thirty-five years old. She said that she's willing to compromise, but the more we talked, the more it seemed like she had a fixed idea in her head of the man she wants to be with. She has to be with a guy who's over six feet tall. She's five feet five. So I told her that about 15 percent of men are over six feet tall, and 80 percent of women want them. Most of that 80 percent won't compromise. Do the math! How can 80 percent of women get 15 percent of men?"

He asked me to try it myself. "Write down the characteristics you're looking for," he said, "then calculate the percentage of men out there who meet those criteria."

We did it together on the phone. We multiplied the numbers— estimated percentages of men who are smart enough, sophisticated enough, funny enough, family-oriented enough, successful enough, kind enough, attractive enough (have hair, are physically fit, give me butterflies), are currently single, kid-friendly, emotionally available, in my age group, and live in Los Angeles—and it came to about *5 percent* of the local male population.

Then we did another calculation. Even if 5 percent meets my desired requirements, what are the odds that I'll meet theirs? How many of *those* men are looking for a 41-year-old? My viable dating pool suddenly dwindled down to about one percent. Oh, and if I want someone who shares my religion? According to Evan, Jewish guys are about 2 percent of American population and about 6 percent of the population in Los Angeles. I'd have to factor that in to the measly one percent of men of any religion who could be potential matches. The final calculation: .1 percent.

Wow. Was I really that picky? Were other women?

Apparently. Evan said some women he's worked with have even more specific criteria that bring the numbers down. Things like, *I'm a huge dog person and the man I'm with has to feel the same way about animals.*

"Frankly," he said, "if someone puts up with your obsession, you're lucky." Evan believes that it's one thing for a partner to accept your interests. It's another to ask them to feel the way that you do about them. And the more requirements you have, the lower the percentages go.

No wonder it seemed like there were no men out there. According to my criteria, there weren't.

These percentages may not have been scientifically precise, but they made sense. Given that I wanted someone who wasn't just smart, but well-read; who wasn't just cute, but had to have hair; who wasn't just age-appropriate, but had to look no older than 42, one in ten thousand available men who would date me seemed about right.

"It's going to be very hard to find someone unless you stretch your criteria a bit," Evan said. "The more you stretch, the more guys you'll let through your filter."

"But what if I have a filter there for a reason?" I asked. "You can't just date anyone."

"Maybe your filter is too narrow," Evan said. "How many guys have you been out on a date with recently?"

I didn't have to answer. I knew he was right. It's not that there's only one guy in ten thousand out there for me. It's that I'm over-looking guys who might make those percentages higher.

So in the five weeks left before Evan's wedding, he was going to help me learn to broaden my filter. We agreed to meet Mondays at noon, but first, he asked, did I have any dates lined up? If he was going to coach me, we'd need to find me some men.

I told him about Wendy, the matchmaker, and how she hadn't found a new prospect yet.

"No problem," Evan smiled. He was going to take me into the trenches of online dating.

The Less-Is-More Effect

Honestly, I was never any good at online dating. I'd either rule out guys based on one criterion (too into punk music) or I'd try to be "open-minded," only to realize that I couldn't get excited about these guys once we started a correspondence. In the end, I kept searching for the same qualities I'd always looked for—but which never ended in my finding the person I wanted to spend my life with. I started to wonder, did I even know what I wanted?

A few weeks before I called Evan, I'd spoken to Dan Ariely, a behavioral economist at MIT. He'd written a book called *Predictably Irrational: The Hidden Forces That Shape Our Decisions*. I told him about my situation. He said he'd heard it all before—in fact, he'd studied it.

"The idea that people know what they want is quite ludicrous," he said right off the bat. According to Ariely, not only are we confused about what we want in the moment, but we fail to take into account that our desires change through time as we deal with life circumstances like illness, financial issues, or children.

If we don't know what we want, he said, dating can be hard, but online dating is even harder. After all, Internet profiles make what you're looking for seem objective (based on data in the profile) when actual connection is extremely subjective.

It's this illusion of objectivity that dooms us.

"The less you know about a potential mate before you meet, the better," Ariely said. "It leaves less room for the fantasy to build. When online daters meet in person, they have so much prior information that there's little room for discovery. And once you see a flaw in the other person, the fantasy is ruined. So instead of giving the person a chance, you go home and log on to the computer to find someone else who looks good on paper."

I told Ariely that when I'd done online dating, I always wanted to get a lot of information upfront so I didn't waste my time. In fact, I wouldn't respond to profiles if they didn't have enough information. Was I doing it all wrong?

Ariely said yes: Knowing too much about a person sight unseen makes it harder to become interested in him. In one study, he told me, online daters were given traits of a potential partner, like the ones you'd find on an online dating site. When participants were given a higher number of traits, they perceived the person to be less similar to them than if they were given a smaller list of traits. The more traits you have knowledge of, the more information that gives you to rule someone out.

It's what he calls "the less is more effect": If you describe yourself in more ambiguous terms in your profile, you'll be more likable.

"If you write, 'I like music,' and I'm reading your profile, I immediately assume that you like the kind of music I like," he said. "But if you tell me specific music you like, we might have different interests, and that's less attractive to me."

Online Jugglers

It's not just too much information that makes online dating confusing—it's too many choices. Aren't there five new "matches" that arrive in your e-mail box each day? Even if none of them is remotely interesting, doesn't it still give you hope that of the next five, one might be The One?

Match.com, I noticed, seems to encourage daters to keep as many irons in the fire as possible. As soon as you send an e-mail to a potential mate, the "mail sent" confirmation screen automatically flashes the message, "Take a look at other members with profiles like [the person you just e-mailed]"—then shows you several *more* people who might interest you. Before the first person even *receives* your e-mail, you're given new choices to consider.

When that happens, Ariely said, we short-change people in a way we wouldn't if there were fewer options. In one study, he and his colleagues got data from an online dating site and looked at people they labeled "jugglers"—those who were managing fifteen or more communications at once.

"The jugglers were writing very bad-quality e-mails to each other," Ariely said. "If you had to write twenty e-mails, how good could they be? So they probably seemed less interesting to the people they e-mailed, because of these rushed, bad-quality e-mails."

At the same time, he said, because the stakes are so low, we have a hard time letting people go. If all it takes to keep someone in consideration is an e-mail, why not correspond with that person, and ten others? In the real world we may be considered too picky, eliminating people prematurely before getting to know them, but in the online dating world, we might be casting too wide a net, unable to eliminate anyone.

"When these people over-juggle," Ariely said, "they don't have the attention to give to the one person who would really work best for them. But because they don't know who that one person is, they keep juggling and end up with nobody."

That's exactly what happened when Ariely followed these jugglers' outcomes. He looked at people who'd exchanged phone numbers or set up dates, and found that people who juggled less not only wrote longer, more thoughtful e-mails—they also ended up going on an actual date. The jugglers, meanwhile, sat home at their computers, juggling.

Okay, so what happens once people meet? Ariely didn't follow these particular subjects, but he did find, more generally, that these kinds of meetings don't go as hoped for because of all those exaggerated expectations.

"But they never learn from this," Ariely explained. "Each time, they don't stop and think, 'I'll have more realistic expectations next time.' Instead, they overexaggerate every time!"

That's because despite the level of detail in these profiles, it's very hard to tell what a person is like from what is essentially a catalogue. Or as he put it, "It's like reading the ingredients on a box of food and imagining what it would taste like."

And that's assuming the list of ingredients is accurate. Part of the problem with online profiles is that we don't always have perfect insight into who we are, or the ability to describe ourselves well in a questionnaire. I remember looking at my personality assessment on eHarmony.com a few years ago and feeling like it didn't capture who I was at all. Was that because I answered their questions with a lack of insight, or because their assessment couldn't quite capture the nuance of my temperament? I was left with a very postmodern dilemma: I wouldn't want to date the kind of guy who would want to date the kind of woman this test revealed me to be. I'd become the Groucho Marx of online dating.

To avoid these problems, Ariely and his colleagues created a different kind of online dating site. Instead of having a profile, each person was represented by, say, a red square or a green triangle, and you'd move around a virtual space. If you were in close proximity to someone, you could start talking. You could wander through an art gallery together and talk about the exhibit. You got to know each other's personalities. You basically went on a virtual date in this virtual world—not knowing anything about each other.

Then, Ariely said, these people all had to go to a real-life speed dating event. At the event, some people had been on Ariely's site before and some hadn't. When it was over, each participant was asked who they'd like to go on a second date with. The results? "They were twice as likely to want to go on a second date if they met through our site," Ariely said.

"How tall you are and what your hair color is—that's not what matters, even though people say it is," he explained. "I think in dating the issue is that we don't know what's important to us."

The M&M Test

I was starting to think that I had no idea what was important to me, either, especially when I ran my dating history by Eli Finkel, a newly married social psychologist at Northwestern University. I told him that I'd always sought out certain types of men, but they didn't necessarily make me happy in the long-term. Was it possible that I didn't know what traits I actually wanted in a mate?

"If you're like most people, then yes," he said.

Finkel told me about an experiment he'd done with his colleague Paul Eastwick to see if the characteristics that people *said* they required in a partner were really what they ended up finding important.

First, they asked single people to report on how much they were looking for certain characteristics—from physical traits to earning potential to warm-heartedness. Subjects rated these on a scale from 1 to 9, in terms of importance. Then they had these people do speed dating. After the meetings, you'd rate each person in the room on the characteristics you'd said you were seeking. Then you'd rate your romantic interest in each person. And if later you went on a date with one of these people, you'd report on how much you enjoyed the date.

Turned out, people's stated preferences didn't do a good job of predicting who they wanted to go out with or had a good time with.

According to Finkel, "There was a lack of correlation between what people said they wanted on the questionnaire, and what they actually picked when they met a real, live person."

Why is that? How can we be so out of touch with what we really want?

Finkel explained it using my favorite candy from childhood, M&M'S.

"If you ask people why they like M&M'S," he said, "they might tell you it's because of the candy shell. But if you give them another candy with the same shell, they won't like it as much as the M&M. So it's not the shell. It must be something else that they like about the M&M."

In other words, we know *that* we like the M&M, but we can't explain *why*.

What does this have to do with dating? Everything, Finkel believes. "People can accurately tell you *what* they like, but not *why*. So if a woman says, 'I'm attracted to this man,' that's accurate. She *is* attracted to him. But if she says it's because he makes money, that might not be the accurate explanation. It might actually be because he's generous."

That's the mistake many of us make: Our must-haves and deal-breakers are the "what," when they should be the "why."

Eastwick, Finkel's colleague, explained it to me like this. You might think, "I'd like to meet somebody who is a lawyer and makes a stable living." But really, you'd be just as happy with somebody who's a composer and works project to project. How can that be? Eastwick says it's because you really wanted someone cultured and intellectual. You thought you wanted a lawyer because he has a stable career, but really it was that kind of *mind* that appealed to you.

Eastwick believes that the "what/why" problem is compounded by another problem: having standards that are too specific. He brought this up when I mentioned a friend who's an art historian at a local museum and wants a guy who "gets" the art world.

Eastwick laughed. "He may not need to be into art to the same degree she is. It sounds like what she really wants is someone intelligent and thoughtful. So if the guy is interested in politics and watches C-SPAN, that's a trade-off she'd probably be happy with."

No wonder Internet dating seems so hard. If we aren't accurate about what we want, we're probably looking for the wrong things.

It's not surprising, then, that according to a 2005 Pew study on American online dating habits, roughly half of the singles who had tried online dating had actually gone on a date as a result, and only about a third of those had formed long-term relationships. So if only a fraction of that third of a half got married, the odds weren't great. But it wasn't impossible. I knew several people who married someone they'd met online.

The question was, how could I increase my odds? I was counting on Evan Marc Katz, the dating coach, to help me figure that out.

8

Mondays with Evan

Session One: The Percentages

"Just tell me," I said to Evan when we were sitting by my computer at our first dating coaching session, "do you think I'll find someone I'll be happy with if I do this?" Evan was asking me to "drill down" to what was really important in a spouse, and I was having trouble.

Evan had told me to sign up with two dating sites the night before. Now, we were filling in my search preferences with an eye toward realistic percentages.

On the desired height range, I wanted to check off 5'10" to 6' tall. Evan reminded me that I'm 5'2" and, he said, the average height of the American male is 5'9" or so.

"How important is height for long-term happiness?" he asked. He had a point. I moved it down to 5'7". Evan pushed further.

"What does it matter whether a guy is a head taller than you or two inches taller?"

He suggested broadening the range to 5'5", but I typed in 5'6". I knew it shouldn't matter, but it did. I couldn't picture myself with someone 5'5".

"I don't want to date someone I wouldn't marry," I explained.

"You don't know who you're going to marry until you date them," he replied. "You could meet someone who's five feet five and cool and quirky and the height wouldn't matter."

I left it at 5'6", and Evan raised an eyebrow. "You aren't facing the reality of the percentages."

"The reality sucks," I said.

"The reality doesn't suck," Evan said. "If you didn't have the fantasy, the reality would be just fine."

Next we selected my desired age range. I was proud of myself for choosing 35 to 48 years old.

"See, I can be flexible," I said. "That's a fourteen-year range."

Evan laughed. "People are always flexible on the end that doesn't matter. They're flexible on the younger end instead of where it really counts, which is on the older end. It's not a real sacrifice to say I'll go out with someone younger or taller. How about increasing it to fifty-two?"

I typed in 50. This kind of thing went on for another ten minutes, with me "stretching" as far as I could in every category and Evan shooting me dubious looks.

Then we were ready to start a search.

I tapped on my keyboard and dozens of men popped up. I checked out a few and ruled out one who looked interesting but listed "any" as the desired education level for his prospective mate. In other words, his partner's highest level of education could be high school.

"Why would someone with a graduate degree want to date

someone who only has a high school degree?" I asked. "Obviously, he doesn't want to date his equal. He doesn't want someone smart."

"Or maybe," Evan said, "he'd prefer to date someone highly educated but he's being open-minded because he thinks he might meet a smart woman who took a nontraditional path and didn't go to college to get where she is now. I don't think he consciously said, 'High school—I need one of those!' I think he just clicked on the 'any' button. Maybe he's simply being nonjudgmental. You're judging him for being nonjudgmental?"

I guess I was. By disqualifying a guy who doesn't discriminate, was I being overly discriminating?

We looked at another profile—a guy who was reasonably cute, age-appropriate, and had a thoughtful profile. But when I read what he was looking for in a partner, I gave Evan the thumbs-down sign. This guy talked about romantic baths together, romantic walks on the beach, romantic Sunday mornings, romantic this and that. I figured he wouldn't be a good match for me, a single mom with little time for that kind of romance. I was looking for the kind of romance that comes in day-to-day family life, in a contented domesticity. I needed someone who understood the mundane life of a parent with a toddler.

Evan smiled. "You're taking this as a literal representation of who this person is!" he said. "He probably spent five minutes answering the question in an idealized way. Just because he didn't say, 'And if you're a single mom, I'll rub your back after you finish cleaning up the puke,' you're not even going to consider him? If you dissect every single person this way, nobody's going to be qualified to date you."

I thought about my percentages and moved Mr. Romantic onto my "hotlist." Then I clicked on the next profile. The guy wasn't super-attractive to me, but he was doctor who does transplants and, given my own background in science, he seemed really interesting.

I read more. He grew up on the East Coast. I liked that—check. He'd been married before—check. He had kids—check. His hobbies were boating, motorcycling, travel, sports, bingo, and canasta—bzzzz!

"Bingo? Canasta?" I said. "He's only forty-five, but he acts like a sixty-year-old. What *is* canasta?"

"You're nixing this guy based on his hobbies?" Evan asked.

"It's not just the bingo. Motorcycles are the biggest turnoff to me," I explained. "It's a whole subculture I find really unappealing. And look—he says he 'reads' books on tape. He doesn't even read, and I'm a writer."

I could tell that Evan had been through this before with his clients. He raised his eyebrows, flashed a knowing smile, and waited for me to finish my rant.

"You're trying too hard," Evan said. "You're micromanaging this in a way that's going to handicap you. Your evolution to finding a happy relationship is in understanding that we can't change the men out there—they are who they are—so something has to give on your end. I'm not telling you to go out with this guy, but he's a perfect example of a guy who's not being given a chance."

I shook my head. "Bingo and motorcycles and books on tape? We're not compatible."

"You have no idea if you're compatible," Evan said. "What you have to push through, because it's not going to come naturally, is your laundry list of credentials and how it's supposed to look. You can be happy with someone who has most of what you're looking for."

Just then I spotted a guy who was exactly what I was looking for.

"Oooh," I said, clicking on a cute 40-year-old. I read on. He had an interesting profile. He was funny. He had a creative but stable-sounding job. I liked what he wrote about what he was looking for in a partner—it pretty much described my personality.

"There's just one problem," Evan said.

"What?" I asked. This guy looked really promising. What could possibly be wrong here?

"His desired age range is twenty-eight to thirty-five. He says he wants kids."

"I have a kid," I said.

"He's not looking for someone with a kid. If he were, he'd have a higher age range. He wants someone to have his own biological kids with."

"But if he met me, we'd probably like each other. We seem to have similar personalities and interests. Why shouldn't I just e-mail him and see if he replies?"

"You can do that," Evan said. "But what would you do if someone who was fifty-five e-mailed you? You're the equivalent to him of a guy who's fifty-five to you. You're just a few years out of this age range, but a critical few years if he wants kids. He probably won't e-mail you back. It's not a good use of your time. What you need to do is focus on the people who are looking for someone like you. It doesn't matter who you're looking for if he's not looking for you."

"It just seems so unfair to be ruled out that way," I said, even though I routinely ruled out guys that way.

"You think you're above the rules because you have a lot going for you," Evan said. "But it doesn't work that way, as you've probably noticed. This is a slog, it's a lot harder than it used to be, and I agree, it isn't even fair. He probably *would* like you in person. But he'd probably also worry that you were too old to have kids with him. So you can try to buck the rules and end up frustrated, or you can try to work within what's realistic in terms of percentages and find the right guy for you."

SAYING YES INSTEAD OF NO

Evan clicked over to a feature on Match.com called "reverse search"—it shows guys who meet your search criteria, but who are also looking for someone like you. Not surprisingly, none of the guys were in the 35 to 45 range. The youngest I saw was 46.

"Here's what I want you to do for next week," Evan said. "I want you to pick one guy out of every twenty that appear on your reverse search list. That's just 5 percent of the guys who meet the desired traits you chose earlier today."

That seemed pretty doable, but Evan had one more suggestion. When there are things I find unappealing about a person, I should try to be more accepting than judgmental. If a guy writes a long, awkward e-mail, for instance, it doesn't mean he's a dork. Maybe he was nervous, or is new to online dating, or cares enough to take the time to send a personal note instead of a snappy pickup line.

"Look for reasons to say 'yes' instead of 'no,'" he reminded me. "Screen in rather than constantly screening out. Always ask yourself this: If an interesting guy were right in front of you, would you honestly turn that person away because of a few pounds or inches, or a sentence in a profile that you don't like? If so, that's fine. Just don't complain when you can't find anybody suitable because you've eliminated every potential guy on a technicality. Because if these guys eliminated people on technicalities, they probably wouldn't date you, either."

Ouch. I hadn't thought of it that way before. I'd been so focused on whether I was interested in a guy that I barely considered whether he'd be interested in me. So Evan told me to write down all the reasons someone *wouldn't* want to date me—all the things a potential boyfriend would have to put up with if he chose to be with me.

I jotted down a few things and handed them to Evan. He looked over my list.

"That's it?"

"What?" I asked. "Am I missing something?" I'd already written that I'm short and neurotic and like a lot of personal space.

"Um, I don't know," Evan said. "Maybe that you're a perfectionist?"

I didn't see what was wrong with that. Isn't that a good thing?

Evan told me I was making a classic mistake: We think we're such a good catch that whatever is "wrong" with us won't be a problem for a potential mate. We think, *yeah, I'm a perfectionist, but that means I'm conscientious!* Rarely do we think, *Yeah, I'm a perfectionist, and that makes me really rigid and hard to live with.*

Which is why, he continued, many people list things that actually sound positive: *I'm too ambitious (instead of I'm ruthless). I'm too honest (instead of I'm insensitive). I'm too giving (instead of I'm needy). I'm too independent (instead of I'm a workaholic). I'm too analytical (instead of I'm too judgmental).*

"Think about what someone would *really* have to put up with to be with you," he said. I gave it another shot, and soon I came up with things like: *I'm overly sensitive. I can't cook anything other than pasta. I can be pathologically indecisive, which always drives boyfriends nuts. I get stressed out easily, and when I do, it's never a pretty sight. I have several profoundly annoying habits, like insisting that my things stay exactly where I've placed them, even if they're in someone else's way. I won't use a cell phone because I think they cause brain tumors, so if you want to reach me, I'll have to be near a landline. And the list went on . . . and on.*

No wonder I'd screwed up my dating life: I wanted to feel secure and relaxed in a relationship, but if I was with someone truly as flawed as me, I'd feel dissatisfied because he was so different from my ideal. And if this flawed person was excited about me, I'd say he was coming on too strong or, worse, seemed desperate. But the second someone closer to my "ideal" happened to want to date me, I was constantly on edge, trying to be "on" and entertaining, and feeling insecure because those men always had countless women vying for their attention. The flawed men always seemed too excited about me, and the idealized men didn't seem excited enough.

I knew that looking at my flaws was important in accepting other people's flaws, but suddenly, seeing them there in black and white, I wondered why anyone had ever dated me at all.

"That's good," Evan laughed. "So next time you're about to rule out some guy because he's not your ideal, try to focus on the good things about him, because some guy is going to have to focus on the good things about you, even though he may have wanted someone more easygoing or taller. Every time you start to dissect some guy, note that he's willfully ignoring all of this in order to go out with you. We want to be tolerated for our moodiness, but we want someone who's never moody. We want to feel attractive even when we let our bodies go, but we want someone who's fit. Doesn't that seem hypocritical?"

It did seem hypocritical—I wanted men to accept me for who I was, but I wasn't willing to accept them for who they were. In the past, I'd always focused on what compromises I'd have to make to be with someone else, but I didn't seriously consider the second part—that being with me wouldn't be winning the lottery either. And no wonder. Like most women, I had friends constantly telling me what a great "catch" I was, that any guy would be "lucky" to have me, and that I should never compromise when choosing a mate.

But Evan said that what many women look at as "compromise" is really just plain old "acceptance."

Of course, he wasn't suggesting that I have a personality transplant and suddenly become Ms. Go-With-The-Flow. He was simply suggesting that in order to reduce the number of filters I used to screen men out, I'd have to change my perspective. It's easy to find the things you dislike about a person, but it's more productive to find the things you like.

He told me about a psychologist named Judith Sills, who wrote a wonderful book called *How to Stop Looking for Someone Perfect and Find Someone to Love*. In her book, Sills says that every person is a package deal, or like the blue plate special at a diner. There are "no substitutions." You have to take the annoying habits and unpleasant features along with the rest of the meal. You may have to deal with a metaphorical side dish you aren't crazy about. "If you require that someone fulfill your perfect picture," Sills writes, "you're in for a long-term relationship with your fantasies."

That's exactly what Evan was trying to tell me. As he got up to leave, he reminded me of my assignment: Pick one out of every twenty guys who met my search criteria and who were also looking for me. E-mail three of them. We'd compare notes the following Monday.

9

It's Not Him, It's You

I was sitting at my computer trying to pick one of every twenty guys on Match.com when my friend Lisa called and asked what I was up to. I told her about Evan's assignment and suggested that she try it, too. Lisa, who is 35 and single, groaned. She said it sounded like a good plan, but she was completely burned out on dating—online or otherwise. She didn't want to talk about dating tonight. It just made her more panicked about still being single.

"Let's talk about movies, books, global warming, the latest episode of *Weeds*—anything but men," she said.

How different this was from two years earlier, when Lisa was 33 and all she wanted to talk about was men. Or, rather, one man—her boyfriend. Lisa had been dating Ryan for a year. He was a 33-year-old lawyer, and she was smitten. They had a lot of fun together, they shared the same goals for a family, and they seemed compatible as friends and lovers. In fact, Ryan had been making comments about marriage. But something didn't feel right.

"He just doesn't fuss over me," Lisa said toward the end of that first year together. "It's not the way I'm used to being treated in a relationship."

At the time, I completely understood what she meant: She didn't feel *adored* by her boyfriend. He told her he loved her, but he never said that he was *the luckiest guy in the world* to have found her. He said she was pretty, but not *the most beautiful woman he had ever met*. He brought her Tylenol when she had the flu, but not flowers for no reason. He was consistently sweet and loving toward her, but he wasn't demonstrative. He didn't put her on a pedestal the way other boyfriends had. Never mind that she didn't put him on a pedestal either. That was the guy's role. He was supposed to court *her*, right?

One day, after another marriage comment, Lisa shared her doubts with her boyfriend. "I just don't feel that you're totally in love with me," she said.

"But I am!" he insisted. He couldn't understand why she felt that way, and Lisa couldn't explain it—it was just a feeling, but one she couldn't let go of. Each time she brought it up, he would seem perplexed, and she would feel rejected. He would then attempt all kinds of romantic gestures to prove his love—leaving a chocolate kiss with a sweet note on her pillow in the morning, calling in the middle of the day just to say he loved her. Lisa was charmed by these gestures, but she also didn't trust them: "I want him to *want* to do these things," she'd said at the time. "But now he's only doing them because I *asked* for them."

Still, Lisa tried to feel reassured because even if the gestures felt forced, it was sweet of Ryan to make the effort. But then, two months later, Lisa and Ryan were at an engagement party and the groom-to-be said in a toast to his bride-to-be that he could never love anyone as much as he loved her. That got Lisa thinking, and when she and Ryan were in the car on the way home, she asked him a question: "If something happened to me and I died young, do you think you could love another woman as much as you love me?"

He thought about it for a minute. "Well, it would be different from the love I have for you," Ryan replied.

"Different, as in you loved me more?" Lisa asked.

"Different as in . . . different," her boyfriend said. As he reached for her hand, he asked, "Why does it matter? I want to be with *you*, not some hypothetical other woman. I don't want to think about you dying. I love *you*. It would be hard to meet someone I love as much. But if I died, I'd expect that you'd fall in love again and it would be different from our relationship, but that you'd go on and live your life."

Three weeks later, Lisa broke up with him.

"I wanted him to be absolutely crazy about me," Lisa said now, two years later. "The fact that he could imagine loving another woman as much meant, to me, that I wasn't the love of his life. I wanted him to say, 'I could imagine getting remarried, but I'd never love her as much as I love you.'"

I asked Lisa what would happen if the hypothetical situation were reversed. If she'd married Ryan, and he died young, could she imagine falling in love again?

There was a long pause. "Yeah," she admitted. "I think I know, intellectually at least, that you can fully love more than one person in your lifetime. But in my heart, I want a guy to feel that way about me and only me anyway."

At the time, I'd backed her up completely. Now, though, as I thought about what Evan called my "unreasonable expectations" when I clicked through online profiles, suddenly I felt that Lisa was being unreasonable, too. And yet, in other areas of our lives, we were considered generally reasonable people. So what was going on here?

Too Good for an Ordinary Relationship

Dr. Michael Broder, a Philadelphia-based psychologist who specializes in relationships, thinks that many single women today bring a dangerous sense of entitlement to dating. Wanting to be adored in that fantasy way, he believes, is another unreasonable requirement on some women's already unreasonable checklists.

"I hear all the time, 'If I can't have a guy who is this, that, or the other thing, I'd rather be alone,'" he told me. "So I say, 'Okay, but be prepared to get your second choice. Because with that sense of entitlement, that's what you'll probably get: being alone.'"

For these women, he said, not only is the imagined guy a fantasy, but so is an actual relationship. After all, there's a limit to what a relationship can provide, and Dr. Broder feels that women in this frame of mind are looking for a relationship from the perspective of what the guy can provide *for them*—a "me-me-me thing"—instead of wanting something more reciprocal.

One of his patients, for instance, had recently said to him about her current boyfriend, "Why should I be with a guy who's less successful than me? I might as well be alone!"

Dr. Broder says he sees a heightened sense of entitlement that previous generations didn't have. Our mothers might have wished, but certainly didn't expect, that their husbands would constantly want to please them, be attracted to them, entertain them, enjoy sharing all their interests, and be the most charming person in the room. Instead, they knew that marriage involved failing health, aging, boredom, periods of stress and disconnection, annoying habits, issues with children, and hardships and misunderstandings of all sorts. But many women today seem to be looking for an idealized spiritual union instead of a realistic marital partnership.

"You end up with the type of woman today who sees herself as too good for an ordinary relationship," Dr. Broder said. "But ask happily married women about their marriages, and they'll probably tell you they're pretty ordinary."

So how did "ordinary" become the kiss of death in dating?

IS HE IN MY LEAGUE?

Maybe it has to do with our egos. For all the talk about women suffering from low self-esteem, Dr. Broder says that many take the "girl power" message of *I'm fabulous!* so far that nobody's good enough for them.

I thought about the 29-year-old acquaintance I'd set up on a date a few years ago with a guy who, I told her before the date, reminded me of her.

"He's cute and loves old movies," I said. "He's a lot like you."

So she went on the date, and came back insulted.

"How could you have said that he's like me?" she asked.

I had no idea what she meant.

"You didn't tell me he was so scrawny!" she explained. Well, so was she.

"And he has that weird hair," she said. He does, but just a year earlier, she had a purple streak in hers. I asked what she was expecting.

"I guess someone more dynamic," she said. "I mean, we could talk about old movies and he was sweet, but when you said he was like me, I was expecting someone more . . ." She trailed off, but I knew what she was trying to say: "Do you think this guy is at my level?"

Well, yes. Yes, I did. And I also thought that if she could see herself accurately and not as Angelina Jolie—she might have really liked him. They were both cute-ish, nice, and perfectly enjoyable people, but they wouldn't blow you away with their looks or charisma when they walked into a room. They were ordinary people.

Like most of us. (He, of course, is now engaged to someone a lot like her, but without her attitude. She, of course, is still single.)

The more I talked to Dr. Broder, the more I wondered if this level of self-involvement was a large part of what makes it hard to find a guy. Can it get to the point where we think we're so special—so uniquely exceptional and appealing—that we lose perspective entirely? I used to think, *yeah, I have high standards, but I can't help it if I have good taste.* (Speaking of good taste, never mind that the guys I *have* chosen haven't always turned out to be so fabulous, either.) Our generation of women is constantly told to have high self-esteem, but it seems that the women who think the most highly of themselves are at risk of ego-tripping themselves out of romantic connection. The more highly we think of ourselves, the more critical we are of perfectly good guys.

It's almost like being an Olympic judge who gives men a "husband" rating: Everyone starts off with a 10, and then the judge deducts points for anything less than perfect. He's not funny enough? Take off two points. He's got a unibrow? Take off another one. Wouldn't a better way to date be starting off at zero and *giving* people points for assets like kindness and warmth instead?

I've always mentally deducted points when deciding whether to date someone. If, for example, I wanted someone smart, funny, and cute, but he turned out to be smart, funny, cute, and nerdy, I'd forget that I got the "smart, funny, and cute" and focus instead on the nerdy. I'd focus on the disappointing aspects instead of feeling lucky to have found the positive ones.

That's what entitlement can do.

You're Both Dysfunctional

Toning down the attitude doesn't just help in dating—it makes marriages better, too. That's what Gian Gonzaga, a psychologist and senior scientist at eHarmony.com who met his wife while working in the famous "marriage lab" at UCLA, told me. His research, which involves studying six hundred couples over the span of several years, focuses on relationship satisfaction and the predictors of marriage success.

"Happily married people believe that their partners are better than the average person, even though that's statistically impossible," Gonzaga explained. "We call those 'positive illusions.' It's not that people don't complain about their spouses or have disagreements. It's that at the end of the day, they still see them as superior to most of the people out there."

In dating, he said, this works the opposite way for many single people who can't seem to find the right person. Instead of viewing the people we're dating through a positive lens, we view *ourselves* as superior. That's why people often attribute what's lacking in a relationship to their partner. But Gonzaga says it goes both ways.

"We tend to be attracted to people who are similar to us in terms of emotional stability, intellect, and competence," he said. "So if you date people who always seem dysfunctional, you're probably equally dysfunctional. If this person is neurotic, you probably are, too. To attract the kind of person you have in your mind, you have to *be* that kind of person. It's not that all the guys you dated weren't good enough for you. People need to realize that they bring their own selves into the equation."

In successful relationships, Gonzaga said, couples appreciate each other's good points instead of focusing on the flaws—because we all have them. A woman in Indiana tried to tell me the same thing. Laura, who has been married for twelve years, observed: "We women like to imagine ourselves as goddesses who are worthy of a man's total worship and devotion, and we are incensed when he fails to give us that. Unfortunately, we get bed hair, body odor, wrinkles, thickness in the middle, and bad attitudes. We would not easily excuse such things in men, yet we expect men to overlook them in us."

I HAVE TO TALK ABOUT *SEX AND THE CITY*

I know, I know—it's become such a cliché to talk about *Sex and the City* that I almost don't want to bring it up. But I can't resist because it seems related to this attitude of entitlement.

On the one hand, the media made a huge deal when the movie based on the mega successful book and series earned nearly $200 million in the United States alone, because it showed that audiences would pay to see strong women on the big screen. But I think it also showed something else: that we can't seem to tell the difference between "strong" and "self-centered."

In case you were one of the few single women who missed the movie, Samantha tells her wonderful boyfriend, who stood by her through breast cancer, that she's leaving him because, "I love you, but I love myself more"—and the entire audience cheered! Now, this was a boyfriend who was loyal and loving and hot and put up with her demands and went through cancer with her, and she decided to leave him because she's in love with *herself*. And this was supposed to be empowering? Reverse the genders (she sticks by him through a grueling bout of prostate cancer; he bails!), and I'm betting the entire audience would have booed and called the guy a total ass.

Samantha isn't the only character with a raging sense of entitlement. Carrie is a nightmare Bridezilla who's outraged when her fiancé tells her he'd be happy to marry her at City Hall. He says he cares not about a wedding day, but about being with her every day.

So what does she do? Carrie and her equally self-absorbed friends go off to Mexico on her would-be honeymoon and—guess what?—complain about men. Her circus of a wedding day didn't go as planned, and now she's on her honeymoon without her beloved husband-to-be. Is this "strong" or "spoiled"?

The TV series wasn't much different. Each week, the characters would dissect various men. There was no room for imperfection, and if the guy didn't also feel that his girlfriend was perfect, well, obviously, she should dump him.

"If you're not totally in love with me and crazy about me," Carrie once told Big, "and if you don't think I'm the most beautiful woman you've seen in your life, then I think I should leave."

Any rational adult knows that back on planet Earth, few men think the woman they're with is the most beautiful person they've seen in their life—and vice versa. But like the SATC gals, many women expect men to fawn over them as though they're queens. That's precisely why these otherwise attractive heroines seemed to have everything but the man. They treated love the way 16-year-old sophomores do, forgetting that 16-year-old girls aren't exactly ready for real-life marriage.

"Do you really think there are a lot of women out there like Carrie?" my friend Elizabeth, a single 31-year-old editor in North Carolina, asked me. Before I could reply, she went on to describe a guy who would write her sweet notes and who she was sort of falling for through his writing.

"He listens attentively to my daily trials and asks me lots of questions about my life, which, I find, most guys are not good about doing," she said. "He also responds to all e-mails and texts quickly and wittily. He seeks out cool concerts for us to go to. He told me I was exactly what he was looking for. What girl doesn't want to hear that?"

But, she continued. "At the same time, he just seems sort of awkward with me, and his place is plastered with Tar Heels stuff. It seems juvenile. It's like a high school boy's room, minus the pinups. It feels like the sports equivalent—Tar Heels porn. He doesn't go hiking. He doesn't speak a foreign language. None of those things seem to fit my idea of the guy I wanted. Am I that girl?"

Grounds for Dismissal

Maybe a lot of us are. My friend Mark, a divorced dad, sent me an e-mail exchange he'd had with Melanie, a never-married woman he met online. They seemed to click, so he and Melanie were making plans to meet in person.

Melanie

From: <Melanie>

To: <Mark>

Sent: Friday, June 13, 2008 2:21 PM

Subject: Re: Checking in

Mark—what about tomorrow Sat. @ 11 am?

Mark

From: <Mark>

Date: Fri, 13 Jun 2008 23:30 PM

To: <Melanie>

Subject: Re: Checking in

Works for me. Meet you in front of Aroma?

Melanie

From: <Melanie>

To: <Mark>

Sent: Saturday, June 14, 2008 7:36 AM

Subject: Re: Checking in

I've lost interest. You are dismissed.

Mark

From: <Mark>

Date: Sat, 14 Jun 2008 07:43 AM

To: <Melanie>

Subject: Re: Checking in

Seriously? What happened?

Melanie

From: <Melanie>

To: <Mark>

Sent: Saturday, June 14, 2008 7:58 AM

Subject: Re: Checking in

Didn't hear from U til almost the next day, indicating I was not a priority . . . That does not work 4 me.

Mark

From: <Mark>

Date: Sat, 14 Jun 2008 8:10 AM

To: <Melanie>

Subject: Re: Checking in

Well, I guess that'll teach me for not having a BlackBerry and being away from my computer yesterday from noon 'til late night, attending my son's college graduation ceremony and dinner with him afterward in Irvine. Because when you don't respond to someone's e-mail within a few hours, it couldn't possibly be because you're away from your computer, gotten into an accident, on a trip someplace, attending an important event, etc. The only possible reason is that you've placed the one who's e-mailed you into a low-priority status. Thank you for that insight that only jumping to conclusions can provide.

Melanie

[NO RESPONSE]

I asked Mark if he ever heard from Melanie again. "A few days later," he said, "she apologized and said she'd been under stress, and perhaps had overreacted—but still didn't want to meet."

According to Melanie's e-mail, "The momentum was lost."

Mark said this kind of self-centeredness is common. "There was also the childless woman I was dating, who gave me an ultimatum," he said. "I could either accept my children's invitation to a Passover seder with them at their place—or be with her and her relatives on Passover. If I accepted my children's invitation, I could forget about continuing the relationship with her."

What did he decide?

"You'll be stunned to know that she and I are not together anymore," he said dryly.

I asked other women what they thought of Mark's e-mail exchange with Melanie and the ultimatum from Mark's former girlfriend. Words like "insane," "inflexible," and "selfish" came up.

Still, we had to admit that, in a twisted way, we could understand why these women felt shafted: a dream guy wouldn't leave the woman waiting by her e-mail for nine hours. A dream guy would want to be with his beloved on a holiday more than with anyone else. (It's okay, of course, for a woman to prioritize her children over her boyfriend—and if he requested otherwise, *he'd* be considered selfish.)

The problem is, a dream guy doesn't exist (precisely because we've *dreamed him up*) and, even if he did, is this really the guy we'd want to be with? A guy who doesn't have a life except for us? A guy who doesn't spend the holidays with his own children?

Of course not. But imagine the conversations that Melanie and the Passover Chick, as she came to be known, had with their girlfriends about why it was necessary to dump Mark.

"What a jerk," they probably said, as their friends nodded and sipped their wine at yet another all-girl bar night where they searched for eligible men.

YES, HE'S WITH *HER*

Melanie may seem extreme, but many of us who carry around this sense of entitlement in dating don't even realize it. One woman who has been married for five years told me an interesting story.

When she was single, Danielle went to a married friend's dinner party. She was seated next to a guy she liked talking to very much, only to learn that the woman on his right was his fiancée. The woman was less attractive, charming, and witty than Danielle was. (I believe this: Danielle is very attractive, charming, and witty.) After everyone left, Danielle was hanging out with her friend who'd given the party, and complained that she was tired of meeting men who were already taken. She couldn't understand why all these other women managed to end up with great guys, but Danielle was still alone.

"What does she have that I don't?" Danielle asked, about the woman engaged to the guy she was interested in. Without missing a beat, her friend shot back: "Two things. One: compassion. And two: his love." Compassion, her friend said, is what leads to love.

Her friend had seen Danielle get excited about guys over the years, just like she was about that night's dinner party guest, only to find something "wrong" with him a month or a year later. This was a wake-up call for Danielle, who realized right then that if she continued to judge potential mates and always find them wanting, she would end up alone. The next guy she dated, she ended up marrying.

"After that conversation, I approached my next relationship completely differently," she told me. "I focused on appreciating what I liked about him, and being compassionate about the things I thought were wrong. And I realized I hadn't been appreciative of my boyfriends in the past."

Danielle admitted that she hadn't been aware of how her sense of entitlement affected her relationships. "I used to think, 'I'm just not getting what I want,' and break up with a guy. Then I realized, when I met my husband, that if I went in with this attitude of expecting things from him instead of appreciating who he was, I would be sabotaging myself. I made a conscious decision to feel pleased by what he offered to the relationship, instead of complaining about what he didn't. And I realized that I had no right to complain about something if I wasn't giving it in return! He said to me one day, 'I like being romantic, but I don't see why I have to be exclusively in charge of romance in this relationship.' And I realized that I expected all the romance to come from him, when maybe it would be nice if it went both ways, you know?"

As Dr. Broder explained, too often in dating we expect to be given a lot of things from men—constant compliments, vacations, meals, 24/7 emotional support, romantic gestures—and those men who don't meet our standards in any of these departments get the boot, unnecessarily.

One woman I spoke to broke up with a guy because she felt

that her boyfriend didn't call and check in enough during the day. Never mind that he was a doctor, which made it difficult to break away. She wanted someone who was "more available." The funny thing is, she thought the problem was that *he* needed to change. It never occurred to her that *she* might need to become a little more understanding. It never occurred to her that she might actually be happier and grow as a person if she made some changes on her end of the relationship.

A barber in Montana told me that this attitude is turning men off.

"I have boatloads of eligible men as clients," he said, "but many of them have told me that they're ready to write off dating entirely. They say that the modern American woman brings nothing to the relationship except this deep-seated hunger for him to be her everything—unless something better comes along."

Or as a 29-year-old single dentist in Atlanta put it: "Women are always asking, 'Where are all the good guys?' And I say, 'You can't see them with your nose in the air.'"

I thought of all the conversations I'd had with single friends over the years about how there just weren't enough good men out there. But now I was starting to discover something else. Maybe there were plenty of good men, but we were turning them off with our over-the-top expectations.

Maybe we needed to *get over ourselves*.

It's a humbling realization, but I knew it was true. I needed to get over myself. I, too, seemed to be suffering from this modern malady. It seemed clear that if I wanted to meet someone, I'd have to stop complaining about the men who were out there and focus instead on making better choices.

But how?

PART THREE

Making Smarter Choices

The perfect is the enemy of the good.

—Voltaire

10

Don't Be Picky, Be Happy

Here are two actual questions posed to *Slate* magazine's advice columnist:

> *Dear Prudence,*
>
> *I have a dilemma. I've been dating this guy for a little over two years. For a while I thought I should marry him . . . he's intelligent, ambitious, kind, and we don't fight or argue very often. But there are things about him that make me think we're not meant for each other. I've recently moved in with him, bringing with me all my belongings, as well as my two dogs and two cats. I love him, but I don't feel like this is even close to the fairy tale relationship I've always longed for. I guess what I need to know is, is there even such a thing as a fairy tale romance? I know I will always be loved and taken care of with him, but is that enough? Would I be*

settling if I agree to marry him? My last relationship lasted way too long (five years), and I knew we were never going to marry. I just don't want to waste five years with another man, only to decide it isn't meant to be. Do you think I should talk to him about it?

—Wondering

Dear Won,

Talk to him and say what? "Could you please be a little more like Prince Charming?" Unless you have a concrete idea of what he could do to help your fantasy along, like flowers every Friday or poems on your pillow, Prudie would not suggest you share with him your desire for a fairy tale romance. The qualities of his that you mention—intelligence, ambition, kindness, and a minimum of arguing, would certainly sound like Prince Charming to a boatload of women. And, my dear, he even welcomed your livestock when you moved in! As to your question—is there such a thing as a fairy tale romance? Prudie would say yes, and in fact she has had one. Alas, they do not endure. Fairy tales are to romance what fireworks are to the night sky. They are transient states . . . and while temporarily thrilling, not what one builds a life around.

—Prudie, historically

Hi Prudence,

After my eight-year marriage ended, I spent some time alone, followed by a series of dates with men who looked great on paper (well-educated, same tastes in books, music, art, etc.) but who were boorish, socially awkward, or downright boring in person. Now comes Mr. (Quite Possibly) Right, whom I've been seeing for nearly a year—a guy who is kind, appreciative, a great listener, and a fabulous lover. My only persistent qualm is that, with him, I miss the caliber of intellectual engagement I enjoyed so much with my ex. Mr. (QP) R is open to attending the museums and performances that interest me, but it's clear that I can't expect any new insights on these experiences from him, and that I'll always need to be the one seeking them out. I love my new beau and don't want to undervalue his many excellent qualities, but as we reach the one-year mark, I do worry I'll grow restless in a relationship that doesn't stimulate me intellectually. Am I focusing too much on a minor deficit, or does this sound like trouble waiting to happen?

—One Nagging Doubt

Dear Nagging Doubt,

I'd have a different answer if you wrote that you had met a man who's kind, appreciative, a great listener, and a brilliant cultural critic—but a total dud in bed. Obviously you and your former husband could talk about the latest Tom Stoppard until the wee hours, but that didn't keep the whole relationship from turning sour. You don't say your new guy is unintelligent, just that he's not interested in the same artistic pursuits you are. So what? If you want some lively discussion about a play or museum exhibit, invite another couple along to talk about it afterward over dinner. Or go to a show with a friend who shares your zeal. Probably your beau

*could write to me that you and he click in so many ways,
but all his previous loves have been fabulous skiers and
accomplished birdwatchers, and he wonders if over the
long-term he will be dissatisfied settling down with
someone who never will match their skills at these pursuits. Wouldn't you want to say, "Don't throw away
what we have because of skiing!"? But if you want to
begin your search again to find that so-far-undiscovered
person who suits you in every way, it sounds as if a
less picky woman will quickly find that Mr. (QP) R is
perfect.*

—*Prudie*

According to a social scientist named Barry Schwartz, there are
two kinds of people in the world: maximizers and satisficers, and
these two advice-seeking women seem like classic maximizers. In
fact, they sound like a lot of single women, including me.

This isn't a good thing, especially when it comes to dating.

In his eye-opening book *The Paradox of Choice: Why More Is
Less*, Schwartz explains the difference between maximizers and
satisficers like this: Say you want to buy a new sweater. You decide
that it needs to be well-fitting, stylish, not itchy, a pretty color, and
in your price range. Say it even has to go with a specific outfit. A
satisficer walks into a store or two, finds a sweater that meets all of
these criteria, and buys it.

She's done.

A maximizer, on the other hand, walks into a store, picks out a
sweater that meets all of these criteria, and thinks, *This sweater is
nice, but maybe I should look at that cute store down the street. Maybe I
can find something I like better. Maybe I can find something on sale.* So
the maximizer hides the pretty sweater on the bottom of the pile

(so that nobody else buys it) and goes to check out another store (or five).

Now, you might think that the maximizer will end up with a better sweater—after all, she's looked at more possibilities—but that's not necessarily the case. A satisficer isn't looking for the absolute best, but she does have high standards. The difference is, she stops when she's found something that meets those high standards.

She wants something stylish, and she's found it, so she doesn't wonder if she can find something *more* stylish at another store. She wants something in her price range, and she's found it, so she doesn't wonder if she can find a *better* value at another store. She wants a flattering fit, and she's found it, so she doesn't wonder if she can find an even *more* flattering fit at another boutique.

A maximizer, on the other hand, will spend another three hours or three days looking for the perfect sweater, even though she may not find anything better, leaving her to buy the sweater she'd hid under the pile on the display table. (If it's still there, which by now, it probably isn't. A satisficer has already bought it!)

But let's say that the maximizer does find a slightly cuter sweater, or a slightly less expensive one. Will she be happier with her purchase than the satisficer is with hers?

Probably not, Schwartz says. That's because while a satisficer is content with something great, a maximizer is content only with the absolute best. And since you can never be sure that you got the absolute best—you can't see every sweater in the entire city; new styles will appear in store windows the very next week and you may like one of those better—the whole process is fraught with anxiety.

Meanwhile, think of all the time and energy wasted on making this decision, all for 5 percent cuter, or ten dollars cheaper that, in the long run, won't really matter. Instead of having agonized for all that time, you'd be warm and stylish, and probably even get a few compliments.

But now, because you've put so much effort into finding the perfect sweater, the stakes are even higher for you to have picked *just the right one*. It's like women who say, "I've waited this long for Mr. Right, I'm not going to settle *now*." The longer you wait and the more you search, the "better" the sweater—or the guy—is going to have to be. You don't want to have gone through all that struggle and turmoil only to end up with a "good enough" sweater or a "good enough" guy just like the one you could have had and enjoyed years earlier. Which is all the more reason to buy the cute enough sweater and choose the good enough guy the first time around.

But Is a Guy Like a Sweater?

Okay, a sweater isn't a relationship, obviously, but whether it's about a sweater or a romantic partner, satisficers tend to be happier in life than maximizers. Satisficers know when they've found what they want, even if it's not perfect. Maximizers either keep looking for someone better and never choose anyone, or they choose someone but will always wonder whether they've settled. They don't understand that not getting 100 percent of what we want isn't just "acceptable"—it's normal.

When I called Barry Schwartz at Swarthmore College, where he's a professor, he explained the maximizer's predicament like this: "You're continually looking over your shoulder to see if there's something better. And the more you look over your shoulder, the less good you'll end up feeling about your partner or a potential partner—even though he's probably just as good, on balance, as the people you're looking at."

This is why, like those women who wrote to *Slate*'s advice columnist, a maximizer can date someone for years and still not know if she wants to marry him. She says she has to "be sure." But Schwartz says it's not that she's "not sure" how she feels about this particular person. It's that she's not sure if *someone better* might come around the bend. After all, will another year—after two years of dating—really provide some crucial new piece of knowledge about her boyfriend, some undiscovered quality he'd been hiding all along? Or will she spend that year in the same state of ambivalence that she spent the year before?

Instead of wondering, *Am I happy?*, maximizers wonder, *Is this the best I can do?* They experience what Schwartz calls *regret in anticipation of making a decision.* As he puts it in his book: "You imagine how you'll feel if you discover that there was a better option available. And that leap of imagination may be all it takes to plunge you into a mire of uncertainty."

The Husband Return Policy

Some people deal with their fear of buyer's remorse by hedging their bets: They live together so that they can decide later whether to fully commit. They buy the proverbial good enough sweater as long as it has a return policy. They may say that living together provides more information about how compatible they are in the long-term. They may even say that they care so much about having a successful marriage that they want to do everything they can to make sure it's the right one. But does living together provide such clarity?

The Centers for Disease Control and Prevention puts the divorce rate of people who live together before marriage at 12 percent higher than those who didn't cohabitate before marriage. And according to a study published in November 2008 by the sociologist Daniel Lichter of Cornell University, divorce rates for women who had lived with more than one man were twice as high as those who hadn't.

What's going on here?

Schwartz has some theories. He feels that people who live together as a "test run" might tend to be maximizers, people who want to be sure they're getting "the best" but then are never truly satisfied. Moreover, the very act of having that return policy mentality—"If it doesn't work out, we'll move out"—might make people less satisfied if they do go on to get married. He told me about a study cited in his book that found that people are more satisfied with nonreturnable items than they are with returnable ones.

"Almost everybody would rather buy in a store that permits returns than in one that does not," he writes in *The Paradox of Choice*. "What we don't realize is that the very option of being allowed to change our minds seems to increase the chances that we *will* change our minds. When we can change our minds about decisions, we are less satisfied with them."

But, according to Schwartz, "When a decision is final"—like, say, marriage instead of cohabitation—"we engage in a variety of psychological processes that enhance our feelings about the choice we made relative to the alternatives."

In other words, the longer you spend being indecisive—thinking that any given guy can be returned for another—the more likely it is that you'll focus on his faults, and nobody will measure up. One guy might seem great, but compare him to another guy who's smarter but more passive, and *both* choices start to look slightly less appealing. The first guy seems less smart, the second guy seems less proactive. It's easy to choose between "pretty good" and "completely wrong"; it's crazy-making to constantly choose between two pretty goods. Compared side by side, two pretty goods might start to look like two mediocres.

As Schwartz put it, "Our powers of interpretation can turn great things into mediocre things."

Every "8" Becomes a "6" over Time

So let's take another look at the woman I mentioned at the beginning of the book, the one who wrote to me and said she wasn't looking for a perfect 10—an 8 would be great. She was, in fact, already dating an 8. Remember her dilemma: *But what if I want a different 8?* She knows she needs to compromise, but in the back of her mind, she's wondering if she can compromise for something *better*. Maybe she can. There's certainly a difference between "being realistic" and being with the wrong person. But it's also possible that she was suffering from the problem of too many choices starting to make all the "pretty good" choices seem less appealing.

Or, Schwartz told me, there's still another possibility: Maybe she was tripped up by a psychological process called "adaptation."

"We get used to things," Schwartz said, "and then we take them for granted." It's kind of like how you can walk into an air-conditioned room on a really hot day and think that air-conditioning is the best thing in the entire world, only to forget it's there an hour later. You get used to it, and it's not so wonderful anymore—it's expected. It used to be a 10, but now it's just a 5.

Similarly, for the woman who wanted a different 8, her 8 may now have become a 6.

"Any new person will look better temporarily," Schwartz said. "The thing she has to remember is that every eight becomes a six over time. You can trade your six for a new eight, but eventually that eight will become a six, and you'll be trading him in for another eight, too." If, however, you fully expect the novelty of the 8 to morph into the comfort of the 6, you won't be disappointed. And by recognizing that you'll adapt to any person you choose, picking "the best" instead of "pretty good" won't seem as important either.

Schwartz's point is that satisficers don't end up with a sweater that's less good than they should have; nor do they pick a guy who's less good than they should have. They're happy because they know that good enough *is* good enough. They realize that nothing is perfect in life—not jobs, not friends, not sweaters, and not spouses—so taking the best available option and appreciating it makes sense.

Toxic Maximizers

To be fair, single men can be maximizers, too. Who doesn't know the guy who dates a string of seemingly wonderful women but can't commit to any of them? Still, Schwartz said the problem isn't these men, per se. It's that many women waste their time going after these men while overlooking satisficer men who can make them happy. Often maximizer women are dating maximizer men, only to find them wanting or to have them find us wanting. Two picky people don't make for a great couple.

That's part of the reason it's often an illusion that if we just wait long enough, we'll meet Mr. Right. The logic would be that the people left later on are "better" because they were so discriminating (after all, nobody was good enough so far). But just the opposite is probably true. The people who got married younger, who knew how to compromise and negotiate and sustain a marriage, are likely less demanding than those who felt they couldn't find anyone good enough. They tend to be better partners and parents. They're probably much more enjoyable to live with over the course of fifty years. All the more reason not only to seek out a satisficer, but to *be* one yourself.

"People often think they have to choose between two qualities, like looks and intelligence," Schwartz told me. "But you'll probably be happy with someone who has an acceptable degree of both." In other words, nobody's asking you to choose between the guy who's a 3 on looks and an 8 on intelligence and another guy who's an 8 on looks and 3 on intelligence. Most of the time, we're faced with a guy who might be a 6 on looks and a 7 on intelligence but an 8 on lifestyle and personality—nothing extreme on either end, but overall a pretty appealing person.

Maximizers consider this settling. They want an 8 on everything. Satisficers consider this a good deal. Ironically, it's the maximizers who, years later, look at the satisficers—with their husbands and families and contentment in life—and say, "I wish I had what *she* has." Well, it was there for the taking. The maximizers simply passed it up.

After all, satisficing isn't about settling for someone who doesn't have the qualities you're seeking. It's about finding someone who is *enough*, as opposed to someone who is *everything*.

MARRIAGE: THE GAME SHOW

When I asked Steven Martin, a demographer at the University of Maryland, why the number of single women is rising in every age category, he said he didn't have the data on why, but he had a personal theory. He believes that many women look at marriage this way:

Let's say you assume you'll have twenty relationships in your life. With every one, you're trying to decide if, say, Guy #3 is better than the possibility of the next seventeen. Some women might go for #3, but always wonder if numbers 4 through 20 would have made a better match. Others might pass on Guy #3 and end up with Guy #20, but spend an awful lot of time wondering if passing up Guy #3 was a big mistake. Others will simply stop getting asked out and end up alone. That's the thing about choice: If you don't choose anything, eventually you're left with nothing.

"I think there's a lot of wistfulness and regret out there," he said.

There sure was for me. All that second-guessing hadn't helped me to make better dating choices in the past, and it wasn't going to help me make better ones in the future. There will always be another nice, warm sweater in another store. And if there's one thing I knew for sure, it's that I didn't want to freeze to death while searching endlessly for the perfect one.

Mondays with Evan

Session Two—The Wrong Assumptions

"You need to do something about your gag reflex," Evan said when he came back the following Monday for our dating coaching session. He wanted to know why I hadn't been able to pick just one out of every twenty men the computer had matched me with. Why, we both wondered, was I having so much trouble letting go of my maximizer tendencies?

Partly, there was the reality of what I was facing: My matches weren't what they used to be. Against Evan's advice, I'd e-mailed the cute 40-year-old from our last session, the one whose desired age range went up to 35. As Evan predicted, he never responded.

I told Evan that, as a sociological (not to mention masochistic) experiment, for one day the week before, I'd changed my age to 31, and I got responses from several potentially interesting men. But when I listed my true age, 41, the most promising guy who wrote me was a 53-year-old former gym teacher whose idea of a vacation was gambling in Las Vegas, but who had a sense of humor and loved kids. Nothing was different in my profile except for my age: the photos, the essays, even the fact that I had a child were the same! I wanted to become a satisficer, but I was finding it a lot harder with the matches I was getting at 41.

"Of course it's harder," Evan said. "But think about it this way: Your market value may be lower than it was ten years ago, but it's also a lot higher now than it will be ten years from now. So I'd like you to try to reserve judgment upfront. Because I don't want to be having this same conversation with you when you're fifty-one and wondering why you turned down all the guys you could have had at forty-one."

Actually, I'd made that mistake already. A few days before, I e-mailed a cute, scuba-diving 40-year-old lawyer with a great profile. I was excited when he e-mailed back—until I opened the message. He reminded me that five years earlier, he found me online and sent me a note. We exchanged a bunch of e-mails, and then had a phone conversation—all of which he thought went well. But when he asked me out at the end of the call, I mumbled something awkward about how I didn't think we were a match.

As I read his e-mail, I vaguely remembered this, but I couldn't understand why I hadn't wanted to meet him. It was probably a ridiculous reason—like, I didn't feel immediate "phone chemistry" and therefore assumed that a date would be a waste of time. Now he was the most interesting guy I'd seen online. But he wasn't receptive to reestablishing contact. This time it was his turn to say, "No thanks."

So I knew Evan was right—later on, I'd regret not considering the guys available to me now. Still, I found it insulting to get e-mails from guys who were so old that I could be their daughter.

"Why is it insulting?" Evan asked. "Let's say that you're Harvard.

You get twenty-five thousand applications each year. Harvard doesn't feel insulted when somebody with a low GPA or poor SAT scores applies. They simply send a note saying, 'Thank you for your application.' They don't get mad at the people who applied but aren't qualified. But the more important difference between you and Harvard is that Harvard accepts nine percent of their applicants each year and you don't even accept nine percent of your applicants. Right now you're accepting two percent."

It was true. Of the fifty matches I viewed, I'd e-mailed only one—the guy I'd "hotlisted" at our last session even though I thought he might be "too romantic." We e-mailed back and forth a few times, then he simply disappeared. So much for romance.

"Let's take a look at your matches," Evan said. "I'm sure we can interest you in a few more."

THE GAG REFLEX

Apparently, I had a pretty loose gag reflex. The first guy Evan clicked on, I ruled out because his favorite movie was *You've Got Mail*.

"What kind of guy lists a Meg Ryan chick flick as his favorite film of all time?" I asked. "It's not just one of many movies he likes. It's his *favorite*."

"I'm going to give you a little electroshock every time you get judgmental," Evan said. "Besides, I liked that movie."

"You did not!" I couldn't believe it. An irreverent guys-guy like Evan?

"I did!" Evan said. "Actually, it's one of my favorite romantic comedies. Does that make me un-datable?"

"No, but that's because it's an aberration. You don't have sappy bad taste—I know what other movies you like. You're not a *You've Got Mail* kind of guy more generally."

"Then how do you know this guy isn't like me?"

Well . . . I didn't. I couldn't argue with that. I added Mr. Chick Flick to my hotlist.

"Oh, and one more thing," Evan said. "I was kidding. To make a point."

I wanted to kill him. "So you don't like *You've Got Mail*?"

"Never saw it."

"I hate you."

"Yeah, but it made you think, didn't it?" Evan asked.

"I still hate you."

Evan flashed a victorious smile. "Just doing my job, darlin'. You can't rule out a guy based on different taste in movies. It doesn't mean what you think it does. Maybe he wrote that because he thought it would impress women and make him come off as a sensitive guy. Or maybe he thinks Meg Ryan is hot. Who knows? You need to stop making the wrong assumptions."

It's a Profile, Not a Life Story

Evan told me that my problem was this: I was making up entire life stories about these guys based on one or two pieces of information. If a guy went to a fancy school, I assumed he was sophisticated. Not necessarily true. If a guy liked cheesy movies, I assumed he had bad taste in everything, or that we had completely different vibes. Not necessarily true again. If a guy couldn't spell, I assumed he wasn't smart, despite the fact that my friend Joy was married to a highly intelligent bad speller. In fact, she'd met Dave on Match.com, but before Dave posted his profile, he asked a writer friend to proofread it so it appeared error-free. Once Joy got to know Dave, she learned that he couldn't spell at all, but by then she also knew how smart he was.

"I almost missed out on meeting my husband, because if I'd

seen his profile with all the spelling mistakes, I never would have replied to his e-mail," Joy told me. "Besides, there's no correlation between great spellers and great boyfriends. All of the great spellers I used to date were slightly tortured guys, and none of them turned out to be great boyfriends."

That's exactly why Evan was saying assumptions are so dangerous. "Being a bad speller doesn't make someone a bad husband," he said. "There are different kinds of intelligence." I knew he was right. I mean, if there were online dating sites in Einstein's time, what would his essays have looked like? I thought about my friends' very smart and competent husbands—I had no idea if they could spell.

Evan suggested that if I wanted to find more hip, literary guys with cleverly written and correctly spelled profiles, I could check out Nerve.com—but that it skews younger and it might not be as relationship-oriented. He said that Match.com was a good choice for me because it's like the mall—everything's at the mall. Nerve is like a trendy boutique. Match has it all—from McDonald's to Bloomingdales.

"What about this guy?" Evan said, clicking on another profile.

"He's not attractive," I said.

"Really? He's got a nice smile."

I laughed. "That's like saying, 'He's got a mouth.' Do you know anyone who doesn't have a nice smile? Everyone has a nice smile, unless they're missing their front teeth."

"What's not attractive about him?"

On second glance, there was nothing unattractive about him. He was just kind of average-looking. Besides, he left the income question blank.

"He has no money," I said. "I can't support another adult. I already support myself and my son. I need to be with someone who can support himself. It says he's self-employed and he's hiding his income."

"How do you know he has no money?" Evan asked. "You're making another assumption that may have no basis in reality. I know many men who leave it blank because they don't want women to e-mail them just because they make a lot of money."

"Then they probably won't get a lot of e-mails from women," I said. "Think about it: Men don't want women to e-mail them for their money, and women don't want men to e-mail them for their looks. But if women don't post a picture, men won't e-mail us! When we hide our pictures, men assume we're not attractive. When they hide their income, we assume they have no money. We all make assumptions."

Evan let out a loud sigh. "Assume all you want," he said, "but you might pass up a guy who's financially stable but didn't feel like telling everyone his income. Look at this guy. He has a graduate degree in business. I'm sure he's not poor. Your MO is 'Shoot first, ask questions later.' But you might be shooting at the wrong target."

"Happy" Doesn't Mean "Gay"

How, I asked, could I know what the right target was? Wasn't I supposed to use these profiles as screening devices? I couldn't e-mail all ten thousand men on the site. I had to make assumptions based on what they wrote.

"Yes," Evan said, "but often your assumptions are misconceptions. *All guys who like bingo are grandpas. All guys who like books on tape don't read actual books.*

I knew that Evan was giving me good advice, but by now I was in a bad mood. It seemed so clear that I'd looked for the wrong things in a man when I was younger, and now, instead of being happily married to a good guy, I was spending my Monday lunch hour going through online profiles with a dating coach. I was tired of looking for The Guy and trying to figure out what it "meant" that he liked bingo or "read" books on tape. Trying to figure out what anything "meant" made me dizzy and depressed.

"See this guy?" I said to Evan, as I clicked on a profile. "This guy looks okay. But you know what? I remember him from ten years ago. What's wrong with him? Why can't he find a girlfriend? He's been on this site for ten years."

"So have you—just not every second for ten years," Evan replied. "You've had three long-term relationships in that time, and come back twice after the breakups. Maybe he has, too. Maybe he just broke up with someone he's dated for two years. You have to stop making these . . ."

"Assumptions!" I said. "I know."

It did seem that a lot of my assumptions were off and I was going to have to keep them in check if I wanted to meet anyone. So I went to my hotlist to show Evan the men I'd seen some potential in. The first was a marketing guy who seemed smart and interesting and had a clever sense of humor. He had thinning salt-and-pepper hair and he was on the "wide" side. He definitely looked older than his stated age of 46. But a message popped up that he was no longer on the site. I couldn't believe it.

"Even he's gone!" I told Evan. "That's amazing. *He* found someone!"

"Proof that some women are less judgmental than you are," Evan said, hoping to make me laugh. "Or maybe he's just taking a break because he'll be traveling for three weeks."

Evan clicked on another guy. "He seems interesting," Evan said. He did, but his picture gave me pause.

"He looks gay, doesn't he?" I asked.

"He looks happy!" Evan said.

"Yeah, but doesn't he look gay?"

"With his daughter in his arms? Probably not."

He looked totally gay to me. I don't care if he'd been married and had a kid. Maybe he got divorced because his wife left him after she discovered he was gay.

"There you go making up these life stories based on nothing more than a profile," Evan said. "Maybe he *is* gay—but nothing in his profile screams 'gay' to me. Is he the most macho-looking guy? No. But that doesn't make him gay. I know this is hard and that as a forty-one-year-old woman on Match.com, you're going to get a lot of commitment-phobes, players, financially unstable guys, unattractive guys, socially awkward guys, bitter divorced guys, much older guys, and guys who don't want kids than you would have ten years ago. Look in your in-box. I'm not telling you anything you don't already know. But are all the good ones taken? Not quite. It's just that you're not going to find them by making assumptions."

Finding Out if He's an "Eh" or an "Ugh"

Evan believes that people make assumptions precisely because dating is so exhausting. They want to know right away whether a guy is The One, even though the only information they have is a one-page profile.

"You want to read the last page of the book before you read the first page," he said, "but you can't. *I just want to know if he's smart. I want to know if he'll commit.* Women want to know what's going to happen. *If I meet this guy, he's going to be like this.* So you make assumptions about the last page of the book, but you have to read the book to know how it really turns out."

Or as my friend Kathy put it, "You know nothing about potential until you sit down with them. And even then, you still don't know that an initial 'eh' is a definite 'ugh.'"

Evan clicked around and landed on a 43-year-old single dad with two young kids. He was age-appropriate—and he was open to dating someone his own age (but also, I noticed, someone as young as thirty). He had some kind of accounting job. He was young-looking and reasonably cute. He referenced a quote I liked.

"I know—he didn't spell-check!" Evan said, as I was about to speak. "But let it go, okay?"

"No problem," I said. "I'm trying to be open."

"You're trying, but twenty minutes ago you ruled out a guy because of his favorite movie."

I reread the single dad's profile. It was pretty standard and normally wouldn't have caught my eye. My instinct was to assume he was boring, but my instinct hadn't found me a husband yet.

"You have two choices," Evan said. "You can let more people into the mix who could possibly make you happy. Or you can hold out for that two percent of men who you *assume* meet your requirements, and hope that coincidentally, someone in that two percent feels that you're in *his* two percent. And even then, the people you assume to meet your requirements might in fact not be the right fit for you. Look at your ex-boyfriends. Something to think about for next week."

As soon as Evan left, I wrote to the single dad. After a couple of e-mails—the usual questions asked between strangers—we spoke on the phone. It wasn't that my conversation with Mike had gone fabulously. In fact, if I'd turned down a date with the cute scuba-diving attorney just a few years earlier simply because he didn't knock my socks off over the telephone, I had even more reason to turn down a date with Mike.

On our call, I found out that he was a Deadhead—at 43—not my scene at all. When he learned where I'd gone to college, he replied, "Ooooh, you're one of those smart people!"—implying, I guess, that he wasn't. He constantly used puns—in an annoying way.

But there were also good things. We had the same political sensibilities and the same dedication to being a parent—he to his two young boys. He worked as a business consultant but had worked as a producer years before, so he also had a creative side. He was easy to talk to. He was kind and understanding of my schedule and offered to travel quite a distance in rush hour traffic to meet me near my house. So when he asked if I wanted to meet in person, I didn't hesitate. I said yes.

We had a date for Friday night.

The Men Who Got Away

NOW that I was about to meet Mike, I started to think about men I wouldn't date because of assumptions I'd made.

Several guys came to mind, and the more I thought about men I never dated, the more I noticed that I'd also made assumptions about men I *hoped* to date. If I assumed some guys were wrong for me, I also assumed some were perfect, sight unseen.

So to see how accurate my assumptions were, I decided to track down a few men from my past.

Andy—The Guy I Assumed Wasn't Cool Enough

I met Andy when I was 32 years old and had just moved to a new city. One of my friends had me call him so that someone could show me around. The first time we had coffee together, we talked for three hours and could have talked for thirty. He was smart, interesting, and extremely funny. There was an immediate sense of comfort, but in an "old friend" kind of way rather than a romantic way. Andy wasn't my type. He was somewhat stocky and had a goatee. He was slightly nerdy. He was really into computers.

Mistake #1: I assumed he wasn't what I wanted in a husband. A week later, when he expressed romantic interest in me, I said that I didn't "think about him that way."

Meanwhile, Andy and I became close friends. We totally "got" each other. We finished each other's sentences and knew what the other person was thinking. We made each other laugh. We shared witty banter, wordplay, the minutiae of our days, and views on everything from politics to relationships, but to me, we were more like buddies than anything else. Not once did I think, "I want to date Andy." I just felt incredibly lucky for our friendship.

Soon I started dating a guy I considered "cool"—he was artistic, exciting, and alluringly unconventional. Around this time, Andy met a woman who was pretty, smart, and kind, and before long, he and Jodi began dating exclusively.

About a year and a half later, my cool boyfriend and I broke up (turned out that what made him exciting also made him unreliable; what made him fascinating and unconventional also made the idea of getting married and having kids with him impractical), and Andy struggled for a while with whether Jodi was The One. Was she stimulating enough? Did they share enough similar interests? Should he look for someone more quirky, like he was? He was 34 now, and ready to be married, but he didn't want to marry the wrong person. Occasionally he'd say, "Where can I find someone like you?" but we always laughed it off, like a big inside joke. By then I had a new boyfriend, and I thought I was falling in love.

One night, Andy asked if I'd meet him for dinner, and I knew something was up. "I have some important news," he said in an e-mail. I figured that he'd finally broken up with Jodi. Instead, when we sat down at the restaurant, here's how he announced his engagement: "Jodi and I are getting married. We want the same things." It seemed comical at the time; I'd never heard a more unromantic way of saying, "I'm getting married!" I remember saying "Congratulations" but secretly feeling bad for him and thinking that he'd settled. I remember feeling that I would never settle like that. I remember thinking that without an initial period of giddy excitement to sustain them through the ups and downs of a marriage, Andy and Jodi would surely get divorced.

Mistake #2: I assumed that Andy was a maximizer like me.

To my surprise, over the next nine years, Andy seemed truly content. After I moved back to Los Angeles, I'd get e-mail updates with links to photos of him and Jodi and their three children, and instead of feeling sorry for Andy, I felt envy—and confusion. Was he really as happy as he seemed in the photos? Didn't he feel lonely in a marriage with someone he'd once described to me as "bland"?

When I asked him about it now, he explained it like this: "She's bland in ways that aren't important in the big picture," he said. "I'm a talker, and I love the banter, and I'm intense about things, and she's just not. It mattered more when we were dating. It still would be nice to have in a spouse, but it has so little to do with the day-to-day of marriage that it matters very little now."

Is his marriage perfect? No. But he wasn't expecting it to be. "A lot of my friends get married and when they don't have the kind of mythical marriage they'd envisioned, they become dissatisfied—like, 'Hey, I didn't sign up for this. This wasn't in the brochure!'"

Andy knew he wanted to marry Jodi, he told me, because while they didn't have intense emotional fireworks (there was definitely physical chemistry), there was a sense of calm and comfort in their courtship. They'd grown up in the same area, their parents knew each other casually, and they had similar upbringings.

"When I saw pictures of her growing up and compared them to

pictures of me growing up," Andy said, "it was almost as though we were in the same pictures. That made it feel right. That made it feel like home. She had a lot of the qualities I was looking for—ethical, professional, solid family upbringing, attractive, kind. About the stuff that wasn't there, I thought, is this really going to be important five years from now?"

Andy believes that people who are adaptable have better marriages, because priorities change so much over time. "The children milestone was a big pivotal moment for me," he said. "Once you become a parent, you realize it's not all about you anymore. Being with a good mom to my children became a much higher priority to me than having the most scintillating dinner partner."

When Andy was dating Jodi, he remembers, he was at Blockbuster and had spent an inordinate amount of time reading all the DVD covers, unable to decide which movie to rent. When he finally picked one, he'd wasted so much time that it was too late to watch the whole movie. So, he started thinking to himself, "Are you going to shop for the perfect movie or rent one and go home and watch it? How long are you going to stay in Blockbuster before you just choose a film?" He realized, he told me, that wondering if he could do better would be torture because anytime you think you have the opportunity to upgrade, you trade one *known* negative thing for an *unknown* negative thing.

"It bothered me that Jodi didn't have certain qualities I'd want, but I also figured that I could spend the rest of my life coming up with reasons that I shouldn't be with person A, B, C, or D. The older I get the more I realize how short life is, and I feel very lucky with my life now. My wife and I may not share witty banter, but we share the incredible bond of watching our kids reach milestones together. And it's uncanny how similar we are when it comes to parenting. Maybe I wouldn't have been on the same page in terms of day-to-day life with someone more exciting, and maybe we would have fought all the time. I'd much rather be in my marriage than that marriage. I made a conscious decision to take inventory of the things I like and value in Jodi, and the things that aren't there aren't worth being miserable about. I have friends who do the whole 10 p.m. Googling thing—*what about that girl from high school?* And while it's tempting, you have to remember that the Internet is just a modern-day Harlequin romance filled with real characters."

Now the comment Andy made years back in announcing his decision to marry Jodi—"We want the same things"—struck me differently. The reason his family Web site photos make me so envious is that I, too, hope to find someone who wants the same things I do. Ironically, the qualities about him I used to find nerdy are the qualities I find appealing about him now. His movie trivia quotes seem endearing and would be great fun to share with kids. His penchant for a cappella singing and amateur filmmaking have been put to hilarious use in his family home videos. His lack of slickness is what makes him such a trustworthy and honest partner. And, incidentally, he's lost the weight and the goatee, and he sure looks cute to me.

I'm not saying that Andy is my soul mate or that it would have worked out if we'd dated. I'm simply saying that I wish I'd entertained the possibility when the possibility still existed. Looking back, I can't believe that there was a man in my life I adored spending time with, and who wanted the same things in life that I did—and I didn't even *consider* dating him. Even today, he's still one of my favorite people to talk to. If I could go back in time, I'd date someone like Andy in a second. Not because I'd be settling, but because different things are important to me now—and should have been all along.

Matt—The Guy I Assumed Was Perfect

To say that Matt was my ideal guy is an understatement. He was brilliant, creative, quirky, successful, handsome, and self-deprecatingly funny—on paper at least. I'd never met him, but I'd read an article about him in a glossy magazine, and I thought, *That's the kind of guy I'd love to date.*

Of course, I recognized how delusional it was to fantasize about a total stranger, but the truth is, I still wanted to end up with someone like Matt. If you'd asked me back then if I thought that was realistic, I would have said no, but on some level, I would have been lying. In my dating life, I constantly overlooked men like Andy in order to hold out for men like Matt.

Nearly ten years later, I was cleaning out some old boxes in my office, and I came across the article I'd ripped out of that glossy magazine when I was 31. I was about to throw it away, but after talking with Evan about misguided assumptions, I Googled Matt to see what had become of him. He was now 45 years old and, as the article predicted, he'd become a well-known and celebrated architect. He was still very handsome. He had a son. And there it was, on his company's Web site—his e-mail address. I sent him a note telling him about my book, and asked if I could talk to him. He wrote back a funny note and said he was game. Wow, I thought. My dream guy is *nice*, too.

I assumed he had it all—looks, personality, talent, charm, and a loving family. I assumed his wife had hit the jackpot.

And indeed, when we first spoke, my assumptions seemed spot on. Matt was just as charming, thoughtful, engaging, and interesting as I imagined him to be. The thirty minutes I'd requested turned into three hours. He was exactly the kind of guy I always went for. But—get this—he wasn't married. He'd never been married. His son was the result of an accidental pregnancy with a former girl-friend. He was single and available.

How could this be? How could a guy who was so appealing on so many levels not have found a partner? The more we chatted, the more it became obvious. He was a toxic maximizer. Nobody was good enough for him. Not the girlfriend who became pregnant (she was "fascinating and intelligent" but "she was sensitive in ways that bothered me" and "her hands were so big—I wasn't attracted to that") and who is now happily married (presumably to someone who can deal with sensitivity and large hands); not the girlfriend who was "wrong about small things a lot of the time—like which direction to go on a road trip—which spoke to a lack of competence"; not the girlfriend who had a different way of communicating than he did. Maybe he and these women were truly incompatible, but he did stay in two of these relationships for five and seven years, respectively.

So there must have been some positive aspects to these rela-tionships, right?

"It's not like I can't stay with someone," Matt explained. "But at the time, it felt like I would be settling if I did. I've never had trouble finding people I enjoy being with and who want to be with me. It makes you live in this world where you think, I can throw this one back into the sea and find another."

Now, at 45, Matt told me that most of his friends his age are married with kids and the question of why he, too, hasn't gotten married is one he asks himself often.

Could it be that he just hasn't met the right person? Or that he hasn't been realistic enough?

"I think I'm realistic," he said, after a long pause. "I've always been attracted to very intelligent, capable, accomplished, insightful, open, positive women. But I don't say I would never date a divorced woman, or someone with kids, or have any rules like that."

I asked if he would be interested in a woman who was intelligent and insightful but perhaps less accomplished. Hypothetically, yes, he said. But honestly, he wasn't so sure.

"I think I've gotten less good at settling," Matt admitted. "I've waited all this time and I'm not going to settle now. A lot of my friends have been divorced."

I used to think that way about divorced couples, too—but I hadn't considered that most people don't go into marriage thinking they're settling. Most go into marriage believing that they've found The One. I doubt that the divorce rate is high because the people who supposedly settled are calling it quits. More likely, the divorce rate is high because the people who thought they were madly in love are realizing that they'd been looking for the wrong qualities in a spouse.

In fact, it occurred to me as I was talking to Matt that the very qualities I was attracted to when I read his magazine profile a decade earlier probably correlated with personality traits that wouldn't necessarily make for the kind of family-oriented husband I was seeking now. An ambitious, brilliant, creative guy can be a great dinner companion, but a guy who works seven days a week, sees his son just two weeks per year (and commented that, were he to have more children, "I think I would get bored with infants"), and has little tolerance for imperfection wouldn't be such an appealing spouse. His personality and impressive mind might be exciting in a boyfriend, but they're rarely compatible with someone who would be happy basking in the routine day-to-day of domestic life. All the experts I spoke to said that shared values were more important than shared interests, and while as a couple, Matt and I would likely never run out of things to talk about, as parents running a household together, we'd also likely never run out of things to disagree about.

At one point in our conversation, Matt asked an interesting question. He was talking about his seven-year relationship, and how despite his wanting it to work, too many things bothered him about his girlfriend. "This comes down to a bigger issue," he said. "How much should people change to make a relationship work?"

I'm not sure if he was talking about himself, his girlfriend, or both. But I found it curious that—like so many single people—he viewed the problem as being one of needing to change rather than needing to accept. Because as my married friends have often said, it's not about changing the other person; it's about accepting things about the other person that you'd like to change, but can't.

Later, Matt told me that he'd tried online dating, and I asked to see his profile. It was like catnip to me. A few years ago, if I'd seen his essay online, I would have been setting the wedding date by the time I hit the "send" button on my e-mail. But when it comes to the kind of spouse I'm seeking now, if I had the choice between someone like him and someone like Andy, I'd definitely pick Andy. And I wouldn't look back. Ten years ago, if someone had told me I'd pick Andy over Matt, I would have found that absurd, if not impossible. But here I am—still single, along with my former Fantasy Guy.

Jeff—The Guy I Assumed Wasn't Brainy Enough

Back in 2006, when I was trying out some scientific-based dating sites for an article I was writing, I dismissed a guy whose profile appeared in my in-box. Why, I asked in the article, would the dating site have matched me—an avid reader attracted to literary types—with the guy whose essay read as follows:

> *While I do read books, I have a notoriously short attention span for them. As a result, partially read copies of numerous really good (so I'm told) books are scattered around my apartment. When these get set aside, it's because I've gotten sucked into magazines . . . Every few days, the magazines lose out to DVDs.*

I assumed we weren't a match and dismissed him without so much as an introductory e-mail. But then, one day, he sent me a note saying that he was reading the *Atlantic* and was stunned to come across his very own online dating profile in print. Isn't it funny, he remarked, that he was reading one of the country's most esteemed literary magazines when he learned that I'd written him off as not literary enough?

"I thought that was hilarious," Jeff said three years later, when I called him up in Northern California to talk about the misunderstanding. Jeff was a year younger than me, highly educated, and worked as a software entrepreneur. We had a lovely conversation about, believe it or not, books he had recently read! He was funny and self-aware and we seemed to have a lot in common, both in terms of values and interests. But now, of course, he had a girlfriend (who, not surprisingly, was in her early thirties).

Jeff told me that he understood why I'd jumped to conclusions based on his profile, and said that he, too, has learned not to make assumptions when it comes to romantic relationships. With his current girlfriend, for instance, he said it used to bother him that they had different senses of humor.

"I used to think that sense of humor was a pretty strong indicator of compatibility and how your brains think," he said. "And in some ways that's true—the things that excite us intellectually are different. I like puzzles and games and trivia. Those things aren't terribly interesting to her. There's a bit of sadness that I can't share that with her, but over the past six months, we've really grown and learned things about each other that have surprised us. We're both really reflective and we communicate well. We can talk about anything and not get defensive. We're both into running, we're involved in community service, and we enjoy and appreciate one another. In other relationships, I was immature. I always managed to find things that were missing."

When I'd first seen Jeff's profile, I'd done the same thing. Instead of focusing on how attractive, smart, and funny he seemed, I saw one negative—that he didn't love books the way I did—and ruled him out. The worst part is, it was a false assumption. His profile simply didn't reflect how well read he was, or how curious he was about a certain kinds of reading material. And in the end, even if he hadn't been well read, how much would that matter in the long run if he was smart and interesting in the ways I discovered on our phone call?

As with Andy, I'll never know what might have happened with Jeff. But this isn't about Jeff or Andy or Matt anymore. It's about not making this mistake with the next guy.

Pulling Another Sheldon

I realized, of course, that I'd done the same thing with Sheldon, the Ivy League–educated single dad that Wendy the matchmaker had tried to set me up with a month earlier. She'd challenged each of my false assumptions, but by the time I came to my senses, Sheldon was dating someone else.

Meanwhile, Wendy tried to find another guy for me, but of the men she looked into, the never-married guys wanted to meet childless but fertile (read: under 35) women only, or they didn't want kids at all. The divorced dads she could find tended to be men in their fifties and about to launch their kids into college in the next few years, and they weren't interested in getting involved with a woman with a toddler. (Nor were they interested in meeting a fertile woman with no kids but who wanted them—they were done with little kids.) Wendy only worked with people she vetted for the important qualities—kind, responsible, stable, marriage-minded, of good character. So that ruled out the guys who weren't looking for anything serious, didn't have their shit together, or were emotionally questionable (still not over the divorce, depressed, immature).

Sadly, she'd come up dry.

I started to wonder where all the divorced dads my age were. I mean, given the national divorce rate, there had to be tons of them, right? Wendy told me that the younger divorced dads exist, but they don't stay single very long, and the divorced moms do, which leads to an excess of single women. Wendy also encounters divorced dads who don't want to marry again or even commit to a long-term partnership because they've been taken to the cleaners by an ex-wife—but they still want the companionship of a girlfriend.

Plus, when it comes to kids, younger single dads are marketable because women value a man who loves his children. Younger single moms are a liability because men devalue the idea of dealing with somebody else's children.

Ten years ago, I had no idea that dating would get this hard, but now it was finally sinking in. Or so I thought.

That same week, Julie Ferman, the matchmaker who owns Cupid's Coach, graciously offered to do a free match for me. I was thrilled. So I filled out a Cupid's Coach profile and made an appointment with her.

ANOTHER GUY GETS AWAY

The first thing Julie did on the day of our appointment was ask me a lot of questions that weren't addressed on the profile: What kind of guys did I date in the past? What worked? What didn't? What was my family like? What was my childhood like? What was important to me? What was I passionate about? That took about an hour. Then she started clicking on her computer. *Tap, tap, tap.* She was going through her matchmaking database.

"I'm looking for my top five candidates," she said, clicking away. "I don't present more because it's too overwhelming. If I give people too many choices, it becomes a Match.com experience, so what's the point? Then a year has gone by and they've spent the money and nothing has changed."

I looked at the computer screen. Five men smiled back at me. Two were very cute. Two looked really old, but, in fact, they were only a few years older than me. I probably look "old" to them, too. It's a phenomenon I've noticed since I turned 40—everyone in my age bracket looks old to me because when I picture myself, I view a mental image of me at 30. I haven't recalibrated the image to reflect what I look like today.

It's a problem, because I'm just not attracted to middle-aged men. I'll meet a guy or see his picture, and I'm pretty sure that if I'd fallen in love with that same guy when he was in his twenties or thirties, and we'd had a family together and gone through our days together for ten or fifteen years, I'd still be attracted to him, because the essence of him would be stored in my mind. It's like the 70-year-old woman who still thinks that her 70-year-old husband is handsome and dapper, because he once was, and that's the man she sees when she looks at him, even all these years later. But to meet the 70-year-old without the shared history, without the shared youth, without that mental image of forty years ago to hold on to, it's hard to get all hot and bothered.

I know I need to get over this. Of the men Julie showed me, the first guy I picked—a thirty-something, boyish-looking, never-married, no-kids screenwriter—was probably the least appropriate candidate for me. She told me she'd put him in there because she didn't know me the way she knows her regular clients—she hadn't gone through the full process with me—and she thought she'd give me a broad age range to learn more about my preferences. But the more we talked about the screenwriter, the more she tried to steer me to a guy I'd overlooked: Sean.

Sean, she told me, was an Eastern philosophy kind of guy who was very successful in his business: pest control. That's right—pest control. On the one hand, I thought, I'm really afraid of spiders, so maybe this could be a match. On the other hand, I never really saw myself with a guy who kills bugs for a living. He was bald, but youthful-looking and definitely cute. He didn't look 46. He lived an hour away. He wasn't Jewish. He was more than a foot taller than me. And would a true Eastern philosophy kind of guy be killing bugs anyway?

I wasn't sure. I went back to the cute, young, Jewish screen-writer.

Julie persisted—strongly, but in a girlfriend-y way. "If you were my sister, who would I tell her to stop everything and meet? Sean! I found my sister her match and I take full credit for their marriage and kids!"

I tried to imagine dating Sean and talking about our days at dinnertime.

"So, how about those roaches?" I'd ask. I couldn't picture it. The screenwriter, on the other hand, had written that he liked *This American Life* and *The Daily Show*. He was funny. And did I mention how adorable he was?

Julie told me that I should be open to the other men she'd selected. There was Chris, a 45-year-old business owner who was divorced with a teenager. He had that handsome classic movie-star look, which isn't at all my type. I go more for quirky.

I know, I know—I ruled out a guy because he's *too* attractive. Could I be any pickier? Apparently, yes—I also didn't think he was intellectual enough because he owns a construction supply business and went to San Diego State. (So much for not making assumptions.)

Then there was Robert, a freelance talent manager who was more laid-back than ambitious. He was also 5'6", but that wasn't a deal-breaker anymore. I was letting go of the height thing. The real issue was that he seemed middle-of-the-road and not very brainy. I needed brainy.

Jon was brainy. He was a 50-year-old Jewish biomedical device entrepreneur who was Ivy League educated and athletic. He wrote smart, sincere essays. But he didn't seem to have a sense of humor and he lived a good hour and a half away. Logistically, how would we date? Finally, there was Scott, a divorced 49-year-old environmental lawyer who lived near me. He had amazing essays, but he also had two teenagers, was Catholic, and looked old to me.

Julie pushed for Scott, too—we were intellectual equals, had similar sensibilities and interests, and were really into raising our kids. But of the options, I selected the screenwriter.

I don't have to tell you how this ends. Like the character in a horror film who hears a noise in the basement in the middle of the night and knows she should call 911 and get the hell out of the house instead of going down the creaky stairs straight into DAN-GER, I had Julie connect me with Mr. Hottie Screenwriter. We spoke on the phone. He was funny. He was creative. He shared my pop culture references. He was warm and kind. But he had to work several freelance jobs to pay the bills, lived in a studio apartment in an iffy part of town, and had no experience with or interest in little kids. He went out to clubs at night and hung out with his young single friends 'til all hours. We both seemed to enjoy the conversation, but the longer we talked, it became increasingly clear that we were at different phases of life. Neither of us asked to meet.

Meanwhile, I didn't pursue any of the other candidates Julie had picked for me until a few weeks later, when I took a second look at Scott's profile.

This time, as I read through his essays, I felt as though I'd been bonked on the head. He was exactly the kind of guy I'd been saying I couldn't find. It wasn't just that he shared nearly all of my interests. It was that he seemed to be someone I'd really like spending time with. So what if he looked older, his kids were teenagers, and we didn't share a religion? We had similar values. We had similar lifestyles and goals. We both prioritized parenting. We both were intellectual and creative (he was a photographer on the side). I loved his self-deprecating sense of humor. He was looking to get married again.

This wasn't news: Julie had told me all this the day she presented him to me, but I was blinded by the young, Jewish screenwriter—a "type" I'd always gone for, and even dated, but never said "I do" with.

I e-mailed Julie and told her of my interest in meeting Scott— only to hear back from her a few hours later: Scott was now seeing one of her other clients. He was off the market. *Of course he was*, I thought. I'd pulled another Sheldon!

What the heck was my problem? On a rational level, I knew I was making choices that wouldn't lead to happiness in the long run. I knew that what the experts were saying was absolutely true. But there was this irrational side of me that seemed to take over, leaving me frustrated and disappointed in myself. How many more times could I let this happen? When, I wondered, would I learn my lesson? I worried that if I didn't learn it soon, I'd be alone forever.

Something had to change. And that something, obviously, was me.

14

Mondays with Evan

Session Three—The Lowdown on Alpha Males

On Friday night, I arrived at the coffeehouse a few minutes early for my date with Mike, the Deadhead single dad I'd e-mailed at my last dating coaching session. I was sitting at a table and sipping a latte when I heard a voice say, "Lori?"

I looked up and, to my surprise, Mike was incredibly handsome—something that didn't come across in his online photos. He was chivalrous, offering to bring me more coffee or buy me some dinner. He asked if I wanted to sit outside because it was so noisy inside. At our little outdoor table we talked about the election, parenthood, and our work. We even realized we had an acquaintance in common.

Evan was right about not making assumptions: It turned out that Mike's being a Deadhead meant that he liked Grateful Dead music, not that he drove a van with stickers all over it and spent his days stoned. He didn't use puns in person; maybe he'd been nervous on the phone. He seemed bright, even if he didn't consider himself "one of those smart people" and admitted that he'd never been a good student. The judgments I'd made sight unseen weren't really accurate.

But still, I told Evan at our third dating coaching session, we didn't seem like we were on the same page in the bigger picture. Mike was very laid-back about practical matters and career aspirations. He was really low-key. He didn't seem very goal-oriented. He just wasn't . . .

"He's not an alpha male," Evan interrupted.

"Well, yeah," I said. "But I don't think I necessarily go for alpha males. I'm not into investment bankers or race car drivers or super-macho guys like that. I'm drawn to intellectual guys. A doctor, or a lawyer, or a scientist who's doing interesting research, or a playwright whose work I respect. He's not someone who just clocks in at the job. He's passionate about what he does."

"Exactly," Evan said. "Alpha males. They're attractive to so many women, but then these same women complain that these guys are hard to date. Meanwhile, they won't date guys who aren't alpha males. They won't date the shy guy, or the guy who's not a leader. Confident, successful men inspire confidence in women."

I agreed. There's something very attractive about a man who's competent and confident. Who can start a company, win a trial, or cure an illness. Who makes a plan, makes a living, and takes the initiative. Who's athletic enough to beat up the imaginary bad guys. Who, I'm embarrassed to admit, can protect us from the world, even if we don't need protecting.

A Nice Guy with Balls

I remembered talking to a single 35-year-old woman, an advertising executive who told me that five years earlier she'd broken up with a guy who taught music to toddlers because his job seemed so wimpy. He ended up marrying someone else and he turned out, of course, to be a great father because he genuinely loved kids. None of the lawyers or bankers she's dated since has worked out. She doubts that these alpha male boyfriends would have been as good a spouse or father as this teacher. They weren't flexible enough, and that led to frequent arguments, but the music teacher, who was mellow, seemed *too* accommodating. It bugged her. Why didn't the teacher have stronger opinions about day-to-day things? Why was he always saying, "If you want to do that, sure, fine with me"?

"It's not a rational thing, but if he'd run the music program, I might have felt differently," she said of her ex-boyfriend. "At least he'd seem more, I don't know, powerful. And I always had the idea that I would grow up and marry someone who made at least the same amount or more money than I did—and he made a lot less. Also, he had all that free time when he wasn't teaching and I'd be working. It just seemed like he would be a Mr. Mom, and I would be bringing home the paycheck and working year-round in the corporate world. I know this sounds bad, but I was embarrassed to bring him to the office Christmas party and to have him tell people that he taught two-year-olds how to bang on plastic drums."

Evan said he hears this story all the time: Women complaining that the attractive alpha males are egocentric or unreliable, but that the nice guys don't turn them on.

"Women say they want an alpha male who's nice," Evan said. "Or maybe a nice guy with balls. They want someone to make them feel excited and safe, simultaneously."

As the advertising executive put it, "I want an ambitious guy who has the qualities that also make a guy who teaches toddlers so appealing—warm, sensitive, generous, nurturing. But I want him to have those qualities at home, and the ambitious qualities out in the world. If that makes any sense."

It did to me.

"But have you noticed," Evan asked when I brought this up, "that these men are very, very rare?" And even if you find one, he added, is that really what you want? Evan said that alpha men are like the bad boys we dated when we were in our twenties. But instead of dating the rebellious rocker who's on the road thirty weeks a year, now we date the charming, never-married 40-year-old who works sixty hours a week, so we always seem to come in second to his work and his freedom.

The nice guys, on the other hand, are . . . nice. They want to please women. They're happy to do what the woman wants. And some women, Evan said, don't want a man to be that nice. They want him to lead, to drive the car, to make decisions instead of always saying okay to whatever plan they come up with.

"But the leaders," Evan said, "can be the most arrogant, most difficult, most combustible guys around. It's hard to find a person who puts you first but also has the kind of personality that likes to take the lead."

Evan told me about a client of his who got annoyed with a guy she'd just started dating. He took her to a place with loud music, and when he sensed that she wasn't happy, he asked her where she wanted to go instead. This was a double turn-off. Not only had he picked a bad place to go, but then he wanted *her* to pick a better alternative to his mistake. Why couldn't this guy just make a decision—and a good one?

Evan said it's a typical complaint he hears from female clients: They want leaders who care about their feelings and can also read their minds. Or they want the guy to be the president, as long as they also have the veto power.

"The only problem," Evan said, "is that you'll find yourself arguing with the alpha guys you date, because often it's his way or the highway. You want him to want to please you, but you don't respect the nice guys who *do* try to please you."

Often Evan finds his clients listing off qualities that rarely co-exist: an incredibly driven guy who also has a lot of free time to take a spontaneous day trip; a handsome charmer who also won't attract other women's attention at a party.

"You may want both qualities," Evan explained, "but you have to pick which is more important. I think when you look at it that way, the answer is fairly obvious. And by the way, these alpha males may not be looking for the qualities you have either."

ALPHA MALES DON'T MARRY *ME*

What the heck did that mean? Why wouldn't an alpha male want to date me?

"Well," he said, "what happened when you dated men like that in the past?"

I told Evan about a couple of alpha males I'd been attracted to in the past. The trial lawyer who seemed to want to win every argument out of court, too. The successful entrepreneur who was used to having his employees meet his needs and wasn't willing to give halfway in a relationship.

Evan nodded. "When we're dating, we often look for people who are mirror images of us," Evan said. "A successful woman will usually seek a successful man. But that very quality which makes them successful creates friction, which is how you end up with two strong-willed people who can't stop arguing. Two people who demand all the attention. Two people who put their jobs before their relationships. But instead of looking for someone who complements us instead of competes with us, we just keep trying to find 'better' versions of ourselves, to our own detriment. A guy can be a leader in other areas, but it might not be at the office."

"Are you saying that ambitious women shouldn't date their equals?" I asked.

Evan shook his head. "I'm saying you have to find an equal whose strengths complement yours. The traits you find impressive in men don't necessarily translate well in the context of a marriage: ambitious, competitive, opinionated."

"But these guys always get married," I said.

"Yeah, but do they marry *you*?"

I tried to think of alpha males I knew and who their spouses were: full-time moms who had given up careers (and liked it that way), women with flexible low-key careers, and, come to think of it, a lot of people in the helping professions, like nurses. Unfortunately, none of that described me.

"Think about it," Evan said. "What does an alpha male get out of dating you? The world revolves around him at work. He likes intellectual stimulation and opinions. He likes challenges. But he already has that all day. What he can't get at work are warmth, support, nurturing. You may be able to provide that, but you're also not the most easygoing personality, and he wants his life at home to be easy. And you want a guy who can lead, but who can also compromise and let you lead. That might create conflict between you two."

So, Evan said, I had a decision to make: Did I want to go out with Mike again?

"You have to decide what you want more," he explained. "Do you want the type of guy you've gone for in the past, even though that hasn't worked out so far? Or do you want to try getting to know Mike, who's a nice guy and a great dad, but isn't super-ambitious? I'm not saying Mike is the right guy for you. He may be completely wrong for you. I'm just saying that you might not have enough information from a first date to know."

He had a point. We'd been on only one date. I'd always used first dates as some kind of test that guys either passed or failed. Passing meant that sparks flew. Failing meant anything else. But maybe I'd overestimated the importance of a first date. After all, I had a good time with Mike—he just didn't "wow" me. I probably didn't "wow" him either, but I'm guessing he asked me out again because the date went well enough. Why not go on a second one?

How much stock should we put in first dates, anyway?

15

What First Dates *Really* Tell Us

"Ooh, so you really liked him!" my friend Lucia said when I told her I was going on a second date with Mike. I tried to explain that I didn't like or not like him. I was basically neutral.

But Lucia, who felt "breathless" when she first met her husband, thought I was being coy.

"Are you just protecting yourself?" she asked. "I'll bet you like him a lot more than you're letting on."

I didn't, but Lucia had trouble understanding why I was going if I was so blasé. As far as she was concerned, why bother?

CHANGING THE STORY

On some level, I also wondered "why bother?" Of course, I knew happily married people who didn't have great first dates, but somehow I expected a memorable one when I met my spouse. I've certainly not been above reading into things on a first date. Once I was really excited after meeting a guy because we discovered that we both ate the same obscure brand of chocolate chip cookies for breakfast ("How weird is that? It's destiny!"). But that didn't mean we were soul mates; it just meant we had the same poor nutritional habits. By date three, we realized we had little in common besides those cookies. Still, the more I heard people tell these stories of how they "just knew" when they first met, the more I bought into the idea that these kinds of beginnings make for happier marriages.

Diane Holmberg, a Canadian researcher and professor who studies relationships, says that's not true and, in fact, the first date stories I hear might not even be that accurate. She's found that married couples often change their courtship stories over time. In her book *Thrice Told Tales: Married Couples Tell Their Stories*, she and her coauthors analyzed how couples described their courtship in the first, third, and seventh years of marriage. It turns out their stories weren't consistent.

"I selected a set of couples who showed a major drop in their overall marital well-being," she explained. "I then selected a second set of couples who were matched with the first set in marital well-being that first year, but stayed stable over time. I then looked at how couples talked about the early stages of their relationship."

By the third year, she found, the stable group's courtship stories had gotten *more positive* than they'd reported that first year, while the less happy group's courtship stories had gotten *more negative* than they'd been in that first year. But remember: That first year, these courtship stories had been *identical in tone*. In other words, happy couples described the early stages of their relationship more positively over time, while couples who became less happy described those early stages more negatively over time.

These weren't just first-date memories—they covered first dates up to the proposal—but it does show, Holmberg says, that there's a kind of revisionist history going on.

Is Lucia's first-date story accurate? I don't know—I didn't know her ten years ago when she met her husband. But either way, I knew I had to change the way I viewed the first date as the forecaster of my future with each guy.

Grace, who has been married for six years, knows that first dates can be misleading.

"I literally heard a voice when I met my husband," she told me. "It said, 'You will marry him and have a son.' Every time I was near him, the world stopped and I felt so connected to him."

They do have a son now, just like the voice said—but the connection didn't prove lasting and they're in the process of getting a divorce.

"The bottom line is that I really didn't know him," she admitted now.

On a recent episode of the radio show *This American Life*, I heard the story of a couple who had this incredibly romantic love-at-first-sight meeting and a movie-worthy courtship, only to be followed by a marriage far more difficult than either expected. It got so hard that they almost split up, but instead chose to work through their differences to create what's now a strong marriage. In an interview, the man commented that because he and his wife had such an amazing love-at-first-sight story, people always want to hear about that—but in his view, they're asking the wrong question.

"Everyone always asks how we met," he said, "but nobody ever asks how we stayed together."

I Wouldn't Return His Calls

Then there's Julie, who had no fireworks whatsoever when she met her husband, Jeff. In fact, she didn't even want to have coffee with him. They first met not at a romantic restaurant, but in an intensive care unit in North Carolina, at a patient's bedside. Julie was the doctor, and Jeff was the nurse.

After their bedside meeting, Jeff left a couple of messages on Julie's answering machine, but she didn't return the calls because she didn't feel there was a polite way to say, "No thanks." She was sure she had no romantic interest in Jeff, and because they might run into each other at the hospital, rejecting him felt awkward.

Then, one night, as Julie was getting ready to join friends from work at a baseball game, Jeff called for what he later said was his third and final attempt.

"It was the perfect gracious response to the date I didn't think I wanted to go on," Julie said. "I invited Jeff to join the group from work—all folks he knew anyway." In other words, the perfect non-date.

But as they sat on a grassy knoll in the outfield, they lost track of the game completely.

"We chatted like old friends," she said. "We laughed about similarities in our upbringing. He was comfortably familiar. Neither of us dated anybody else after that night."

They've been married for twelve years.

"Jeff was the package that arrived at my doorstep a couple of times," Julie said, "but it wasn't until he was unwrapped and just sitting there that I could see what a treasure he was."

THE FROG PRINCE

Helena Rosenberg, a psychotherapist in Los Angeles with an expertise in counseling single women seeking mates, calls men like her own husband Frog Princes—people you don't naturally think of as your potential mate on first glance but who turn out to be princes as you get to know them.

Jennifer, who is 36 and met her husband seven years ago, is married to a Frog Prince.

"I was at a party and I didn't even notice Danny," she said, referring to her husband. "I noticed another guy. I dated the other guy and became friends with Danny. Soon I realized that Danny was the more impressive guy. He just didn't have the kinds of attributes that can be seen from across the table on a first date. The best husbands are the ones who have these unseen qualities, the kind of things you'll see over time, like kindness, patience, generosity, and honesty."

Scott Haltzman, a psychiatrist at Brown University and the author of *The Secrets of Happily Married Women: How to Get More Out of Your Relationship by Doing Less*, told me from his office in Providence that it's important for women to learn this when they're just starting to date.

"My own clinical observation is that first impressions are not a strong predictor of marital success," he said. "I've got a seventeen-year-old daughter, and she'll say she went out with a guy and he was boring. I say, 'Great, boring's good! Better that than bad boys. If you didn't feel a sense of danger or a wave of nausea, go out again. People mistake the nausea for interest, but if you can objectively tell yourself that a guy has some good qualities, go out again. It can take several dates just to figure out whether there's something interesting about this person. And then you may find you're truly attracted to him."

That reminded me of something Anne Meara of the comedy team Stiller and Meara once said in a *New York Times* interview about her thirty-plus-year marriage: "Was it love at first sight? It wasn't then—but it sure is now."

He Looked Short—in a Headshot

By now it sounds obvious: First meetings tell us very little. But I'm guessing that if *Cosmo* ran a quiz consisting of first-date stories, and then asked readers to guess which led to happy marriages, which led to unhappy marriages, and which led to no marriage at all—many of us would fail. Take the story of Tracey and Phil. She wouldn't even meet the man who became her husband because, when she Googled him, he looked short—*in a headshot.*

Tracey, who is now 32, told me over the phone from Philadelphia that her mother knew Phil's mom, and wanted to set them up.

"My mom said he was a good guy who came from a good family, and that he had graduated from law school and was practicing," Tracey explained. So she went to his law firm's Web site and, based on the two-inch headshot, assumed that Phil was short.

"I didn't believe my mom when she said Phil was tall," Tracey explained, "because she's not interested in height. She was looking for someone who would be a good companion. I want that, but I have to be attracted, and my type is tall guys."

Meanwhile, Phil had similar reservations. "My mom said that Tracey was very bright and had a master's from NYU. She said she was a good person and she had pretty eyes, so I assumed that meant the rest of her, well . . . not so much."

When they finally did meet—at a holiday party in their hometown over a Christmas break—they both felt vindicated. Even though Phil turned out to be 6'5", neither of them was impressed.

"I felt stupid that I assumed he was short," Tracey said. "But there definitely was no spark. I didn't have that instant, *Wow, I want to talk to him* feeling."

Phil was equally lukewarm about Tracey. "She had big curly hair, and that was not a good thing. She looked like a poodle."

After some friendly but unmemorable conversation, Tracey,

who is naturally outgoing, asked for Phil's business card. She thought Phil was a smart, decent guy and maybe they'd get together the next time they were in town.

"I had no romantic expectations not only because there seemed to be no chemistry between us, but also because we lived in different states," Tracey said. She was living near Washington, D.C., and he was living in New Jersey. "I was definitely not interested romantically, but I thought since our families knew each other, he might become a friend."

When Tracey did eventually call Phil, the conversation went surprisingly well. "If she hadn't called me," Phil said, "I wouldn't have sought her out." But suddenly they found themselves talking on the phone, long-distance, consistently for a month.

Phil was calling her daily, but Tracey *still* didn't see this as having romantic potential. "I still just thought he was a really great guy and I was making a really good friend," she said.

Phil wasn't sure what to think, but over a long weekend, Phil went to visit his mother in Maryland and, on the way home, stopped through Tracey's neighborhood to meet her for dinner. This time, there was more interest, but neither had that struck-by-lightning feeling. The attraction, Tracey said, was "more mellow."

"We'd been talking on the phone for about a month," Phil said, "so I knew her better. She looked better, too, but only because I knew her better."

"I felt the same way," Tracey added. "We'd become friends. And that added to the attraction. If we hadn't taken the time to get to know each other, I still might have felt nothing."

After that, the two had several conversations each day. Phil would drive down to D.C. every weekend he could. Despite the distance, or perhaps because of it, Tracey and Phil used to joke that they talked to each other more than most couples in the same location do.

"He was always accessible," Tracey said. "That meant a lot to me. Other boyfriends I had were attractive and successful, but what I was missing was that they didn't treat me well. They weren't nice people. They looked good, had good jobs, came from decent families—but weren't decent people. They were arrogant. Phil was always nice to me, always there for me. I never had to wonder if he was going to call me back or worry about any of those games."

Now that they're married, they seem like typical blissed-out newlyweds, but they're also quick to say that they each had to make some compromises.

"She's a great person because I see her as a true partner, an equal," Phil said. "She's equally smart, has a great sense of humor. We have fun together. She makes me better and want to be better. But I also think that she's overly sensitive sometimes. If I had my ideal list, maybe that wouldn't be on it. We work through it, though, because we're truly interested in understanding each other."

Tracey cops to being too emotional, and says that she appreciates how patient Phil is with her. If she could change one thing about Phil, it would be that he's not as "on it" as she'd like.

"He likes that I'm type A, because I keep track of all the bills and things that need to get done," she said. "But I don't like how laid-back he is all the time. In a perfect world, I'd like to see him have a little more urgency with things. Sometimes I feel like I want to put a Post-it on my forehead so he'll remember things and not procrastinate. But he puts up with me, so fair is fair. We're a team."

Phil and Tracey had that romantic energy I crave—finishing each other's sentences, being gentle with each other's vulnerabilities, having enough comfort to laugh at their respective less-than-appealing qualities. How sad it would be, I thought, if they hadn't gotten past their first impressions.

Tracey thinks about this, too. "I tell my friends who are single that if the person is reasonably cute and seems like a good, smart person, you have to go on a second date, even if he's not your type or the date was boring or you didn't feel anything. And if they protest, I say, look at me and Phil."

THREE HUNDRED FIRST-DATE MISTAKES

He's not my type. The date was boring. I didn't feel anything. These are just three reasons women give for never seeing a guy again. Evan Marc Katz, the dating coach, told me that the list can get outrageously long.

"I sent out an e-mail to women because I wanted to find out for men what guys were doing wrong on first dates," Evan said. "I thought I'd get a list of a few things: *The guy didn't pay. He was rude to the waiter. He didn't ask about her life.* But they sent back three hundred things! I didn't even know there were three hundred things I could do wrong on a first date. Ten, maybe. But not three hundred! Imagine how picky you have to be to be able to name so many things that would make you not go on a *second date*.

"But they said things like, 'He shouldn't talk in any other voice, even if he does the greatest Austin Powers impression in the whole world' and 'He shouldn't tell her that nothing will stop him from watching the big game' and 'He shouldn't wear a brown belt and black shoes, or vice versa.' I tried this with men, and they only named a few things that wouldn't lead to a second date: *She wasn't attractive enough. She wasn't stimulating enough. She wasn't warm.*"

For women, he said, the problem seems to be that we don't realize we're just on a date. As Evan put it, "A woman thinks, 'Is he my husband?' That's a much higher bar than just, 'Should we go out on a second date?' A guy will ask you out on a second date if he thinks you're cute and he had fun. From what I've seen, women are much more judgmental in a first-date situation."

CONFUSING GOOD DATERS WITH GOOD HUSBANDS

Dr. Michael Broder, the therapist in Philadelphia who spoke to me about entitlement, said that those unreasonable expectations start at the first date.

"Almost everyone knows someone who's happily married but where there weren't sparks flying at the beginning of the relationship," he said. "But a lot of women go on a first date and say, 'I need passion upfront and if it's not there, have a nice life.' They don't want to wait to see if something develops on a second or third date. They want it all, right now, and they don't have the patience for guys who don't make the best impression immediately. He either dazzles her or she doesn't want to see him again."

Dr. Broder believes that women often confuse good daters with good husbands and, conversely, bad daters with bad husbands. We forget that the guy who is awkward or too quiet or not funny on a first date might be acting that way because he's excited about you, not because he's a moron. In fact, he could turn out to be a really cool guy. The guy who doesn't wow you with his smooth dating skills might wow you as a loving husband. The smooth operator, on the other hand, might not turn out to be such a great husband. Courtship skills, especially on a first date, aren't a good predictor of what kind of husband a guy will make.

That's why Lisa Clampitt, the New York City matchmaker, told me that if a client is on the fence after a first date, she'll strongly encourage a second. She doesn't require it, but she makes it clear to both parties beforehand that if the interaction is "neutral," you can't go wrong with a second try. Sometimes people are nervous on first dates. Sometimes they feel as though they have only one shot, like in a job interview, and they're too focused on landing the second date to relax on the first. But if the second date is a given, the first interaction can be more natural. And even if the first interaction is natural but the sparks aren't there—like with Mike and me—she feels that the dynamic often changes on a second date, and you may view each other differently once you've already met.

If, on the other hand, the first date is "super-negative," Clampitt talks to her clients to understand why.

"Sometimes, I understand," she said. "At the same time, I don't want them to be unreasonable and miss an opportunity."

I asked her what advice she'd give to a friend of mine who went on a first date with a guy she described as cute and smart and well-traveled, but who "wasn't a fabulous conversationalist." As my friend put it, "The date was a bit like twenty questions. There were some awkward 'what next?' pauses." She didn't want to go on the second date.

Clampitt sighed through the phone line. "What do people expect when they're meeting someone for the first time?" she asked. "That you'll have the same comfort level that you do with people you already know? Sometimes a first conversation flows easily, but often, it's not until the second or third or fourth date that it starts to feel more natural. We give our coworkers or potential new friends the benefit of the doubt when we meet for the first time, even if those first interactions aren't super-exciting. Why not potential mates?"

Clampitt says that you can't tell much from these early exchanges, so while she's not asking you to marry the guy, she's just asking you to spend another *two hours* with him to see if you have a good time.

"Love should increase over time, not start at a high," she said. "Real love is developed over time. It's about learning to trust, bond, and build family together, with or without children. So I'm in favor of not overthinking yourself to death in the beginning. Women, especially, tend to rule people out too quickly. In my experience, it's the women who won't go on second dates more than the men."

Clampitt wasn't the first to point out that women tend to be pickier than men. Was this true—not just on first dates, but in general? I thought about the three hundred things women said that men do wrong on first dates. That seemed pretty extreme.

So I had to find out: Are women really pickier?

Are Women Pickier Than Men?

"Oh, come on," I said to my friend Kyle, a married journalist in New York, when we were talking about picky daters. I didn't believe his theory: that if a woman is basically attractive and normal, most men will give her a chance.

He explained it like this: "If a girl seems like she isn't going to have too many unexplained crying jags or have too many antidepressant prescriptions or want to endlessly discuss the minutiae of the relationship, or go through our e-mail or Google the names of our exes, that's a huge plus for us. It's like cha-ching! Yahtzee! Touchdown!"

He may have been half-kidding, but there was some truth there, too: Men do have slightly less stringent requirements than women.

In a 2007 *Time*/CNN poll, 80 percent of men and women said they thought they'd meet their perfect mate eventually. But when they were asked if they would marry someone else if they didn't find

Mr. or Ms. Perfect, 34 percent of the women said yes, compared with 41 percent of men.

Lisa Clampitt, the New York City matchmaker, wasn't surprised. Her male clients are often more open-minded than the women. If she asks a guy to move his upper age limit from 30 to 35, he usually will. If she asks him to consider 5'2" instead of 5'6", he'll probably do it.

"Men are open to different styles, whereas women have a hard time with that," Clampitt said. "They have a lot of rules about who they'll date and who they won't. They can't let go of their ideal guy."

Dan Ariely, the behavioral economist at MIT, studied more than twenty thousand online daters and also found that women were pickier than men. Basically, if a woman was above a certain threshold of physical attractiveness and seemed warm, the guy was interested. The men didn't microanalyze dating prospects for income, education level, what kind of work they did, height, or race to the degree women analyzed men in those categories.

"Women have a more concrete picture in their minds of what the guy is going to be like," Ariely told me. "Men have more of a vague notion, and they're not so rigid about the details."

Okay, but that's about initial attraction. Once they were in relationships, I knew plenty of men who nixed women for what I considered to be lame reasons. Ben, a 45-year-old banker, told me that he'd broken up with one girlfriend because her ankles were too thick, another because they didn't share the same taste in furniture ("I felt we could never agree on how to make a home together"), and another because, believe it or not, they were "too similar."

Too similar?

"We had a lot of fun," he explained, "but I ultimately realized we weren't different enough to make the relationship interesting long-term." When I asked Ben what sorts of issues girlfriends might have had with him, he cited things like lack of attentiveness to their stories, being a terrible procrastinator, and letting his body "go to pot" (yet he couldn't deal with his girlfriend's ankles?).

A cute lawyer broke up with two women whose company he enjoyed very much, except at dinner parties: one was too talkative ("She dominated the conversation") and the other was too shy ("I always felt responsible for keeping the conversation going for her"). He didn't seem to realize that if he got married and had kids, he wouldn't be going to as many dinner parties and that how much he enjoyed his wife's company one-on-one would become most important.

"I'm looking for just the right balance," he explained. "Kind of like the Three Bears." (I guess women aren't the only ones who believe in fairy tales.)

"Well," Ariely said when I shared these stories, "sometimes it's less about being picky and more about having intimacy issues. Both men and women can have intimacy issues, but in general, in psychologically healthy people who also want to get married, women make more calculated decisions than men. Less is needed to make men fall in love. Ask men and women what percentage of people they'd date, and women will give a much smaller percentage. Why? There's the evolutionary story. But I think there's also a cultural one."

From an evolutionary perspective, he said, women have had to be particular because they needed someone to help them raise their babies. In more recent times, though, cultural standards seem to have made women inordinately picky—and not just about the baby-related things like income and good genes. To check that out, I asked dozens of women what they wanted in a partner, and got all the usual responses: someone attractive, funny, smart, kind, and financially stable. But if I probed just a tiny bit more, they also wanted—actually, *required*—a partner with a dynamic emotional life, a guy who would listen to her feelings and share his feelings the way their girlfriends did. When I asked why, several people said they want a guy who is emotionally complex because, to them, that signifies a thoughtful and reflective person.

That seemed legitimate. But don't men want a thoughtful and reflective partner, too? Yes and no, Ariely said. He believes that men tend to view emotional complexity differently: emotionally complex women seem neurotic and high-maintenance to a lot of men. A woman's idea of complexity might be a man's idea of instability.

Melissa, who is 33 and admits to being "emotionally complex," thinks Ariely is right.

"People say men settle for women who are just not challenging," she said, "but that's wrong because I think that's what many men *look for*—the easy-going wife, the adoring wife, the low-maintenance and unchallenging wife. The wife who doesn't overthink things. Which makes men *seem* less picky. But are men less picky, or do men and women just want different things?"

One-Stop Shopping

The guys I spoke to think they do. They feel that women often expect a lot—and men can't live up to it all. Kyle, the journalist in New York, said that back when he was dating, women wanted to find both the tall, wealthy guy and the emotional equivalent of a gal pal.

"Women want their men to be gay and straight at the same time," he explained. "This creates a lot of frustration with men, and resentment. Straight men don't want to talk about fashion or nitpick over people's personality foibles the way gay men do."

That reminded me of a conversation I had with a close friend one night, when I said that I wanted what she had with her husband—they seemed like the ideal combination of lovers and best friends.

"Actually," she said, "my best friend is you."

She explained it like this: "If I told my husband even half of what I tell you, he'd die of boredom and tune me out, and then we'd get into a fight about how he's not listening to me. Besides, instead of nagging him every day, I complain to you!"

I was confused. "If I'm your best friend," I asked, "does that mean your husband isn't?"

"Maybe," she smiled. "But I still love him more than you."

It's a distinction she said she couldn't make even a few years back. Then one day, frustrated that her husband wasn't as interested in emotional topics as she was, she had a realization. "I thought, even our best friends don't meet all our needs. That's why we have *many* close friends, not just one. So why does a husband have to be an uber-friend who meets every need and shares every interest? Who can handle that kind of pressure?"

It's a lesson she thinks more single women should learn.

I remembered, too, what my friend Andy, one of the "men who got away," had said about his wife.

"I think one-stop shopping is overrated," he told me. "I get passion at my office with my work, or with my friends that I sometimes call or chat with—it's not the same, and, boy, it would be exciting to have it with my spouse. But I spend more time with people at my office than I do with my spouse."

I asked if he considered that settling. "Not at all," he said. "She has a lot of the qualities I wanted in a spouse. And I was tired of looking for all the things she's not."

Most men I spoke to seemed realistic about the limitations of one human being providing total fulfillment for another. As Kurt, the engaged guy I spoke to back at the bar in Los Angeles put it, "Men don't care if you watch football games together, but women won't marry you if you don't want to hear the minute details of their book club meeting."

I was starting to think about the issue this way: Men and women both have to compromise to be with a mate, but they compromise differently. For married men, the biggest compromise is sexual monogamy. For married women, the biggest compromise is not having emotional monogamy. In other words, the compromise is not having one all-encompassing emotional connection, and having to get some of that connection outside of the marriage. It's having to accept that one human being can't provide a level of emotional intensity that most men don't want in the first place.

I CAN BE LESS PICKY—IN THEORY

Annie is 34 and out there dating again. For three years, she was married to a handsome, smart, funny, and exciting guy who was a great boyfriend, but turned out to be a terrible spouse. In retrospect, she feels she overlooked the warning signs. She'd always been picky, but after her divorce, she was trying to date differently.

"What's changed the most is that I still want to have positive feelings about the guy and find him interesting, but it doesn't have to be like 'I've never felt that way' or 'my toes are tingling.' I had that with the guy I married, and I know it can be misleading."

Now, she says, she realizes that other qualities are more important.

"I'm trying to be more appreciative of kindness and good company," she told me. "Things that are very basic, but that I didn't used to focus on as much as I should have. I just want someone relatively smart, very kind, financially secure, and who wants a family *now*. I'll redo the math on the physical stuff. I believe that, but sometimes I go back to my old ways."

Recently, she said, a married friend wanted to set her up with a lawyer at her husband's law firm. She looked at his Facebook page and thought he was cute but didn't like what he wrote.

"He had this typical corporate lawyer bio," Annie said. "I thought, Ugh—how boring. My friend didn't say he was a dullard, but she didn't say he was interesting either. She said, 'What's the downside of meeting him? He's a great guy.' But I thought, 'Do I want to make small talk about spicy tuna rolls with this guy?' Everyone says that I need to change my attitude and just go and see if we have fun."

I asked Annie how she would feel a few years from now if she's still single, knowing she wouldn't even go on a first date with a guy *because she didn't like his corporate bio*.

She thought about it for a minute. "When I'm 35, will I go out with this guy if he's still available? I'm not sure. I'm not there yet. But if in two years I wouldn't—then I would think it's *my* problem versus this is me trying to honor myself. Then it's just me being self-sabotaging." Annie says it's not just the biological clock that would motivate her to change. It's that most of her friends are in happy marriages and she wants what they have, too.

"I want to go through life with someone," she said. "And I know that means I have to let go of some fantasies I have, and that everyone compromises. In theory, I'm absolutely on board with being less picky. But in practice, I'm having a hard time with it."

Like Annie, 39-year-old Jocelyn is on board in theory only.

"I'm not a monk who can sit alone in my cell just waiting for the whole perfect scenario," she told me. "I know that life is imperfect. But I just know that I require a certain emotional depth and insight in a guy, and if I can't be with someone who truly appreciates my nuances, I'm not going to be interested in the long-term."

Evan Marc Katz, the dating coach, says that most women he works with start out like Annie and Jocelyn: *I can't help who I'm attracted to. I want to compromise, but I just can't.* To these women, Evan says, "Fine, don't compromise. Just don't be too surprised if everyone else 'compromises' their way into a fulfilling relationship while you keep chasing a dream that never has a happy ending."

WOMEN WANT MORE

Edna Pollin, a divorce attorney in Denver, told me that from what she sees, "Women are dissatisfied because they always want more." They want, for instance, more romance, more help around the house, more passion. Some want what she called "better income producers." Sure, she said, there are men in midlife crisis who initiate divorce, but more often it's the women who want out, leaving the men confused.

"The men feel like, 'Nobody told me we were having problems. I thought everything was fine,'" she explained.

Maybe that's one reason that, according to a report on divorce put out by the National Marriage Project at Rutgers University, two-thirds of divorces are initiated by women. Pollin said that women often expect their spouses to be "everything" and then feel like something's missing—their soul mate, for instance.

Keith, 36, told me that when his wife asked for a divorce a year ago, she told him, "I love you, but I am not in love with you."

Turned out she was "in love" with someone else.

"I have an MBA, a good job in computer security, a pilot's license, own my own house, am in decent shape, and volunteer teaching GED classes. I go to church. I'm not the exciting roller-coaster ride. I get paid to be cautious and manage risk. I'm not an exciting Romeo. That's what my ex left me for."

I asked Paul Amato, a sociologist at Penn State who studies divorced couples, why women do things like this.

He told me that it has to do with a gender difference in expectations. Often women he studied said they believed that marriage was going to be different—more exciting, or easier. So they think the problem is the husband: They think *he's* become boring, but really it's marriage that's "boring" compared to the romance of the dating years.

I asked some men about their expectations for marriage. Alex, who is 39 and has been married for four years, told me he's fine not getting everything on his wife wish list, because he's deeply in love with his spouse.

"I wish my wife weren't so uptight about day-to-day life," he said. "I wish she were more tolerant of my slower pace in getting things done. And I wish she were younger and sexier, but isn't that always the case in a long-term relationship?"

Graham, who is 34 and in a serious relationship, told me that there are always things he wishes were different in his relationships, but most of them aren't big enough to be deal-breakers. When he's ruled out women in the past, it always came down to different values—career goals, money, safety, religion, parenting for future kids. He never broke up with his past girlfriends over things like this: "I wished I were with someone who liked more of the same things, like playing sports or the same music or theater. I wished she liked to hike. I wished I were with someone who was able to continue to contribute financially even after kids are born. I wished I were with someone who was small enough so I could pick her up during sex. I wished I were with someone who wanted to have sex with the frequency that I do. I wished I were with someone who preferred coming to my apartment in Brooklyn so I didn't have to stay at her place in Manhattan all the time."

As I listened to his list, I thought about all the women I knew who had broken up with guys, or would without hesitation, if the tables were turned: He didn't share an interest of hers, he didn't make enough money, he wanted sex more than she did, he wouldn't make the trek to her apartment. Yet this guy accepted these things.

Graham's current girlfriend is by no means perfect, but to break up, he feels, would be too picky. His girlfriend isn't athletic and doesn't like sports; she's much taller than he'd like; there are some potential sexual issues to work out; she can be dramatic in situations that Graham feels don't merit drama.

"I'm sticking with it," he said, "because the things I do find important seem to be there. She's bright, there's mutual attraction, we laugh and sing together, we have similar values, there's a feeling of mutual respect and admiration."

Jack, a 30-year-old Web designer who's about to get married, told me he felt bad ten years ago, when he was rejected after confessing his romantic interest to his best friend from college. But as he listened to her dating stories over the years, he realized it wasn't personal. He's seen her reject men based on one piece of information ("He went a month without medical insurance—how irresponsible is that?"), one sentence (He said, "All the *girls* I've gone out with"), or one pet name she didn't like ("He called me 'dude' as a term of endearment").

"I enjoy her friendship, but who'd want to go out with someone as judgmental as that?" he asked. "She always puts her finger on the one thing that's wrong with a guy."

I'd been guilty of that in the past, but now I had the opposite problem: What happens when you can't quite put your finger on what's wrong? I was thinking about this after my second date with Mike. I needed to talk to Evan. I needed to get clearer on what really matters.

PART FOUR

What Really Matters

Love is an ideal thing, marriage a real thing; a confusion of the real with the ideal never goes unpunished.

—Goethe

17

Mondays with Evan

Session Four—Wants Versus Needs

At our fourth coaching session, I gave Evan the update on Mike.

"I wish I could say that I liked him more on the second date," I explained. "I wish I could say that his being an attractive, nice, well-intentioned guy who's close to my age and a great dad and is looking to be married again was enough. But I can't."

It had nothing to do with the alpha male thing. I'd pretty much let go of that. Instead, it was just that we weren't connecting more generally. It went beyond these two dates: Even in e-mail exchanges and on several phone calls, I told Evan, the only thing that Mike and I really shared beyond the superficial was our love of parenthood. That's no small thing, I know. But otherwise, our conversations felt forced and the more we talked, instead of developing an easier rapport, we simply ran out of things to say. There's only so much small talk two people who clearly aren't clicking can make.

I told Evan about another guy I'd discovered online. Like Mike, Rick was a divorced dad and an involved parent. From his profile and half a dozen e-mails, he seemed interesting: He was a funny, self-deprecating, intellectual-seeming history professor. We wrote back and forth with a flirtatious ease. We understood each other's references. We seemed to have similar views and lifestyles. There were some downsides—he was fifty and looked his age; his kids were teenagers and I had a two-year-old—but none of that mattered. I was trying not to sweat the details anymore, and I was excited about our connection. He asked to talk by phone and I gave him my number.

He called me that day, but I wasn't home, so he left a message. Then, before I had a chance to call back, he called three more times. I don't mean that I looked at my Caller ID and discovered that he'd called and hung up. I mean that he actually spoke to my voicemail, three times in the span of five hours, and said, as if this were perfectly normal behavior, "Hi, it's Rick from online! Just seeing if we could chat." Then he'd leave his number. Every time.

By the time I got his messages it was late at night. I was going to call him the next day after work, but during the day, Rick called three more times—three!—and two of those times, he left the same message. "Hi, it's Rick from online! Guess I missed you. Hope to hear from you." The day before, I thought he might have been nervous or overeager. I was willing to give him the benefit of the doubt. Now I just thought he was creepy. Who calls someone you've never even met *six times in twenty-four hours*? I didn't call him back.

A few days later, I picked up the phone as I was walking out the door, and it was Rick. "Hey, it's Rick," he said casually, as if we were old friends and I'd instantly know who he was. "How are you?" I explained that I was about to leave but I'd call him back later. At that moment, I honestly thought I'd give him another chance. But when I got home a few hours later, I saw that he'd called and hung up on my machine again! I decided that was too weird.

"He strikes me as a stalker, or at least as someone who has no clue about basic social interaction," I told Evan.

Evan agreed that his behavior was totally creepy. "One of the most common complaints I hear from women is that men don't pay enough attention. But when they pay too much attention—they call too much, they call too soon, they express their excitement too soon—women get turned off. I usually encourage women to give the awkward guys a break. But being open to awkward isn't the same as going out with freaks."

Finally, a situation where it wasn't a case of me being too picky!

EVAN READS ME THE RIOT ACT

Okay, I didn't want to date freaks, but I also wanted to date people I had more of a natural connection with than Mike.

I didn't think that was too much to ask, but when I told Evan that replying to an e-mail from a real estate broker who was wearing a pink polka-dot bow tie would be a waste of time, Evan sighed and shook his head, like a teacher frustrated with a lazy student. Then he looked me in the eye and, for the first time since we started our sessions, completely lost his patience.

"You're listening to me each week, but you're not changing!" he said, raising his voice into a near-yell. "You won't open up to anything other than what you've been open to for the past twenty years! You're like the person who wants to lose weight but won't change their eating or exercise habits. 'But this is what I *like* to eat!' they say. And their doctor would say, 'Fine, you keep eating that—but you won't lose weight!' You have to do something differently if you want different results. The waste of time isn't e-mailing guys like this. The waste of time is *not* e-mailing guys like this. Will he be The Guy? I don't know. But it's like a lottery, and one of these guys might well turn out to be someone you click with. And you'll never find out because you've wasted all your time *not* giving anyone a chance!"

Wow. We both sat there in silence for several minutes. I felt like such an idiot. I kept thinking I was changing, but in reality I was only changing in my head. I wasn't changing that much in my *actions*. Here I was, 41 and single, after years of dismissing good guys for bad reasons—men like Andy and Jeff and Sheldon and Scott. And now, I wouldn't even e-mail a guy who fit a lot of what I was looking for, who wrote me a very clever e-mail, and who might be interested in someone like me, despite my own baggage and flaws, just because of what he did for a living (selling real estate seemed as boring to me as accounting) and what he was wearing (that pink polka-dot bow tie!).

I broke the silence by tapping on my keyboard. I wrote a note to Bow Tie Guy as Evan sat there looking over my shoulder.

The lesson I should have learned from the Creepy Stalker incident, Evan said after I pushed "send," is that the person who seems great based on his profile can turn out to be disappointing as often as the guy who isn't your type turns out to be appealing.

"None of these people are real until you're in a committed relationship with them," Evan said, "You're always projecting something onto them. Stop drawing a picture of The Guy in your head because the real guy won't look like that."

Which is why, whenever I objected to meeting a guy who seemed too serious, or too old, Evan would say, "It's just a date!" Whenever I said that the fact that a guy lived an hour away wasn't ideal, Evan would say, "Nothing's ideal. People expect ideal and they miss out on opportunities to meet the right guy. Even what you think is ideal isn't ultimately going to be ideal. There's no such thing as ideal. So let go of ideal."

WHICH BRINGS US BACK TO MIKE

I was willing to let go of ideal, but what exactly did that mean? Mike was a good guy and at the same life stage, raising small children like me. He was cute and reliable. Yet his whole vibe was drastically different from mine. We had a hard time finding things to talk about. I was intensely intellectually curious by nature and he was very laid back by nature. We weren't connecting.

"I don't think it's unreasonable to want intellectual stimulation *and* a devoted dad," I told Evan. "I have friends who have husbands like that. It's not impossible to find."

"It's not," Evan agreed. "And if those two things are absolute needs, then you should look for that. But then you can't go around nixing guys who are devoted dads and intellectually stimulating because they wear pink bow ties. You can't have everything."

I didn't think I wanted "everything," but when Evan asked me to write down my "needs"—as opposed to my "wants"—I came up with fourteen things. Evan told me that if I wanted to be realistic, I should narrow the list down to three.

I was surprised. Only three?

"The difference between 'needs' and 'wants' is crucial," he explained. "If you have fourteen 'needs,' it means that if a guy has thirteen of the fourteen qualities, he's gone! And even if he's most of these things, you have to remember that a lot of good qualities flip over and become bad qualities. Someone highly intelligent and analytical can also be opinionated and a know-it-all. Someone easygoing may have no opinions or be lazy."

He told me about a client of his who'd had her heart broken by a charming but commitment-phobic man. When she was ready to date again, she went online and sifted through her responses. She was excited about one guy who reminded her of her ex. They went out on a date, he said he'd call, and he didn't.

But another guy did. "In her view, he wasn't the most compelling candidate in the bunch," Evan said, "but he just kept asking her out. Every time my client would go on a date with him, she would have fun. And then she'd complain to me that he wasn't what she was looking for."

He was too short for her. He wasn't rugged enough. But he met her *needs*: He was thoughtful and reliable, he had the same values as she did, and he shared a similar lifestyle. And when she distinguished between her wants and her needs, she fell in love. She thought she wanted the charming, manly-man guy—and maybe on some level she still *wants* that—but what she *needed* was someone fun and thoughtful and reliable who had similar goals and values.

Evan said her story is like that of a guy who gets fired from his job and thinks his life is over, only to realize it's a perfect opportunity for him to create the life he always dreamed of. He wouldn't have chosen to get fired, of course. It wasn't what he thought he wanted, but it made him happier than he ever imagined because it opened him up to a possibility he hadn't considered before.

That's also why so many married people say, "I wouldn't have chosen my spouse on an online dating Web site," because their spouses weren't what they thought they wanted. Until, of course, they met them.

Narrowing Down the Needs

"What you want isn't necessarily good for you," Evan said. "And in going after the person you think you want, you ignore what you really need."

But figuring out what you need isn't easy. If distinguishing wants from needs can seem baffling, he said, sometimes our desires even contradict themselves: *I want someone with strong opinions . . . who never argues. I want someone who's spontaneous and wild . . . who has a stable job.*

Evan told me about a male dating client who couldn't figure out what he needed, either. This guy was around 40, smart, successful, and serious about getting married. He wanted someone smart and mature, but who was easygoing and slender. So he'd go out on dates, and then he'd complain that the younger women with the great bodies were often a little too immature and at a different stage of life, the brainy corporate lawyers were a little too demanding, and the women who were more mature generally didn't have the younger body type he preferred.

How do you get over it? You distinguish between your wants and needs. Evan gave some examples:

You *want* someone creative.
   You **need** someone you can trust.

You *want* someone who shares your love of jazz.
   You **need** someone who appreciates some of your interests.

You *want* someone who is athletic and physically active.
   You **need** someone who accepts you at your worst.

A few minutes later, I was able to narrow down my list to three essential needs: intellectually curious, kid-friendly, and financially stable. That's it.

Obviously, these weren't the only qualities I would be looking for in a partner, but they would be the only basis on which I could rule someone out for a first date. In other words, I couldn't say no to a first date with a guy who wore bow ties but met these three requirements.

Now that I clarified my needs, Evan pointed out that it made sense why Mike and I had fizzled out. He was definitely kid-friendly, but he wasn't intellectually curious and, as a freelance consultant supporting two kids and trying to make ends meet from job-to-job, he was iffy on financial stability. He had many wonderful qualities, but he met just one out of my three essential needs. For a woman with three *different* essential needs, he'd be a great catch.

Making this distinction felt good. I knew this wasn't a magic formula, but it seemed like a better screening tool than my usual, "I'm either excited about him or I'm not." And it sure seemed better than comparing him to a mental list of fourteen "essential" items.

I felt like finally, I was starting to turn a small corner.

That night, the real estate guy in the bow tie e-mailed back and I got more information. He was a 46-year-old widowed dad with an 8-year-old son. "Real estate" meant that he designed houses and sold them, and he seemed passionate about his work. He was 5'6" and balding, but funny and thoughtful in his e-mail. He seemed sophisticated and smart, despite not having been highly educated. He suggested that we talk on the phone, but I took it a step further. If he was intellectually curious, a good dad, and financially stable, what more did I need to know to before agreeing to a first date? Why not just meet?

This may not seem like a big deal, but it felt like real progress for me. I'd made so many mistakes on those first phone calls—jumping to all kinds of conclusions that weren't helpful or accurate. Dan Ariely of MIT had warned me about how misleading those phone calls were—how they only set you up to have unrealistic expectations if the call went well, or led you to decline a date if it went less than well than you expected (like what happened with Scuba Matt).

So in the spirit of changing my *actions*, I suggested that we get together instead. Not for coffee, where I could get in and out in twenty minutes, but for an afternoon hike, where I'd be with the guy for a couple of hours of conversation. I wasn't going to interview him on the date, either. I was just going to try to have a good time.

We set the date for the following Tuesday. Oh—and this is the unbelievable part—his name was Sheldon! I mean, not literally Sheldon, but he had the same name as the guy I'd called Sheldon. I was amazed, and even pleased. Because this time, instead of being judgmental, I thought the universe was giving me a second chance.

I decided to call him "Sheldon2."

A Husband Who Wants to Get Married

When I told my friend Maggie about "Sheldon2" and how I'd narrowed down my needs to just three, she said she'd also gone through that process recently—with her fiancé.

"My mom once told me that one characteristic to look for in a husband is simply someone who wants to be married," she said. "Look for someone for whom the married lifestyle is appealing. I remember thinking that was fairly unromantic—after all, shouldn't *I* be enough to make someone want to commit for life? Aren't I just inherently that great? But I also suspected there was some truth in it."

Like me, Maggie spent most of her twenties looking for an intense connection. She found it in a long-term relationship with an older guy who was in many ways a great match—they were both talented, creative film producers—but the more years they stayed together, the more it became apparent that they wanted different things in life.

"When it didn't work out," she said, "I remember being shocked at this, because I thought love could conquer all. But it can't conquer fundamental differences in what you want your life to be."

Then, at 30, she met Will.

"He didn't seem like someone I would be with *at all*," she said, "and I spent about six months sort of holding him at arm's length because he didn't meet my 'criteria' of what I wanted. He was a scientist and I didn't understand what he did at all for the first three months. He was totally scruffy in a college dude way—he hadn't cut his hair in like six months when I first met him, and he had no actual furniture in his apartment. It was all milk crates and a futon. He was really shy and not good at witty banter."

So Will didn't meet some of her "wants." But, she told me, he met her core "needs": (1) He was interesting and intellectually curious, (2) They had shared values and goals, and (3) He was dependable and loyal.

Meanwhile, she said, "All of our other differences are things that I've come to find fun and interesting." They didn't have many interests in common when they first got together, but they've had a lot of fun introducing each other to new things. She goes mountain biking and hiking with him now, and he likes going to plays with her. They also connected on the practical stuff.

"We both, thankfully, had the same opinions, by and large, about money and kids. These two things I think are the most important externals that challenge compatibility, so I'm relieved for us that we were so much on the same page from the beginning."

What Maggie ended up with is a happy balance of wants and

needs. She learned in her early thirties something essential that I was just learning in my forties: "Love" isn't independent of practical things, and if we want to find a happy relationship, we have to learn how to take those practical things into consideration.

But just how practical should we be in the search for love?

18

The Business of Love

Soon after I spoke to Maggie, a guy named John Curtis offered to send me a copy of his book. It arrived with a heart divided by a ticker tape symbol on the cover, and this quote right above it, attributed to the *New York Times*:

"This provocative, groundbreaking book may be the must-read relationship book of the decade!"

The book was called *The Business of Love: 9 Best Practices for Improving the Bottom Line of Your Relationship*, and if you've never heard of this book, don't worry, you're not alone. When I called up Curtis, a former marriage and family therapist who later became a management consultant, he admitted that using the word "business" in a book about relationships tends to turn people off.

"I had a hard time selling it, frankly," he said from his office in North Carolina. "People want the softer side of love. They blindly move into relationships thinking, 'We're so in love, we'll work it all out.' Then they're fighting all the time because they never sat down to talk about the division of labor, or how to allocate their finances, because it felt unromantic. Well, how romantic is it to argue because you never bothered to come up with a practical plan?"

Curtis's book teaches couples how to create a vision statement for their relationship, outline specific objectives on various dimensions (family, fiscal, leisure, career), generate his and her job descriptions, and decide on compensation and benefits. A marriage has always been a socioeconomic partnership, Curtis said, but societal expectations began to change in the sixties and seventies.

Or as Stephanie Coontz put it in her book *Marriage, A History*: "The older view that wives and husbands were work mates gave way to the idea that they were soul mates." But, she noted, "Only rarely in history has love been seen as the main reason for getting married."

That's why Curtis feels that love alone isn't enough for a successful marriage. "Marriage is like running a business in a lot of ways— who cooks dinner, who picks up the towels, who pays the bills, what is the budget we're working with—and two businesspeople would never start a business without knowing who's going to do this, who's going to do that, what the timeline is for certain goals. If you're forming a partnership with someone—including a romantic partnership— there's more likelihood for success if you sit down together and articulate your shared vision for the partnership early on."

It made sense to me now. What I didn't realize when I chose to date only men who excited me from the get-go (without considering the practical side of things), is that what makes for a good marriage isn't necessarily what makes for a good romantic relationship. According to my married friends, once you're married, it's not so much about who you want to go on a tropical vacation with; it's about who you want to run a household with. Marriage isn't a constant passion-fest; it's more like a partnership formed to run a very small, mundane nonprofit business.

And that, they say, can be really, really nice. Having a solid, like-minded teammate in life is pleasurable in its own way, and for most people, it's certainly better than not having one at all.

Older, Overweight, and Bald (Which They All Eventually Become Anyway)

If this sounds unromantic, when I look at my friends' marriages, with their routine day-to-dayness, they actually seem far more romantic than any dating relationship might be. Dating *seems* romantic, but for the most part it's an extended audition. Marriage *seems* boring, but for the most part it's a state of comfort and acceptance. Dating is about grand romantic gestures that mean little over the long-term. Marriage is about small acts of kindness that bond you over a lifetime. It's quietly romantic. He makes her tea. She goes to the doctor appointment with him. They listen to each other's daily trivia. They put up with each other's quirks. They're there for each other.

"I just want someone who's willing to be in the trenches with me," my single 41-year-old friend Jennifer told me, "and I never thought of marriage that way before."

I hadn't, either. When I was in my late thirties, my long-married friend Renée offered this dating advice to me in an e-mail:

> I would say even if he's not the love of your life, make sure he's someone you respect intellectually, makes you laugh, appreciates you . . . I bet there are plenty of these men in the older, overweight, and bald category (which they all eventually become anyway).

At the time, I thought she was kidding (she wasn't), but now it sounds smart. Thinking about marriage in a romantic vacuum isn't much different from being a naive tenth-grade girl who gets pregnant by her high school boyfriend and goes around telling everyone, "Oh, we love each other, we'll make it work." Love doesn't conquer all in a reality-based world.

If I'd been thinking practically when I was younger, I probably would have been with better-suited men for what I want now—a smart, like-minded partner who will be an involved parent. I knew I wanted that, of course, but I also wanted fifteen other things that were not only idealistic, but antithetical to those very practical traits I sought. For a while my boyfriends had to be "artistic" and "unconventional," but most of those guys had neither the temperament nor the means to help me run the future household I hoped for.

Now I was starting to realize that there's a practical underpinning to almost every aspect of romantic relationships—and it starts with how we date.

THE PRINCE CHARMING PRICE TAG

One night, a married friend and I added up the costs—financial, logistical, and emotional—of dating for a year versus being married for that year, once you're in your thirties. It went like this:

Say you're single and you want to meet someone. You're no longer in school, so on a typical day, you don't encounter available, age-appropriate men as often as you used to. You may have been working in the same place for several years, in which case few new single men come into your orbit. Even when one shows up, he's not necessarily interested in you and/or you're not necessarily interested in him. You may even work in a field populated almost exclusively by women: teaching, social work, fashion, publicity, nutrition, design, fund-raising, publishing. By the time you're over thirty, many people are married, and some have kids, so social events like parties or barbecues happen less often than they did in your twenties, and there are fewer single male guests.

Given that your social life probably involves a lot of dead-end dates, short-lived relationships, and other single women friends (usually talking about how hard it is to meet men), you realize that you need to be proactive. You join an online dating service for a year ($200). When you become burned out on the first site, you may even join a second one ($200). You spend five hours a week corresponding with people and doing searches (cost: whatever your professional hourly rate is plus the emotional exhaustion involved). If you have a ticking biological clock and you're pulling out all the stops, you may even hire a matchmaker (anywhere from $500 to several thousand dollars).

You need to look attractive on first dates, so there's the cost of the wardrobe—skirts, pants, blouses, sweaters, camisoles, coats, shoes, purses, jackets, jewelry. You have to be prepared for everything from a dressy restaurant to a boho coffeehouse to a basketball game or an afternoon hike, in all kinds of weather conditions ($1,000 for six outfits, through four seasons). You need a good haircut every two months ($450 for six cuts with tip). You might also need color to cover the gray roots—welcome to your thirties ($400 for four times). You need an eyebrow wax, and as you get into your mid-thirties, you'll probably need a lip wax for the burgeoning premenopausal mustache ($25 a month). Makeup and skin care products aren't cheap, either ($300 a year). Some women also indulge in manicures ($15 a pop), pedicures ($25), facials ($50), and even teeth whitening ($650). Every date takes an hour of round-trip transportation time, an hour of getting dressed time, two hours of actual date time, and, for some of us, an hour of therapy time to talk about how depressing it is to still be single ($100 a session).

Now, let's say you're lucky enough to meet someone you want to date. I'll call him Brad. You and Brad have "chemistry"! He's smart, funny, attractive, cool, and likes the same music you do. Suddenly you have more wardrobe costs (you can't wear your first- and second-date outfits over and over). Granny panties won't cut it, so you have bra and panty costs (even at Target, we're talking $100, as you'll need several sets). If you're over 35, gravity will be taking a toll, so you may have to splurge for one of those super-duper Miracle Bras ($50 each). Your waxing costs are higher (it's no longer just about the, uh, eyebrows).

Then, two months in, it's Brad's birthday. You're excited about each other. You want his birthday to be great. You either make him dinner ($50 for food, $50 for wine, plus a lot of time shopping, preparing, and cooking) or you take him out someplace (a nice restaurant, a concert—none of this is cheap). You buy a cake and a gift ($100). You two keep dating, so you continue shopping, waxing, getting pedicures. Soon it's the holiday season. Again, you buy him gifts ($75). You're spending more time together, so you're giving up the opportunity to meet other available men while you're still this age and look this good and have this much time left on your biological clock.

But four months later, the relationship isn't working out so well. You're losing interest, he's losing interest—doesn't matter. You break up. Now you have to start over—all that time, money, emotional energy, and lost opportunity spent on yet another failed relationship.

Total cost so far: $2,000 without the therapy, $3,600 with the therapy.

So you go back to trying to meet a guy. You're hanging out online (already paid for). You're asking friends to set you up (cost: time, effort, and humiliation). You're going to bars ($15 for drinks, one hour to get ready, one hour of round-trip transportation, $40 dry cleaning bill for the beer some guy accidentally spilled on your suede boots). You're constantly going to places where you might meet men: dinner parties ($20 for the dessert you brought), ball games ($20 for the ticket plus the annoyance, since you don't like basketball anyway), photography classes ($100), museum openings ($10 for the ticket, only to see that every guy there is gay or married), and library lectures (ditto).

You meet someone! Steve's not your fantasy—he's not very athletic, and you're not feeling as much chemistry as you'd like—but he's cute, kind, smart, and really into you. You invest in that relationship (financially, emotionally, logistically). You meet Steve's parents, you become close with his sister, and spend a lot of time with his family. But after five months, you worry that he's not what you're looking for. He's just not . . . you can't really articulate it, but you're certain that when you meet The One, you won't have these kinds of doubts. So it's back to the drawing board.

Three weeks later, you meet your future husband! Finally, you think, it's happened! You go on to date the guy you're convinced is The One, only to realize two months later that he's self-absorbed, clueless, arrogant, dumb, humorless, dull, mean, afraid of commitment, or just-not-that-into-you.

The costs at the end of one year: $4,000 without therapy. $9,000 with therapy, although you'll probably quit therapy right about now because even your therapist can't keep track of all your dates' names at this point.

SUNK COSTS AND OPPORTUNITY COSTS

What you're left with is what economists call "sunk costs"—all the time, money, and emotional reserves you've invested in something with absolutely no payoff. It's like renting a new apartment every six months, paying the moving costs, decorating it, and throwing all that rent money the landlord's way, instead of investing in a place that you've bought and that will build up equity over the years. Not only do you have start-up costs with each new relationship (the money, time, and effort of retelling your entire life story and imparting information like your favorite pizza toppings, along with learning someone else's), but none of those costs are transferable to the next relationship. By dating for "better," you're losing net worth, and you've gained nothing except the enormous stress of getting older and still being single.

Maybe you're saying, "Wait, there *was* a payoff. I *did* gain something. I grew as a person in that relationship." Okay. But at what point is growing as a person in relationship after relationship as valuable as growing as a person inside a realistic but happy marriage? In your twenties, breaking up is largely about heartbreak and loneliness; in your thirties, it's also about the angst of possibly ending up alone.

Of course, men who can't accept a good enough spouse also have sunk costs—especially if they're paying for more of the meals and entertainment. But what they don't have to the same degree are the "opportunity costs" of the quest for a "better" mate. While you spent time in a relationship that didn't work out, you lost the opportunity to be out there meeting other guys. Men, on the other hand, don't have a closing window in which to have biological kids. Moreover, if they spend six months or a year in a go-nowhere relationship, they don't lose value in the dating market the way women in their thirties do. If anything, men become more valuable in their thirties, and if they start to lose their value around age 50, they can still meet and marry someone ten to fifteen years younger and start a family together.

As any economist will tell you, it's all about supply and demand. The longer you hold out, the more the supply of available men goes down at the same time that their demand goes up and a woman's marital value goes down. The result, for women, is like a really bad dating recession.

The Bachelor Auction

In 2008, a *Slate* magazine article by Mark Gimein used an auction analogy to explain the low supply of men as women get older. If dating is like an auction, you'd think that the stronger bidders—the more appealing women—would "win." Instead, Gimein says, the strong bidders are so confident in their ability to find a guy that they bid *too late*. While the strong bidders wait for the best possible prospect, the weak bidders—the less conventionally appealing women—bid earlier and more aggressively because they know they can be outbid.

So what happens? More and more appealing men, rejected by the strong bidders, are taken off the dating market by the weak bidders. In the end, what's left are the least appealing men—the ones even the weak bidders didn't bid on!—along with the most appealing (but overly confident) women.

After reading this article, I thought about the men older women I know have married over the past few years: a still-trying-to-make-it-in-his-forties actor who works as a temp; a depressed widower with three nightmarish kids; a workaholic who spends all his time trying to start new businesses that inevitably fail—but who refuses to consider working for a company. It's not that these men have no good qualities or that the women who married them are crazy. It's just that the few available men who will also date an older woman require far more of a concession than the men who would date us when we were younger but too cocky to bid in the auction.

"Where have all the appealing men gone?" Gimein writes. "Most of them married young—and sometimes to women whose most salient characteristic was not their beauty, or passion, or intellect, but their decisiveness."

A Year of Marriage

Now, let's say that instead of being single for a year in your thirties, you spent that year married to a great guy (but not some fantasy Prince Charming). What are your costs? You'll have to share a bathroom, but Prince Charming pees on the toilet rim, too. You might have to give up some independence and time alone, but how much quality alone time did you really have between the gym and a full-time job that pays the bills and going to bars or parties looking for men?

You'll still get waxes and haircuts and buy clothes, but you can hang out in sweats and a ponytail on a daily basis and it won't matter so much to a guy who leaves his underwear on the floor and farts in your presence. You don't have to do the upkeep required to be in physical dating condition, which, as you get older, is harder not only because you're probably supporting yourself with a demanding career, but because you're constantly competing with younger and more attractive women for the same men. Your husband may wish that you still looked as good as you did when you were dating, but he's been in love with you for a while, so he'll overlook the tummy hairs.

If you're married, your days are more pleasant because you can relax at home in the evenings and have a companion to talk to instead of running around town meeting strangers and trying to be charming and make a good impression. You'll still do things for the holidays and your spouse's birthday, and you'll still go on vacations, but now you'll have shared lifetime memories as a payoff for all that effort and expense, which is well worth the economic investment. Even if you spend an annual $3,000 on a few outfits, manicures, waxes, haircuts, a weekend getaway, and gifts for your husband, it's a long-term investment. There are no sunk costs, opportunity costs, or the cost of an album full of photos that you'll have to crop in half (to get rid of the boyfriend you no longer speak to) if you want to have any visual memory of your life during that year.

And let's not forget: The money you spend while married is, in effect, both yours and your spouse's. Even if you keep separate checking accounts, there are two people maintaining the household, so you're not sacrificing as much as if these were expenditures from an individual without the economic security and backup of a partnership. These are low-risk investments.

When my married friend and I finished our admittedly unscientific calculation, it seemed that from a cost-benefit perspective, being married over 30 clearly beat out being single over 30. Granted, the sunk costs could be compensated for if you had an unusually high income. The emotional costs could be dealt with if you could vent to a best friend who had the patience of Mother Teresa. But there's simply no way around those opportunity costs.

The biggest opportunity cost, of course, is the possibility that you'll give up a really good guy only to end up with nobody.

SELLING TOO EARLY

That's what happened to Emily who, at 27, broke up with Sam, a nice, loving, and smart but not particularly "hip" technology guy she adored, in order to go out with Jonathan, an irresistibly sexy film agent who shared all of her interests. Two years later, that relationship fizzled out, and she realized that Sam was the right guy for her after all. Meanwhile, once Sam hit 30, his stock shot up in value, he had tons of women who wanted to date him, he didn't forgive Emily for dumping him, and she couldn't get him back (she tried!). Three years later, he was married. She sold too early.

In economics, what she did made no sense. If your goal is financial stability, you don't invest in risky, volatile stocks because they're the "hot" picks of the week. Everyone knows that they rarely turn out to be good long-term investments (like the "hot" men who often aren't as great as they seem).

But many of us play those odds anyway. We take incredible risks, because we believe that everything is reversible, that no one decision is make or break. But when you have a time limit, one bad choice can make or break whether you'll ever marry, whether you'll have kids, whether you'll have more than one kid, and whether you'll marry someone as enjoyable as the person you turned away three or thirteen years earlier. We don't know how to stop while we're ahead, so we give up our best (and perhaps last) chance for marital happiness.

Emily is now 37 and single. She dates a lot of older, divorced men with kids. She didn't realize that holding out for Prince Charming rarely means ending up with a storybook family. She certainly didn't grow up dreaming about marrying a middle-aged divorced guy with resentful kids who don't want a stepmom and an ex-wife who pages him at 10 p.m. to talk about the school carpool the next day.

When she was younger, she thought the price of compromising was too high. Now, though, she's paying an even higher price for having not compromised.

DEPRECIATING ASSETS

I'll be the first to admit that there's something unseemly about discussing relationships from an economic perspective. In this post-feminist era, we say we believe that finding a partner should be a matter of love and love only. But as recently as 2007, a 25-year-old woman in New York, who claimed she was "articulate" and "classy" and described her looks as "spectacularly beautiful" posted a query on Craigslist in which she asked why she couldn't find a wealthy husband. A guy replied, in part, as follows:

Your offer, from the prospective of a guy like me, is plain and simple a crappy business deal. Here's why. Cutting through all the B.S., what you suggest is a simple trade: you bring your looks to the party and I bring my money. Fine, simple. But here's the rub, your looks will fade and my money will likely continue into perpetuity . . . in fact, it is very likely that my income increases but it is an absolute certainty that you won't be getting any more beautiful!

So, in economic terms you are a depreciating asset and I am an earning asset. Not only are you a depreciating asset, your depreciation accelerates! Let me explain, you're 25 now and will likely stay pretty hot for the next 5 years, but less so each year. Then the fade begins in earnest. By 35 stick a fork in you!

In case you think I'm being cruel, I would say the following. If my money were to go away, so would you, so when your beauty fades I need an out. It's as simple as that. So a deal that makes sense is dating, not marriage.

While this guy probably didn't charm the ladies with his viewpoint, many men I asked admitted that he's not far off base. But before women get incensed, we should realize that it's not just men being crass. According to Dan Ariely, the MIT researcher, women give economic value to physical attributes as well.

$10,000 an Inch

In one of Ariely's studies, men's online photos were ranked for attractiveness by independent male and female observers. Then the researchers looked at how much online attention these men got. It turns out that if you're an ordinary-looking guy whose online picture is ranked around the median in attractiveness, you'd need to make $143,000 more per year than a guy whose picture ranked in the top tenth percentile. If your picture ranks in the bottom tenth, you'd need to make $186,000 more than the guy in the top tenth percentile.

"Women care so much about height," he told me, "that to be as appealing as the average five foot ten man, I'd have to earn $40,000 more per year at my height of five feet nine." Ariely found that a 5'4" man would need to make $229,000 more than a 6' tall man to have equal appeal; a 5'6" man would need $183,000 more; a 5'10" man would need $32,000 more.

Of course, the tall workaholic might not make as good a spouse as the shorter involved parent, just as the hot 26-year-old woman might not make as good a spouse as the mature 42-year-old woman. We've all dated based on superficial factors before, and it hasn't worked out. But we want what we want, rational or not. And the dating market proves this time and again.

Which is how this reverse power shift occurs: Guys in their twenties are like women in their forties. Women in their twenties are like guys in their forties.

It's all about perceived value.

You're Only as Valuable as Your Options

That's why Evan Marc Katz, my dating coach, kept reminding me that my view of my own value doesn't matter. In dating, you're only as valuable as your options.

"You can be as picky as you like, as long as you have the option of being that way," Evan said. "When we think we should be in demand and we're not, that's where the friction comes in. What holds you back is that you're trying to be the twenty-seven-year-old woman who's at the top of the dating totem pole. A twenty-seven-year-old can pretty much date anyone—older, younger. But it won't always be this way. That's why no matter how old you are, you can't afford to throw people away on a technicality."

But how do you know where you are on the totem pole?

"It's economics." Evan shrugged. "A gallon of milk is good, but nobody will buy it at ten dollars. The product is priced too high. A lot of women are setting their price point so high that they're pricing themselves out of the market." He says that you can assess your market value this way: If you have an in-box full of responses from men you've e-mailed, you're correctly priced. If you don't, you've priced yourself too high.

"If a guy is forty and cute and makes a good living and wants to get married, it makes more sense for him to be with a thirty-two-year-old than a woman his own age," Evan continued. "But a lot of us don't adjust. We just say, '*I'm valuable. This is what I'm willing to take. I'm only dating guys who are my age. I'm only dating men who are this tall.*' That's a lovely declaration. But you may not have many buyers. I see a lot of younger women overpricing themselves, too, and when they finally price themselves more realistically five years later, it might be too late."

That's exactly what I saw happening: Women under 30 might be dating a great guy, but there's this one thing they think he's lacking. They're with an 8 but they want a 10. Then they're 40 and they can only get a 5! So they gave up the 8 in order to hold out for the 10, only to end up with a 5—or nothing. The 8 would have been wonderful—the 8 is a catch—but it's not until you can only get a 5 that you realize it.

When I was 22, nobody would fault me for breaking up with a boyfriend who was smart, nice, funny, and cute but too into sci-fi. But by the time I was 37, I was seen as greedy, demanding, and overreaching if I wanted just smart, nice, funny, and cute. In fact, at 37, it was hard to find a guy like that in the first place. But it didn't occur to me to take a good deal "while supplies last."

In business terms, Evan says romantic market value works like this: "Saying you should hold out for a ten is like saying that everyone should hold out for a five-hundred-thousand-dollar salary because that's what you're *worth*. Well, if there's only a small percentage of those five-hundred-thousand-dollar jobs out there, there's going to be a *lot* of unemployment. That is, unless someone compromises and finds a lower-paying job—like a seven—that has much better benefits and quality of life."

Evan said that people who don't take their own marketability into account are deluding themselves.

"I would be more marketable if I were a millionaire," he said. "Bill Gates would have an entirely different level of marketability if he weren't Bill Gates. That goes against our ideals of love and being valued for your internal qualities only, and a lot of people find it offensive. Everyone wants to be thought of as special. But you can either pretend it isn't true, or get more realistic about your options so you can actually meet someone."

He was right. If we're really honest with ourselves, many of us probably realize that we aren't 100 percent pure in our search for true love. Attraction is a subtle calculus involving the quality of the romantic appeal but also factoring in the quality of life you'd have with this person.

Most women in their thirties, for instance, would feel very differently about a fabulous guy who's unemployed versus one who's got a lucrative job—even if both men were equally smart and cute and interesting. The discrepancy has less to do with whether the guy has ambition and passion (because the unemployed guy might be working diligently on his music or start-up company but making no money, whereas the guy with the lucrative job might have no passion for his work at all) and more to do with what colors our sense of how we'd feel about being in this situation in the future with a family. Even for the most romantic among us, the practical stuff matters.

Marriage Is a Good Business to Be In

If the economics of dating can seem icky, the economics of a marital partnership seem, to me at least, comforting. Marriage provides an infrastructure, child care, economic security, companionship, and, studies show, better health. It's easier and more fun to go through life as a couple. According to *The Case for Marriage*, a comprehensive summary of research on the benefits of marriage, by Linda J. Waite and Maggie Gallagher, married people are happier overall.

It's certainly a good business to be in, but it's still a business. Just recently I came across an article on MSN Money entitled "Get Real: Marriage Is a Business" by Liz Pulliam Weston. The subhead read: "Put aside the romantic notion that love conquers all—and pull out your calculators. Successful partnerships require a plan, a CFO (usually) and regular progress reports."

In the article, Pulliam Weston talks about the fact that married people build significantly more wealth than singles do; that marriage has not just romantic, but legal and financial ramifications; and that, as John Curtis had said, you need to have a business plan for the marriage.

The MSN article was linked to another called "How to Leave Your Husband," which advises planning an exit strategy before you announce your intention to divorce—all in the service of landing the best financial outcome. So if divorce has an economic component, it logically follows that its precursor, marriage, must, too.

But ask most young singles about the idea that there's a socioeconomic underpinning to modern love, and they're offended. They'll insist that economics in mate selection is a thing of the past, a primitive relic from the days when there was little or no choice in whom you married or whether you married—like in an arranged marriage. But if using practical criteria in picking a spouse is so distasteful, how could it be that so many arranged marriages *do* work?

What do people in these arranged marriages know that we love-obsessed Westerners don't?

19

Love at Twenty-seventh Sight

Jayamala Madathil is an Indian-born researcher at Sonoma State University in California, and she's an expert on arranged marriages. I called Madathil to ask about a study she'd done that surprised me. She compared satisfaction in arranged marriages and marriages of choice—both in the United States—and found that the people in arranged marriages were just as satisfied, if not more so, than those in marriages of choice.

Now, I'm not so out of touch to think that arranged marriages are the solution to women's dating problems, but I found Madathil's study intriguing: Was it really possible that a guy your parents select for you could make you just as happy as the guy you spend years and years painstakingly searching for?

If so, why?

Madathil said that her study didn't investigate why (that's her next project), but she was happy to share the story of her own fourteen-year arranged marriage as an example.

There Was Nothing Wrong with Him

The first thing Madathil told me about her husband is that she's "totally in love" with him—his warmth, kindness, intelligence, how handsome he is. . . . Her list went on and on. The minute she started talking about her husband, she seemed to morph from an articulate scientist into a giddy teenager.

"I'm sorry," she said, "it's just that we have such a romantic marriage. But if I tell you how we met, you'd probably not find it romantic at all."

She was right about that.

"Our families met each other," she explained, "and they thought it was a compatible match in terms of expectations. They decided we could proceed. So my husband and I met, and we liked each other. We agreed on basic values and what you expect from life. Physical appearances matter—I thought, yeah, he looks cute. But he didn't have to be gorgeous. It seemed realistic and possible. So I said, sure."

Just like that. I tried to imagine sitting across from a total stranger and saying to myself, "Yeah, it seems realistic and possible. Sure, I'll marry him!"

In my very American mind-set, I wondered why Madathil didn't want to meet other candidates. After all, she told me that she could have met as many men as she wanted until she found the right match. How did she know to pick *this* one?

"Well, there was nothing wrong with him," she replied matter-of-factly.

That sounded hilarious to me. "There was nothing wrong with him" isn't the reasoning most single American women use when it comes to marriage decisions. (In fact, often we seem to find *something* wrong with a guy.) Besides, based on what she'd just told me, some women wouldn't have gone on even a second date with

Madathil's husband—much less agreed to marriage—because there were no initial sparks.

"I think what's different from the coffee date is that we're not looking for sparks or anything like that," she said. "It's more like on a friendship level, where you meet someone and you know pretty quickly whether you want to hang out with them again. Romance isn't the primary focus in the beginning. It's more about whether this is a good fit value-wise."

She believes that's one area couples in love marriages sometimes overlook.

"I know couples here in America who can date for two years and not know if they have the same values," she said. "They *think* they know, but they haven't really talked about the important issues that would come up in a marriage. In an arranged marriage, all the requirements are laid out in the beginning. There are no games to be played. It is what it is—if you seem compatible, fine. You get married. What's the point of seeing each other a second or third or fourth time? What other information are you going to get?"

Madathil, in fact, was introduced to another prospective husband before she met her current husband, but she turned that first guy down. She didn't marry the first guy precisely because she already had all the information she needed from that initial meeting. If a typical American woman might nix a guy on a first date for any number of superficial reasons—too hairy, chews funny— Madathil told me that she and that first suitor didn't proceed because of major lifestyle issues: He wanted a stay-at-home partner and she wanted to do graduate work and get a job.

"It's a very realistic way of doing things," Madathil said. "We realize there are going to have to be adjustments and you'll have to be flexible, but not on the basic things—career, children, where you want to live. It's seeing the bigger picture. It's not about, "Well, he plays golf and I hate golf, so forget it."

THE COMMITMENT IS LIBERATING

Madathil said that when she and her husband got married, "It's like we started dating at that point—but it's better than dating, because you know that no matter what happens, you'll both be there tomorrow. I don't have to wait by the phone and wonder if he'll continue the relationship. Ironically enough, it's the commitment that makes it liberating!"

The focus, she added, goes from "Is this going to work?" to "How can we make this work?" As Madathil and her husband got to know each other, she liked a lot of things about him. She liked the way they talked about things. She liked how they treated each other. But she wasn't in love with him yet. She fell in love with her husband because of the way they *disagreed* with each other.

"When everything's great, it's easy to fall in love," she said. "But when you disagree—how you come to a consensus is very telling. My husband both met and exceeded my expectations. I have never once thought that I could have found someone better."

How different that was from our culture's view of love, where having disagreements in the beginning of a relationship seems like the death knell. The beginning of a relationship is supposed to be like a honeymoon. A couple is supposed to feel totally in synch. Any deviation from that is a sign that you're not compatible. But Madathil is saying it's not *whether* you argue—its *how* you get through the arguments. And the more practice you have getting through those arguments gracefully, she told me, the less you'll argue later.

Her advice to women who are dating is this: First find a good match, *then* fall in love. Above all, don't think you've "fallen in love" only to learn too late that it's a bad match.

It seemed like good advice. After all, given the American obsession with falling in love immediately, why were so many people getting divorced or feeling empty in marriages that started out as "true love"?

WHAT'S A HUSBAND FOR?

A New Jersey–born attorney and journalist named Reva Seth seemed to have some answers. In her book *First Comes Marriage: Modern Relationship Advice from the Wisdom of Arranged Marriage*, she explains that after years of being in the dating trenches, she realized she was doing something wrong. Eventually, she found her own husband not through an arranged marriage, but by *using the principles* she learned from interviews with hundreds of women in arranged marriages. Her advice is aimed at people like me, people who will never, ever sit down with Mom and Dad and some guy's parents and decide to tie the knot on the spot—but who could benefit from the stories of those who have.

Like me, when Seth was dating she wanted to fall in love and get married, but she'd never really focused on why. So in her book, Seth asks an important question in an era when women can take care of themselves: "What do you think a husband today is for, and why do you want one?"

It's a hard question to answer, if only because it seems obvious. You might say, "I want a soul mate to share my life with."

Okay, a soul mate. What, exactly, does that mean? As Diane Sollee, founder and director of the Coalition for Marriage, Family, and Couples Education, put it, "People think they have to find their soul mate to have a good marriage. You're not going to 'find' your soul mate. Anyone you meet already has soul mates. Dozens of them.

Their mother. Their father. Their lifelong friends. You get married, and after twenty years of loving, bearing and raising children, meeting challenges—then you'll have 'created' soul mate status."

In arranged marriages, the husband question is easier to answer. Your parents are looking for someone to provide contented companionship, children (if you both want them), and the infrastructure for family life. They want someone with qualities like integrity, humility, ambition, and generosity—the things that are going to matter. If a guy can read your mind but he can't hold a job, or if he's incredibly funny but doesn't call when he says he will, is that the kind of guy you want to marry?

I know—you want him to read your mind *and* hold a job, to be funny *and* reliable. But do you want a husband or someone who practices telepathy? Do you want the life of the party or a guy you can count on?

As Seth writes in her book, husbands are life partners, not life savers. A full 50 percent of marital satisfaction is up to you, but many women dating today don't see it that way.

A friend of my mother's who's been happily married for forty years made the same observation: "Marriage alone won't make you happy. A good marriage will bring you much happiness, but it's not your husband's job to provide constant entertainment and stimulation. So many of my daughters' friends expect the impossible of what a husband should be."

Indeed, one 30-year-old woman I spoke to can't decide whether or not to stay with a guy who spends his Sundays watching football. Her boyfriend is a kind, loving, well-educated public defender, but still she wonders if she can live with a guy who sits on the sofa every Sunday for five hours.

"I don't expect all of our interests to overlap," she told me. "But on a Sunday, I wish we could do something together that we'd both enjoy."

In arranged marriages, parents look for someone who is similar to their child—but that doesn't mean a male twin who's musical like she is, shares her obsession with Rollerblading, and has the same favorite restaurants. Spouses *do* have many things in common, but they're common goals, not hobbies: They share the kind of life they want to build together. So what if your husband is alphabetizing his video game collection while you're out on a run? Why is that a problem? How many guys have you dated who shared practically all of your interests but the relationship didn't work out anyway? We all know that "We both love sushi" doesn't make for happily ever after.

In a 2009 *New York Times* "Modern Love" column, Farahad Zama, whose marriage was arranged after he met his wife-to-be for forty-five minutes, writes about how different he and his wife are on things ranging from cleanliness to reading habits to food preferences.

"Would we have gotten married if we had met in the conventional Western manner and dated each other?" he asks. "Or would we have given up on each other and moved on, searching for the perfect 'one'? I don't know.

"But," he continues, "what I am sure about is that our marriage, arranged with other considerations in mind, took us from acquaintanceship to love and kept us together until we realized that our differences are the yin and yang that make our relationship whole. Now we consider ourselves absolutely perfect for each other."

Love Is Timing, a Verb, and a Noun

Zama believes that a lot of what makes arranged marriages work is the fact that the Hollywood version of "love" isn't in the equation. He's probably right. Our Western expectations of what "being in love" means seem to have so skewed what we value in a partner that many single women today, when asked what kind of guy they're looking for, often say, "Someone tall, funny, and successful," instead of "Someone warm, trustworthy, loyal, and who can compromise and handle life's stresses well."

I was starting to wonder if arranged marriages were similar to those of people who say they got married because of "timing." You know, people who were eager to get married and get on with their lives, and the next good enough person they dated became their spouse. It's not an arranged marriage, exactly, but it's certainly entered into with a very pragmatic eye.

"I was ready to be married," Angela, a 35-year-old editor in New York who got married five years ago, told me. "He wasn't my soul mate, but I thought we'd be happy together. Now he's my soul mate. But could another guy have become my soul mate? Sure. It was timing—we were both ready for the commitment and wanted it very badly. We weren't looking for perfection. We were looking for compatibility. And then we fell in love."

Vimal Vora, a 27-year-old Indian American strategy consultant living in New York City, told me that in Indian culture, people treat "love" as both a verb and a noun.

"You love someone by honoring them, cherishing them, caring for them," he said, but to Americans, love seems to be only a noun: "You feel this exogenous wonderful passion. It's this absurd and uncomfortable and irrational and floaty feeling that almost feels like it chose you."

His point was that if you have everything you need in a relationship, but you're just not feeling it anymore, maybe you're focusing too much on whether you're in love (the noun) and not making enough of an effort to love (the verb) your partner. There's an aspect of love (the verb) that's a choice.

Vora feels that you need both the noun and verb, but, as he put it, what we tend to forget is this: "The verb can create the noun, and the noun can inspire the verb."

20

Mondays with Evan

Session 5—The Chemistry-to-Compatibility Ratio

"We're going out again," I announced at my final session with Evan. "But it's weird, because I don't feel the way I'm used to feeling. There was no chemistry, but I'm really looking forward to seeing him again."

Evan smiled. "Isn't that chemistry?" he asked. "If you're excited to see someone again?"

We were talking about my date with Sheldon2, the widowed 46-year-old who designed and sold houses, and who had an 8-year-old son. He's the guy I didn't even want to e-mail, until Evan read me the riot act. I'd ruled him out because he was 5'6" and balding, worked in what I (mistakenly) thought was a boring job, and wore a pink polka-dot bow tie in his online photo.

Now I was telling Evan about our hike.

A week earlier, Sheldon2 and I had met at the bottom of a local trail, where I found him sitting on a rock and listening to his iPod. With his baseball cap, trendy shorts, and Coldplay T-shirt, he looked to be in his late thirties. I might not have noticed him at a party, but when he said hello to me, my first thought was, "He's kind of cute." I wasn't attracted to him in an I-imagine-myself-sleeping-with-him way. He wasn't my physical type at all. But there was something about his cuteness and the warmth of his hello that instantly put me at ease.

If I were telling a friend about our date, there wouldn't be anything exciting to report. A month ago, I might not even have gone a second date with Sheldon2. He wasn't an intellectual—but he *was* curious and smart. He had "a bright mind," a vitality, and mental nimbleness. We didn't share flirtatious banter to the degree I had with boyfriends in the past—but we never lacked for conversation. He wasn't slick—but he was thoughtful. He helped me climb over big rocks and made me laugh. There were no butterflies, there was no good-bye kiss, but the thing is, I had a nice time.

I told Evan about that study on arranged marriages, and how my focus on intense chemistry screwed me up in the past. There was the cute urban planner who flew across the country to meet me, but because I'd built up such a fantasy around him, I found him disappointing in real life. Not that he was actually disappointing. He was smart, funny, interesting, and self-aware, if a bit shy and reserved. As we walked around town, I had a nice time, but given what my friend who put us in touch had said about him, I expected that when we met, there would be some, well, zing. *A nice time* didn't count. It felt like too much effort to keep in touch long-distance, even though he would be moving to my city six months later. But the guys I'd put so much effort into—the sparks guys— were often bad matches for me. (I looked up the urban planner on Facebook recently, and he's married to a psychologist and has a baby girl. He also looked adorable in his photos.)

Now, with Sheldon2, I felt like the John Cusack character when he said about his girlfriend in the movie *High Fidelity*: "She didn't make me miserable, or anxious, or ill at ease. You know, it sounds boring, but it wasn't. It wasn't spectacular either. It was just good. But really good."

And I was starting to ask myself the same question he did: "Should I bolt every time I get that feeling in my gut when I meet someone new? Well, I've been listening to my gut since I was fourteen years old, and frankly speaking, I've come to the conclusion that my guts have shit for brains."

Mine, too. All it took was one look on Match.com to confirm that my gut didn't pick the best guys.

GOING FOR THE SEXY

Evan and I opened up my hotlist picks and e-mail exchanges from the first few weeks of our sessions. Mostly, they were filled with sexy forty-something never-married men who wrote great profiles and either never e-mailed me back, or if we did start a correspondence, seemed to have no history of committed relationships, had a pattern of serial short-term relationships, bragged about themselves obnoxiously, used sexual innuendo in a creepy way, had complicated relationships with their families, were stalled in their careers, or just generally didn't seem like nice, normal, stable husbands-to-be.

Evan said that's typical. He told me he knows full well that single men in their late thirties and early forties are in great demand and can easily get married, and if they've never been married by their mid-forties, often they come with some kind of baggage or issue.

My friend Kayla, who's 36, noticed the same thing.

"At that age, if he seems like a catch, there's a catch," she said. "Never-married men in their forties are bad news—there's something fishy there. I've found they have one of five tragic problems: mommy, addiction, gay, job, or commitment. Divorced with kids controls for the insanity factor. At least it says he's interested in a certain conventional life that I'm also interested in."

By now of course, I knew that divorced dads were probably better matches for me. "But it's interesting," Evan said, "that your hotlist is filled with never marrieds. What does this tell you?"

"That I suck at dating? That I'm a bad judge of character?"

Evan shook his head. "It tells you that you're blinded by what you think of as chemistry. You go for the sexy. I'm guessing that if you were at a party and you had a nice conversation with a divorced guy who was a little overweight and gray and worked in finance and lived in the valley—but he was a cool guy and you liked being around him—you'd probably give him your phone number. Five years ago you may not have. You're learning to let more people through the filter.

"But," he continued, "I'm also guessing that if you started dating this guy, you'd be on the phone with your friends saying, 'I'm not sure if this feels right—he's overweight and gray.' You'd date him, but you'd probably keep thinking that you want someone more creative and who lives closer to you. The trouble we have is reconciling the people we'd pick out of a dating lineup with the people we actually like to spend time with."

LET'S TALK ABOUT YOUR CHILDHOOD

When I told Gian Gonzaga, the eHarmony.com researcher, about my "type," he said that people commonly confuse "chemistry" with their type, and their "type" with someone they have a lot in common with on the surface. But there's a problem with that way of thinking.

"With relationships," he said, "you don't change much in terms of personality or temperament, so your partner won't suddenly become more generous, or more extroverted. But couples do tend to take on the other person's interests somewhat, so that can change over time. People get hung up on what they have in common when what they need to have in common is the 'getting each other' aspect. *That's* the chemistry."

One woman made this exact mistake. In her twenties, Amy, a broadcast journalist, broke up with her long-term boyfriend, a law student, because she thought she had more chemistry with the exciting new guy she met at work. They were both passionate about TV news, and loved sharing their daily experiences with each other. They were both equally obsessed with the industry.

"I ended up marrying the man I worked with in TV news and we've been married for fifteen years and have three children," she said. "But I'm miserable. We have nothing in common that matters. My husband eventually got out of TV news and into PR. He's a videographer and is working freelance and isn't the most motivated guy in the world."

Now, she regrets breaking up with her long-term boyfriend, who became a lawyer. She had more *real* chemistry him. "After the kids grow up," Amy said of her marriage, "we'll probably get divorced and go our separate ways since we won't have anything that holds us together."

Lisa Clampitt, the matchmaker in New York who used to be a social worker, told me that often what seems like "chemistry" might be emotional baggage from childhood. That's why if she sees a client repeatedly going after men who aren't working out, she looks at the psychological roots of the attraction.

"Sometimes what people consider chemistry is actually a replay of what happened in their families," Clampitt said. "So a person who had a workaholic father might grow up to be attracted to someone married or emotionally unavailable, and when someone's available in a healthy way, she doesn't feel the spark."

In these cases, Clampitt focuses on the good qualities the woman is attracted to and tries to blend them with someone healthier.

"I'll say, 'Let's find someone funny and passionate, but who's also communicative and stable and wants kids—even if it seems at first that you won't have as much chemistry with this person.' I remind clients that chemistry sometimes leads to bad decisions."

THE CHEMISTRY ADDICTION

Evan reminded me of this, too.

"What happens when your chemistry is dialed up to ten?" he asked. "What has that been like for you?"

I thought back to those times when I felt the rush with a new guy.

"It was amazing!" I said.

"Was it?" Evan asked. "Or were you checking your voice mail every twenty minutes, unable to focus at work, ignoring your friends and the rest of your life, and generally acting like an idiot?"

It was more like that, I admitted.

"Exactly," he continued. "When the rush is there, you're not acting like yourself. You're nervous and insecure. There's no critical thinking and you make idiotic choices: *I just want to rip his clothes off and breathe his air and so what if he's clinically depressed!*

Evan often encounters situations like these with his clients: The intense three-month relationship that burns out quickly. The passionate relationship that can't survive the incompatible life goals. The intensely attracted couple who also intensely argue all the time.

But when his clients meet wonderful men and don't have that

amped-up level of excitement, they say, "But I'm not feeling what I felt with so-and-so." To which Evan replies, "So-and-so dumped you. So-and-so was married to someone else. So-and-so didn't want kids. So-and-so was irresponsible. How exciting was that?"

It seems so obvious, but how many women are drawn to completely inappropriate men—guys who are too old or too young or unemployed or unavailable—and insist that he is, despite the hurdles, her soul mate? (He rarely turns out to be. Either that or her soul is a liar, cheater, slacker, etc.)

When I've felt that intense chemistry, how often did I overlook things I shouldn't have? How often did I give leeway I shouldn't have and try to "figure him out"—maybe he has intimacy issues, his father didn't love him enough, his mother loved him too much—instead of moving on to someone who could give me what I really wanted?

How do intelligent people make such stupid decisions?

Helen Fisher, a biological anthropologist at Rutgers University who studies the physiology of romantic love, says it might be because romantic love is like a drug addiction. When she put forty-nine people who were madly in love in a functional MRI machine to see which parts of the brain were involved with these feelings, she found that when you feel that strong chemistry with someone, the brain system that becomes activated is the reward system, which is what also lights up when you reach for a piece of chocolate, or a cigarette, or an amphetamine. These cells near the base of the brain produce a substance called dopamine—and dopamine is what gives us that "high." It doesn't matter to your brain whether you're craving a smoke or a lover—the result is the same: longing, obsession, need.

When you've got all that dopamine floating around, she said, it's hard to remember that the high only lasts, on average, from eighteen months to three years. Some people sustain it longer, she said, but even then, the quality of the high changes.

"We just finished a study where we put people in the MRI machine who were still in love after twenty-one years of marriage," she said. "We no longer found activity in a brain region associated with anxiety, and instead found activity in the area associated with calm and pain relief. You're still attracted to the person, you still laugh at their jokes, but that early anxiety is now replaced with calm. If they don't send you an e-mail, you don't sit at the end of your bed and cry."

But if the expected pattern is that crazy early love anxiety leading to calm and security, Fisher says it can also go in the other direction. The calm and security you feel with a person can later trigger romantic love—something most people craving the immediate sparks forget. In fact, it happened to Fisher.

"There was a man who was following me around for some time, and I thought he was a pest," she said. But whenever she hung out with him, she felt totally relaxed and comfortable. "Four years later, I fell in love with him. I never expected that to happen. And I'm still with him ten years later."

Fisher isn't saying that chemistry isn't important. It's just that it helps to know that it might take time to develop. And, as Evan told me, even when it does develop, often we don't think it's strong enough because our ratio is off.

"You should look for a chemistry that's a six or seven and a compatibility that's a nine," he said. "Most of us look for a chemistry of a nine but end up with a compatibility of a four. People are consistently steering themselves into a ditch because of the all-consuming pursuit of chemistry."

Evan said the ditch looks like this: If there's a ton of initial chemistry, it's hard to develop a realistic picture of the person, and if the guy turns out to be unkind, or selfish, or unreliable, it's hard to let go because you're already hooked. But if you get involved with a guy who started out as a friend, as soon as you hit that inevitable obstacle or rough patch, you tell yourself, *I was never attracted to him anyway*. So in the name of chemistry, you give the wrong people a chance and let the right people go.

ARE YOU HAVING YOUR PERIOD?

Martie Haselton, a researcher who studies mate choice and sexuality at the University of California at Los Angeles, told me that what we think of as chemistry might be less about that romantic *je ne sais quoi* and more about hormones. In her studies, she found that the kind of men women prefer changes depending on where they are in their menstrual cycle (how's that for unromantic?).

According to Haselton, women prefer more masculine men on high fertility days of the cycle but on other days, they'll pick someone more on the feminine side of things. So while on high fertility days, they're drawn to behavioral dominance and competitive traits in men, on other days of the cycle, they go for the nice guys.

"What women want is everything," she told me from her office at UCLA. "They want the guy who will be a good long-term partner in a relationship, someone kind, caring, a good provider. These are more feminine traits. But what women also want is a very sexy guy, very good-looking, tall, muscular—the bad boy traits. They don't usually come in the same package. But it's even more confusing, because they find they're attracted to something a little bit different depending on where they are in their cycles."

Interestingly, if a woman is on the Pill, she won't get these cyclical changes. But, Haselton added, "If she goes off the Pill, whoops." Now she may view her nice-guy boyfriend or husband less favorably on high fertility days. These are the days when she thinks, "Something's missing."

I asked Haselton how people end up with good partners despite the fact that we can't control our biology.

"I don't think biology is the problem," she said. "I think expectations are. It's normal to be more or less attracted to your partner from time to time, but now people think there's a problem if they go through a natural phase of 'not feeling it' as much. And they also think they have to feel it intensely, and right away."

Evan, too, admitted that he used to think that way, and now he was a week away from his wedding to a woman he never expected to date in the first place. From everything he'd told me, it was clear that he'd never been happier, that he was in no way settling, and that he and his wife-to-be *did* have really strong chemistry now—it just wasn't the immediate out-of-body kind he'd always been seduced by.

Famous Last Words

As Evan and I hugged good-bye at the end of our session, I was sad to see him go. As much as I'd resisted his advice at first, now I felt I might be lost without it. I told him I didn't want to do anything stupid with Sheldon2 while Evan was off on his honeymoon.

"You know everything you need to know," he said, reassuring me. "It might be hard to make some changes, but I think you're finally ready to try."

I believed him on one level, but I still wanted some final words of wisdom to hold on to. "If there's one thing you want me to remember from all this," I asked, "what would it be?"

Evan thought for a minute, then left me with this:

"There's the way it was supposed to go, and the way it really goes," he said. "You have to keep on challenging yourself. Your way of doing things so far has led you to where you are today. You have to go through a process to have the potential to meet someone you like. It's up to you whether you choose to go through that process."

For the rest of the day, his words ran through my mind. *There's the way it was supposed to go and the way it really goes . . . You have to go through a process . . . It's up to you whether you choose to go through that process.*

It sounded simple but slightly enigmatic at the same time. Then I had lunch with a former colleague, and what Evan said suddenly became totally clear.

2I

Dump the List, Not the Guy

The colleague was Lauren, a 31-year-old TV writer. We were talking about work, when she happened to mention that she'd broken up with her boyfriend of four months. A few weeks earlier, Lauren had said how much she liked this guy.

I asked what happened.

Nothing had happened, Lauren replied. He just wasn't The One.

But what about all those things she liked about him?

"Well, I felt really comfortable with him," she explained. "He was so nonjudgmental and accepting. In vulnerable moments, he always said the perfect thing. Stuff like that made the superficial concerns not matter so much."

Her superficial concerns were things like the fact that he was blond (she's not into blonds); he was her height, 5'8", and she wanted someone taller than her; and he was a bad dresser. Other things bothered her, like how he would lie backward on her bed and put his sweaty feet on her pillow. "Clueless," she said. "I need someone who would know not do that in the first place."

She was annoyed by the way he sometimes spoke like Justin Timberlake even though he had a degree from a top university. She was annoyed that he wanted to have sex more than she did, even though, she admitted, it was the best sex she ever had.

She overlooked these things in the beginning because, she said, "emotionally, he was exactly what I wanted—responsive, thoughtful, and kind. He didn't expect the porn star bikini wax, which was nice. I could be my natural self. He wasn't scared of the heavy things going on in my life—like that my mom had cancer. He was always thoughtful and asking about that, and gave me leeway when my mood was all over the place—he attributed it to my mom's illness. Sometimes, though, I was moody because I just felt annoyed with him."

She didn't think there should be so many annoyances early on in the relationship. There might need to be some small tweaks, but overall, shouldn't this part be easy?

"The key thing I'm pondering is whether I should communicate more about what's annoying me to at least give the guy a chance to improve," Lauren said, implying that the problem was that the guy needed improving. "Instead, I dump the guy thinking I can find someone who fits all of my collective needs in some telepathic way. Probably not a wise assumption."

Lauren was doing the opposite of what Evan suggested—she wasn't willing to "go through the process." She was doing what I'd always done, relying on a rigid mental checklist of what The Guy was supposed to be like.

Forget About "My Type"

Susan Page, a relationship expert and the author of *If I'm So Wonderful, Why Am I Still Single?*, believes in the process, too. A former campus minister at Columbia University in New York, she also served as Director of Women's Programs at the University of California, Berkeley, where she helped found the nation's first university-based human sexuality program. She told me that in her workshops with singles across the country, she's noticed that the biggest impediment to going through the process is what she calls "pseudo high standards.

"People hold back because of some issue," she told me on the phone, "and they never get a real test of what it would be like to be in a committed relationship with that person. Single people would find someone more easily if everything wasn't a test. When you adopt a spirit of goodwill toward something you don't like in your partner, that leads to positive changes in your relationship. But many people break up instead. You should never settle for less than what you need, but that doesn't mean it's going to be everything on your checklist, because you can't know what qualities you'll be attracted to in a particular person."

She learned this herself when she met her husband nearly thirty years ago.

"I was a Methodist minister at the time," she said, "and I assumed I'd be with someone of the same religion, highly educated, professional—a doctor, a lawyer, a professor. Someone who played bridge and loved to sing and dance. Well, my husband is Jewish, a junior college drop-out, an artist, he doesn't sing or dance, doesn't play bridge."

They met at a friend's house one day and started talking. "I asked what he did," she continued, "and he said, 'I'm a studio potter.'

I thought, 'Oh, great. He's a hippie dropout who can't get his life together so he's making mugs and trying to sell them on the street.' I wrote him off at this point. I liked talking to him, but I wasn't thinking this was husband material."

Actually, the studio potter made a good living selling his artwork and even had a show on Madison Avenue in New York. They went out for breakfast a couple of days later, but she still didn't think it would lead anywhere. He just wasn't her type. That seemed to be that.

But Page was an avid folk dancer, and one day, the potter showed up unexpectedly and watched her dance. Afterward, they went to a neighborhood bar and stayed there until 2 a.m. There still weren't any sparks, but some rapport was starting to develop. Then they spent a Saturday at an art museum, and soon, to Page's surprise, she was smitten.

"He had the qualities I wanted that nobody puts on a list," she said.

Page said that a list is like the fantasy we have of finding "the whole package." She often hears from single women that if a guy has 80 percent of what's on the list, he won't make the cut.

"Since when is getting eighty percent considered settling?" she asked. "We create these fantasy men—he's going to have this kind of career, this color eyes, be this age. How specific can you get before you rule out almost everyone?"

Being Surprised by the Pot

I ran the Lauren situation by Page, who said it was an all too familiar story.

"People have a tendency to analyze far too much," she said. "So many times we let our chatter in our brain talk us out of things that might be good for us. The converse is also true—if someone has a lot of things on your list, but your gut is telling you, 'I don't trust this person,' that's more important than the list."

Page told me a story about a guy she'd been infatuated with before she was married.

"He had everything on my list," she explained. "Professional, well-liked, charismatic. Cute, funny, well-established. But I realized early on that he was very narcissistic. I thought, there's no real affection here. I was one more member of his audience. I was infatuated, but I stopped seeing him. It was very painful, but I did the right thing for myself."

Page said that lists may seem like a good way to clarify your thinking, but it's actually hard to make one that doesn't either oversimplify or take things out of context. Even if you make a list of qualities you want, for instance, they aren't all weighted equally (is age as important as honesty?), and with many qualities you want, it's not like people have them or they don't. Often, they have *some degree* of that quality—like sense of humor or financial stability—which may not be at the level you had in mind when you wrote it down.

Lists are also confusing because they're about qualities a man has independently, but fail to take into account qualities he'll have *inside a relationship*. He may be the right age, have the right sense of humor, and have the right job, but what is he going to be like when he's *with you*? How are you going to feel when you're with him? Will you get along well? None of this can be quantified on paper.

Instead, it was from her husband's work as a potter that Page came up with an analogy she finds relevant to relationships.

"In America," she said, "when a potter makes a pot, they put a glaze on it and put it in the kiln and know exactly what it's supposed to look like when it comes out. But when the Japanese make a pot, they put it in a wood-fire kiln that could be any temperature, and when they take the pot out, it's not always exactly like they thought it was supposed to look like. And they say, 'Oh, wow, this is what the fire did to the pot and it's gorgeous!' They believe that there's no beauty in perfection.

"So instead of knowing what the person across from you is *supposed* to be like, ask yourself the pot question, 'But what is it, and is it beautiful?' rather than thinking, 'It's not this and it should look like this.' The question you have to ask is, 'Do I like it?' instead of 'How does it compare to what I thought I wanted?' People can surprise you."

I told her about the enormous list I'd made months earlier when a friend put me up to it. She suggested that instead of making a list of what I want in a man, I should make a list of the qualities my ex-boyfriends had, and then think about how much or how little the checklist mattered to those relationships in the end. When she asks happily married people about how their husbands stacked up on a list, often they admit that their spouses didn't meet a lot of the criteria—but they met more important ones.

"It's about reexamining the usefulness of your criteria," she said. "When you meet the right guy, most people find a list to be misleading, if not completely useless."

BREAKING UP WITH MY LIST

I took another look at my detailed Husband Store shopping list. I thought about how many times I should have dumped the list, instead of the guy who didn't match the list. Case in point: I'd gone on a second date with Sheldon2. When he picked me up and stood there at my door, smiling his adorable smile, he looked even cuter than he had on the hike. Soon a long meal in a funky café turned into dancing at a bar which turned into a walk on the beach, and before we knew it, six hours had flown by. I had more fun with him than I'd had on many of my dates with men who *did* meet my checklist criteria.

So I decided to do it. I was going to break up with my list. But how?

I could just ignore it, of course, but I felt like I needed to do it in a more concrete way. I needed to physically rid myself of all those unreasonable requirements in order to truly open myself up to other possibilities.

I thought about shredding it in the trash, but that didn't seem climactic enough for the occasion. A symbolic gesture seemed more fitting. Should I mail it off somewhere—to a sorority house, as a cautionary tale? Should I bury it somewhere, like a time capsule of misguided dating that I might dig up twenty years from now?

I considered asking some single friends if they wanted to bring their own lists to the beach and burn them together in a big bonfire, but that felt too clichéd, and besides, breaking up with my list felt like something I had to do on my own. As corny as it sounds, I wanted to find a way to represent the personal shift I was making in how I would find a partner. Besides being embarrassing, the whole thing felt too private to share.

So on a cold, cloudy winter day, I got in my car, placed my list— now floating inside a helium balloon with a long white string— next to me in the passenger seat, and headed for the ocean.

It was early morning and the water was freezing. I felt slightly ridiculous, but as I stood there, barefoot, about to release my list into the sky, the most unexpected thing happened. A really cute guy came jogging toward me.

"Hey!" he yelled. I looked behind me to see if he was talking to someone else, but I was alone at the shoreline.

"Hey!" he yelled again. He was definitely talking to me. I

couldn't believe my luck. I released the balloon, then watched the guy run closer. He stopped next to me, breathing heavily from his run.

"Hey," I said.

"What are you doing?" he asked. He had on shorts and a ripped UCLA Law sweatshirt. No ring on his left hand. I stared at his dark, curly hair and his muscular legs. I thought: Could I really be meeting The Guy while releasing my dating checklist in a helium balloon on the beach? How's that for an incredible wedding story?

"Um, I was just sending a message off to sea," I said. I didn't know how to explain it without sounding like a total dork.

We watched the balloon float away until it got smaller and smaller and became a mere speck. Then it disappeared entirely.

He looked me in the eye. His chocolate brown eyes were like magnets. My stomach started doing somersaults.

"Well," he said, "you really shouldn't do that. It's bad for the environment. I tried to stop you."

And with that, he continued his run.

For a split second, I was disappointed. And besides, who made him the balloon police? But then I was glad I'd encountered this guy. Our two minutes together showed me, yet again, just how deeply I craved the fantasy, which rarely turned out to be the reality. Our encounter was like a haiku of a relationship: I'd projected my usual romantic notions onto him and, of course, they didn't turn out as planned. Changing was going to be hard, I knew, but well worth it in the end.

I walked on the beach for a while, then got back in my car and gave the parking attendant my ticket. The sun had finally come out, bright rays on my windshield, and I squinted to find some dollar bills.

"Spring is coming," the attendant said.

"It is," I replied. "A new beginning."

PART FIVE

Putting It All Together

It is not lack of love but lack of friendship that makes unhappy marriages.

—Friedrich Nietzsche

22

The Good Enough Marriage

Now that I was truly focused on finding Mr. Good Enough, I came across something called "the good enough marriage." It was a phrase coined by Paul Amato, the sociologist I'd spoken to at Penn State. Amato studies marriages like these—good marriages, but not perfect ones. And what he found reminded me of the way I'd been dating.

Back in 1980, he and his colleagues developed a study of 2,000 married people. Every two years, the researchers followed up with these couples to find out how their marriages were going. They did this for twenty years. A lot of these couples divorced. So Amato wanted to know, what predicts divorce?

"What we found seemed surprising at first," he told me over the phone, "because we think of couples who get divorced as going through a long, terrible period of fighting. We think of them as estranged and so miserable that they decide the marriage can't be salvaged."

This was true of some couples, but many didn't follow that pattern at all. Up until the divorce, in fact, they seemed to be getting along pretty well. They weren't ecstatically happy, but they weren't unhappy. They frequently went out with their spouses and when asked, said they had very few marital problems or disagreements. On a scale from 1 to 10, they'd rate their marriages as 7s—not 2s or 3s.

"Nothing serious was going on," Amato said. "Their marriages weren't perfect, but they were pretty good. Two years later, they were divorced. These couples were happy enough, but wanted something more."

When the couples in Amato's study were asked why they got divorced, they'd say things like, "We were drifting apart—it's not like when we first got married," or "I didn't really feel like I was growing as a person," or "I thought my spouse was a nice person but not really my soul mate." They were disappointed, but not angry.

"They didn't dislike their spouse," Amato said. "Some people said, 'You know, I still love my spouse, but I just realized we weren't right for each other.' Often they'd found someone else and they thought, 'Now, *this* is my soul mate.' Even though the marriage isn't at all bad, they think they've found something better."

DIFFERENT, BUT NOT BETTER

Just like single women who break up with "good enough" boyfriends because they think they'll find something "better," a lot of these married folks were wrong. Five years later, Amato followed up and found that most people who remarried reported either no increase in satisfaction or that they were *less* happy than they'd been in their first marriages.

"We didn't ask if they regretted it," Amato said, "because most people won't admit to making a mistake. It makes you look like a goofball. So we looked at symptoms of depression and asked them how satisfied they were with their lives, and compared these to the results from five years earlier. Statistically, they were less happy."

This was because even if the second marriage was different from the first one, things traded off. "Different" didn't necessarily mean it was an improvement. I'd read the same thing on the relationship expert Diane Sollee's SmartMarriages.com Web site: "Research has shown that every happy, successful couple has approximately ten areas of 'incompatibility' or disagreement that they will never re-solve. Instead the successful couples learn how to manage the dis-agreements and live life 'around' them—to love in spite of their areas of difference. . . . If we switch partners, we'll just get ten new areas of disagreement."

No wonder the Centers for Disease Control and Prevention re-ports that the divorce rate for second marriages is higher than that of first-timers. Maybe these people have a hard time accepting that a good marriage doesn't mean the marriage has to be good all the time.

Indeed, according to the Rutgers Marriage Project, research using a large national sample in the late 1980s found that of people who were unhappy in their marriages but stayed in them anyway, 86 percent indicated in interviews five years later that they were happier. In fact, three-fifths of the formerly unhappily married couples rated their marriages as either "very happy" or "quite happy."

"Most good enough marriages have the potential to become stronger and better with time, effort, and commitment," Amato said. "I think the 'soul mate' concept has done a lot of harm because it sets the bar extremely high for a 'successful' marriage. Marriage is not about metaphysics."

Inheriting the Expectations

Later, in 1992, Amato and his team interviewed the adult children of the "good enough marriage" couples who split up. They did this three times until 2000. Turned out, some of these kids were having trouble finding their "good enough" partner, too.

"If it was a terrible marriage," Amato said, "the kids bounded back pretty quickly post-divorce. It was a relief from all the fighting. But the kids who had been in these good enough marriage families were quite messed up after the divorce. They suffered from low self-esteem and depression, and they had negative views about marriage. These kids were surprised by the divorce and they couldn't understand it, because unlike the kids in the high-conflict marriage families, it wasn't a relief and they didn't see it coming. The good enough marriages were good enough for the kids, because kids don't care if their parents are being self-actualized. They had stability and ready access to both parents, and they were happy. The fact that their parents were having an existential crisis didn't matter to them."

In adulthood, though, these kids from good enough marriage families replicated their parents' marriages. As soon as problems began to appear in their own relationships, they immediately began to think about breaking up or getting a divorce.

Many of them did.

"They got out quickly as problems of any kind began to arise," Amato said. "Kids from the intact families, when they were married and problems arose, often said, 'It looks like we've got some issues to deal with,' but they didn't get divorced. Yet the kids whose parents in good enough marriages divorced became very cautious about marriage. They were more likely to cohabitate. They didn't feel like they could trust their partners. It was scary to commit because their parents had seemed happy and even then, they got divorced."

Overall, Amato found that these adult children had a low tolerance for problems in a relationship. They grew up believing that if the flame was going out, the solution wasn't to rekindle it, but to find another spark.

A Shift from "Us" to "Me"

I asked Amato where this idea came from that the minute we feel less than completely fulfilled, we should seek something better.

"My own thinking," he said, "is that it comes from the 1970s. The human potential movement with Carl Rogers and Abraham Maslow talking about how every facet of life should contribute to your personal growth. Maslow put self-actualization above having a good marriage in his hierarchy. So if you don't like your friends, you find new ones. Same with a job. Same with marriage. In the 1960s, there were attitude surveys that involved university students. One study asked, What are the most important reasons for getting married? They said, I want to get married to raise a family, or so I can be economically secure, so I can have a nice home and a yard. And I want to be married to someone I love. But this part about love wasn't the first thing they said. It was fourth or fifth.

"But by the time you reach the 1970s and 80s," he continued, "love is the most important reason for getting married, and the other reasons drop substantially on the list. This whole idea that love is the overriding reason for getting married is relatively new. We now see marriage based entirely on finding the perfect lover. My personal feeling is that you'll be happier if you're more realistic in your expectations of what you can actually get out of marriage."

In his book *Alone Together*, Amato and his cowriter talk about the difference between today's marriages, which are more individualistic, and the pre-1970s marriages, which he calls "companionate marriages," where you looked for a compatible and reliable partner to help you achieve mutual life goals.

"Cooperative teamwork was the definition of a good marriage," Amato said, "but now the focus has shifted to personal satisfaction through the marital relationship itself. *Yes, he might be a good father and a good husband, but will he satisfy my deepest needs for romantic love and personal growth?* The result has been a delay in the age at marriage, an increasing number of women who never marry, an increase in never-married mothers, and an increase in divorces for reasons having little to do with the spouse not being a supportive friend and cooperative teammate."

Choosing someone who is good enough, Amato said, is neither a personal defeat nor is it settling for less. "In most cases," he said, "it is a reasonable and practical strategy for having a happy life over the long run."

I asked Amato about the studies I'd seen in the book *The Case for Marriage: Why Married People Are Happier, Healthier, and Better Off Financially* by Linda Waite and Maggie Gallagher, which showed that one of the strongest hedges against depression—and against unhappiness more generally—is marriage.

Did these findings apply only to great marriages, or did they also apply to "good enough" marriages?

"Being in a dysfunctional, hostile marriage is definitely not good for a person's sense of well-being," he said. "But based on a variety of studies, most people in 'good enough marriages'—nice person, works hard, will make a good parent—are happier than single people. Surveys show that the great majority of single people eventually want to be married, and people tend to be happiest when their lives are congruent with their goals. So single people who want to be married will usually get a boost in happiness when they become married, assuming they don't make a big mistake and marry a psychopath."

In other words, a person doesn't need a fairy tale marriage to achieve this happiness boost effect. Only a good enough one.

Wanting a Boyfriend and a Husband

Amato told me that both men and women have trouble accepting "good enough" partners, but in his work, he's found that women generally have higher expectations than men. He and his colleagues studied unmarried adults in their twenties in same-sex focus groups, where they were asked questions like, "How do you know when you've found the right person?"

With women, he said, the word "butterflies" came up again and again, but the guys didn't use that word. "Guys would say, 'I knew this person was the right person when we'd been dating for six months and she had to go away for a week, and when she was gone, I missed her so much. I thought that I felt happier when she was around. I realized how important she was.' Women talked a lot about chemistry and fireworks."

With married people, Amato also found differences. "Women are more critical of relationships," he said. "We interviewed husbands and wives and the husbands would say, 'Well there's this and sometimes there's that,' and wives would say, 'Tell me where you want me to start!' Men say, 'This comes up, but it's okay that we don't agree on this one thing because it bothers me, but not that much.' But his wife can't let go of it. It might be because of the way girls' socialization involves relationships. Women expect more of friendships, too. They expect self-disclosure and deep communication. Men are more easygoing about both relationships and friendships. They can watch a movie together and that's fine."

I knew what he meant. Earlier that week, a married friend had said, "My husband loves me, I love him, he's a good father, and he's a wonderful person." But now, with two toddlers, she missed the way they were when they were dating. "I want a boyfriend," she said. "But I don't want to give up what I have. So I guess I want a husband *and* a boyfriend!"

I asked Amato if he felt there was any correlation between the higher divorce rate and the longer laundry list of traits modern women seek in a mate.

"Oh, yeah, definitely!" he said. "One school of thought is, the increased divorce rate is because our culture became more individualistic and our expectations for marriage changed—it became a therapeutic relationship instead of a practical relationship. Marriage was supposed to improve us and make us happy. The meaning of marriage changed. Other people say it's demographic, that there are more women in the workforce. They aren't financially dependent on men. My personal feeling is, it's the former. It's about unrealistic expectations."

For instance, he said, more women seem to think that if they feel lonely at any point in their marriage, something's wrong. Then they leave, and they're even lonelier alone, or they marry someone else and are surprised when they also experience periods of loneliness.

"They're not lonely because of the marriage," he said. "They're lonely because it's normal for people to experience loneliness."

Edna Pollin, the divorce attorney in Denver, told me that in her experience, many women who divorce their husbands because they "want something more" aren't going to find it. What often happens, she said, is that her ex-husband remarries (someone much younger), and the new wife gets all of his love, companionship, financial support, and caretaking, while the wife who left him ends up in a one-bedroom apartment with a Netflix subscription and no sign of Prince Charming. Then she finally appreciates what she had, but even if her ex-husband is still single, she's caused irreparable damage and he won't take her back.

Scott Haltzman, the psychiatrist at Brown University, told me that one woman came to him and said she recognized that her spouse was a good husband and father, her parents love him, he'd never have an affair, and he's a good-looking guy, but she just "didn't feel it anymore." She said that she imagined herself divorced and happier.

"So," Haltzman told me, "I said, 'Imagine meeting him at the sidelines at the kids' soccer game, now that you're divorced. Imagine his new girlfriend at his side. Imagine her looking at him with loving eyes and adoration.' She said, 'Okay, I could imagine that.' So I asked, 'Why would this woman be looking at him that way?' and suddenly she listed all of her husband's good qualities that she'd been overlooking. It's a choice to look at that person with the same love in your eyes. We think our relationship is going to be perfect because *our spouse* will make it perfect, but two people are involved."

That's why Amato suggests that people really look at *why* they're thinking about breaking up or getting divorced.

"You can ask a few questions and find out pretty quickly how someone feels about their partner," he said. "'I love him, but I'm not in love with him,' is very different from, 'He's not a good spouse.'" In one of Amato's studies, he looked at couples who now considered each other "good friends." What was important over time, he found, was the ability to resolve conflict in an amicable way, general compatibility, and basic agreement on values and goals, like religion and children and how to raise children.

"A lot comes down to more pragmatic things that keep the marriage going long-term," he said. "This isn't what a lot of single people find exciting. But if they want a long-term marriage, they need to start looking for the things that are going to be important in one."

Amato's research confirmed what so many people in strong marriages seemed to know. Why hadn't anyone shared these kinds of insights with me when I was dating in my twenties? Certainly there were wise people in my own community who could have filled me in.

In fact, there was one final "expert" I had to talk to.

23

A Visit with the Rabbi

The "expert" was my local rabbi.

The more I talked to experts about dating, the more it seemed that part of the problem for single people today was a lack of meaningful connection to their local communities. In the past, when it came to relationship issues, family, neighbors, and spiritual leaders routinely offered commonsense advice to young singles, but now "community wisdom" seemed to come more from reality series, daytime talk shows, and single friends texting with the latest "boy story."

So I wanted to know: What would a rabbi say about things like passion and compromise and picking the right partner? I called up David Wolpe, the head rabbi at Sinai Temple in Los Angeles. He's a hip, fiftyish married guy known for his wisdom, and he'd just been named the number one pulpit rabbi in America by *Newsweek* magazine. When I told him I wanted his thoughts on relationships, he invited me to stop by his book-lined office for a chat. Here's what he had to say.

FEELING *TOO* COMFORTABLE

Me: How important do you think sparks are in a marriage?

Rabbi Wolpe: It's interesting—a lot of people when they're dating come to me and say, "I just want someone I can be myself with. Someone I'm completely comfortable with." But the same thing that you want in marriage, people don't like in dating. The same comfort and ease also translates into, "You're too comfortable and easy with me. You don't try!" So which is it—do you want exciting, or do you want comfortable? What do you want long-term?

Me: What do you think matters most long-term?

RW: The biggest predictor I've seen of whether a marriage will work has nothing to do with sparks, but how similar two people's expectations are. If they have very different expectations in the marriage, or very different upbringings that they haven't really worked through, it's going to be a struggle. And I actually think that kindness, long-term, is the most useful—and overlooked—quality people should be looking for.

DATING ROBERT REICH

Me: You've seen the list of what I was looking for in a guy. If a forty-one-year-old woman brought you that list, would you say, "This girl is dreaming"?

RW: Mm-hmm! I would say that at thirty-one, too.

Me: At thirty-one?

RW: I would even say it at twenty-one, that much more, because, at twenty-one, you're going to be really dazzled by stuff that doesn't matter. You *can* marry somebody who has lousy taste. Who's colorblind, who can't pick a painting out. You could do that and be perfectly happy.

Me: What about physical characteristics?

RW: So, Robert Reich comes along. You're not going to date him? He's four feet ten and a half.

Me: I'm flexible on height within reason, but four feet ten? I don't think I'd be attracted to someone who's four ten.

RW: I understand. But don't you think someone could change that?

Me: Would you say that to a guy? Would you say, "There's this woman, and she's 250 pounds, but she's really special—is that okay with you?"

RW: I think it works this way. Let's say there's a 50 percent chance that you could be with a guy who is five feet nine. That's a height you like, but it could go either way depending on what else he brings to the table. Now, there's probably a 5 percent chance that you could be with someone who's under five-four. But there's *a chance*. To immediately assume—I mean, maybe if you spent an hour with Danny DeVito or Robert Reich, all of a sudden you would say, you know what, this is somebody that I actually could spend my life with—even though the height is never going to be ideal. On the other hand, take somebody who is unkind. There's a *one hundred percent chance* that you won't want to be with him. So I'm saying: What are the real irreducibles as opposed to the very unlikelies? And it seems to me the real irreducibles are the character questions. It seems that Danny DeVito's wife is happy.

MARRIED TO THE MARRIAGE

Me: What do you think single people should think more about when they're dating?

RW: Well, I think that a marriage is like a construction in the sense that, at a certain point in the marriage, you're no longer just married to the *person*, you're married to the *marriage* and everything that it means. The children, the past that you share together, the friends that you have—you're married to the whole thing, so it's not so much about the individual in a vacuum the way it is when you're dating. When I look at my wife, for example, I don't just see my wife. I see my daughter and the life that we built and the friends that we have and the things that we've surmounted to get to this moment.

Me: And people who are holding out for exactly the right guy don't realize this?

RW: When people are dating they don't know that. I mean, even if they know it in theory, they can't know it in practice. In the same way that people have all these plans for their kids, but they don't know what their kids will be like. The fact that we had a girl instead of a boy makes our family a very different family than it would have been if I were to have had a boy. And six months after my daughter was born, my wife had cancer. So we couldn't have more children. This is all part of what went into making the marriage what it is, and you aren't thinking about, "Is he tall enough?" or "Is she pretty enough?" so much. In some ways I think all the qualities that seem so important while you're dating—they get overwhelmed by what happens subsequently if you build a life together.

Me: What do you think of the idea of soul mates?

RW: Soul mates are a beautiful notion to believe in once it happens. But it's a dangerous thing to believe in before you've found the person you've decided to spend your life with. In reality, there are many people we could be happy with—it's just that your soul develops in different ways with different people.

Breaking Up with His Wife

Me: What do you mean you once broke up with your wife?

RW: We broke up once for a brief while, while we were going out. She wasn't my idea of what a rabbi's wife was supposed to be like. She ran a horse farm before I met her. But even though I had a preset role in mind, the person overwrote the role. We got back together because she was just the person that I wanted to be with.

Me: What were you looking for?

RW: I think I probably would've said I wanted to be with an intellectual. But that's not who she is. I wanted to be with somebody who loves English literature. That isn't what she loves, but it doesn't matter. And because I'm a rabbi, I thought I'd be with somebody who was comfortable in formal settings. For the first few years of our marriage, every time my wife and I had to go somewhere that demanded anything other than jeans, it was angst and struggle. In fact, after I met her mother, she told my wife, "That's the first man you've ever gone out with who didn't wear Birkenstocks—he wears shoes!"

Me: That's interesting because the marital researchers I spoke to said that differences might seem cute in the beginning, but ultimately people who are temperamentally similar do better. So why do you think the differences work in your marriage?

RW: We're not together because of the differences—we're together because of our *similarities*. There are deep similarities between my wife and me. We like and dislike the same people—almost a hundred percent of the time. We look at the world largely the same way, politically and religiously. The way we think about raising our daughter is very similar.

So, I would say, though I may not have been aware of it at first, on the deep currents of life we were similar, and on the things that we weren't similar about, we were moveable. The deep similarities overcame the surface differences and the differences didn't matter nearly as much as we built a life together. She said, "I encourage you to do your world—are you comfortable going to those dinners by yourself?" And the truth is, it's perfectly fine for me to go by myself because I'm busy being the rabbi anyway and I go around to the tables and so on, so we worked that out. Early on, I had this fixed idea of what a rabbi's wife would be, and over the years it's changed and become more flexible.

Taking Out the Trash

Me: What Talmudic wisdom do you give couples right before they're going to get married?

RW: The most common thing that I say is not Talmudic. It's actually from early on in my marriage, which is about taking out the trash.

My wife said to me early on, "Will you take out the trash?" And I said to her what I always say when someone asks me to do something, which is, "In a minute." And I came in a few minutes later, and the trash was already taken out. And I was furious! Because I knew, since this is what my mother does, that she had done it to make me feel bad that I didn't do it when she asked me. And my wife was shocked that I was angry because she thought she was doing me a favor. But I didn't believe her for a very long time. This type of thing became an issue between us.

And that's because many people, I think, have an inability to believe that other people work differently. We don't realize that you have to learn someone in the way that you learn a subject. You can't do it only by feeling. You actually have to listen to them and believe them when they tell you how they work. That's a very counterintuitive thing to do because we all trust our instincts about people, but you really can be very wrong. Your instincts are based on people you know, and this person you're getting to know is not your mother or your ex-girlfriends or your sister.

So one of the things I tell young couples is that they need to be open to the fact that they will work differently from each other and from the families they grew up in, and that they have to respect that, and listen to that. In dating, people break up over these things and they miss the opportunity to really get to know the other person. They dismiss people without really understanding them—and then they wonder why they can't meet anyone and why they're still single.

How This All Relates to Sheldon2

The rabbi was right about not dismissing people without understanding them. On our third date, Sheldon2 wore a bow tie. To a movie. It wasn't even the same bow tie he'd worn in his online dating photo. This one was a checkered gray and white number. How many of these did he have?

"I guess I should have dressed up more," I joked when I opened the door and saw the bow tie. He laughed, and told me about his fondness for bow ties, even though he knows it's unusual. Then he explained how it started.

When Sheldon2 was a little boy, his grandfather always wore bow ties, and his grandpa was his best buddy. One day, he told his grandfather, "When I grow up, I want to be just like you!"

"You want to be a dentist?" his grandfather asked, and Sheldon2 replied, "No, I want to wear a bow tie!" That became a running joke. Twenty years later, after his grandfather died, Sheldon2 inherited all of the bow ties—his grandfather had remembered! So Sheldon2 likes to wear them because they remind him of his beloved grandfather.

I was so charmed by this story that it made me like Sheldon2 even more. And to think I almost didn't e-mail him because I thought, "What kind of dork wears pink polka-dotted bow ties?"

After I left the rabbi's office, I felt like I'd done enough asking questions for the time being. Everything I'd been told about relationships over the past several months—from the rabbi, scientists, marriage researchers, dating experts, and matchmakers—I'd seen play out positively not only in my life, but in the lives of women I spoke to.

So while I was off dating Sheldon2, I asked a few of these women to share their own stories.

24

Claire's Story—Getting Over Myself

Claire *was like a lot of women who seem to have everything but the guy. She had no shortage of boyfriends, but couldn't find the one to spend her life with. Then something changed—her. Here's Claire:*

When I was single, people used to tell me all the time that I was bright and attractive, so I couldn't figure out why I couldn't find love. I'd always had boyfriends, but in retrospect, they weren't people I'd want to marry now. I went for very attractive guys. You know, blond hair and blue eyes or your classic dark hair and handsome. I felt good walking down the street with them. My boyfriends were very intelligent, and they made me laugh. I'm an extrovert and I had to be with someone outgoing.

But none of these relationships worked out. One boyfriend drank too much. One was stressed out all the time and didn't take care of himself. One broke up with me because he said I was too demanding, but I don't think asking him to be reliable or honest was demanding. The last one didn't want to have children. When I met him he said he possibly would. I didn't want to hear the word "possibly."

I did a lot of Internet dating, but I was particular. I would write guys off immediately if they talked too much, or snorted on the phone when they laughed. I thought, *I'm not going to be able to live with this.*

When I was growing up, I thought I'd just meet a guy in the supermarket. I'd drop a can of peas and he'd pick it up. We'd live happily ever after. Then you grow up with fantasies like "tall, dark, and handsome," and that prototype unconsciously stays with you and prevents you from seeing beyond it.

WHAT HE WASN'T

I met my husband, Chris, online, when I was 38 and he was 45. I was looking to get married. I was concerned about having children but interested in meeting the right person. I liked his profile. His pictures were cute, but you can't really tell what someone looks like from online dating photos.

On my first date with Chris, we met for coffee and we talked for a while and I thought he was very nice. He was somewhat attractive, but it wasn't like the guys I normally dated. He's short—he's 5'8"—and he didn't have a full head of hair. He wasn't slick like the guys I usually went for. There was no banter, which I found so sexy with other boyfriends. He'd slip up on a word. He was just so different from the guys I'd been excited by in the past. So I didn't think, 'This is the guy I'm going to marry.' I just thought, 'He's a nice guy.' I guess the only way to describe it is that I felt safe with him. I felt like I could trust him.

So I went on a few dates with him, but afterward I'd call my friends and say he's too skinny, or he's not ambitious enough, because he was in the same job for years and he never got a raise. He comes from a small town and is kind of laid-back, and I thought, this is crazy, I'm a city girl. This won't work. But I liked being with him more than with any other guy. I really fell for him about five months in, and we dated for about a year. But I always had my reservations. On my birthday he came over with balloons, and all I could think when I saw him was that he was too scrawny.

I know that sounds horrible, but I had a job where I was dealing with men who made a lot of money and who had stylish suits on every day. I was surrounded by handsome, successful, charming types, but I'd dated that kind of guy before, and being with Chris felt so different. The day-to-day with Chris was so good—we could have fun in the supermarket together, we'd go kayaking, he was always very respectful. But it wasn't exciting in the way I thought love had to be. He wasn't exciting in the way I thought the man I would marry had to be.

There were other things that bothered me. I wondered what was wrong with him if he was still single in his mid-forties. This wasn't a commitment-phobic guy—he really wanted to get married, but couldn't seem to. Later I learned that he'd gotten hurt a couple of times by old girlfriends who dumped him and it took him a while to get back on the horse, but at the time, I wondered why I should want to be with him if none of those other women did. Also, personality-wise, I'm on fast pilot and he processes information on a slower speed than I do. But I came to realize that he can say something very profound with fewer words. I loved that he was grounded. There's something about him that's very calming, and he's just a really good man.

But still, my attraction to him would come and go. I felt that if I had so many doubts, this wasn't the right guy for me.

FORTY AND CONFUSED

At 39, I broke up with him. I thought, *I'm not going to settle just because my biological clock is ticking*. I told Chris this wasn't working. Then I met a guy who was very handsome. I was so attracted to him—I was blinded by the attraction. He was smooth and knew how to seduce me. He had a great apartment in a doorman building on the Upper West Side. He kind of wowed me. But he decided he didn't want to have kids and he couldn't relate to me the way Chris could. Chris won't join me in argument if I'm starting something. He'll wait—he knows me so well. Chris wanted to get back together, and we did.

I was 40 then, and lonely and tired of dating. I was confused about why I'd left Chris and I wished I was more physically attracted to him. It's a very confusing thing when somebody loves you so much and you just aren't there yet. When I saw him again, he had gained weight and I thought, I'm not attracted to him like that. I used to be turned off by how scrawny he was, and now I was turned off by how heavy he was! But I knew that Chris would do anything for me and I shouldn't listen to these other parts of me that seemed so superficial. I looked at women older than me who were single and serial dating and I thought, *I don't want to be them*.

THE STATUS MAN

For six months, I was still ambivalent and I was looking everywhere for validation. I read books, I asked my friends. I had a friend who was single and not in a relationship, and she'd say, "Are you sure you love him?" She would encourage me to be ambivalent, but I think she just didn't want to be the last single person in our circle of friends. Misery loves company, right? My friends who are married always said they truly liked Chris. They thought he was kind, down to earth, loving, and grounded.

But the confusion felt like it was going to kill me!

I remember when we were dating, I met this very beautiful woman at a party. She introduced me to her husband and he was 5'4". I was so sure she would be with a different kind of guy. Later we became friendly and when we talked about men, she said, "I didn't think I'd marry someone three inches shorter than me, but I love him." It was that simple.

So I thought, I have to get over the prototype of the status man, which is a very narcissistic thing.

A Deeper Kind of Romance

Chris is very nurturing. He's very sweet, and that's the kind of thing that kept me with him during my confusion. I love to ski, and he learned to ski so we could do it together. He's romantic, but in a completely different way than I was used to. With Chris, the simple day-to-day things are romantic, not the fast heart-racing things. He'll say, "Let's go look at the moon together," and he'll take my hand in his. I wake up and he's got eggs ready for me and he buys the paper and everything is already there. I think, wow, that's really thoughtful—and that lasts a lifetime.

Not that you don't need passion in your life, but I get that, too, just in a more subdued way. We went running together and he picked flowers and he put them in a vase in our room. He's got a lot of feminine qualities that I used to look down on but that I've come to appreciate. And we have good sex. It's not about how physically attractive I find him in comparison to my other boyfriends because the truth is, I'm never going to find him as attractive. But instead of focusing on aspects of him I'm not as attracted to, I think about how he's got beautiful blue eyes and I focus on that.

One night I was in the bathroom brushing my teeth and I looked into the bedroom and noticed that he was on my side of the bed. I said, "What are we doing . . . switching sides?" and he said "No, I was just keeping that side warm for you." He knew that I'm always cold when I first get into bed. Then I realized that he'd been doing that on other nights and not even telling me. He doesn't have a million dollars, but I think that story is worth a million dollars.

I also think about the nonmonetary things he brings to the relationship—picking up the kids from school, being a real team player in the parenting category. He loves kids. When I met him, he was helping underprivileged kids learn to read and he volunteered at an animal shelter. I still double his salary, and in a perfect world, would my husband be making as much money as me? Yes. But I got a lot of other things I didn't get from the guys who made more money.

We got married a year after we got back together. I wish I hadn't wasted all that time wondering whether he was The One. I wanted to "feel" different, but I thought maybe if I just jump in the water, I'll realize that it's warm and it feels good. And it does! It took me a long time to fall in love with Chris, but I'm absolutely in love with him now. When I was ambivalent, people said, "Ask yourself why you're still there if he's not right."

I didn't get all the things I wanted, but I don't feel like I settled at all. My husband has integrity and cares about his family and the world at large. He is more forgiving than I am and I can learn a lot from him. If we ever started to have problems, he would go to counseling, he would go to workshops, he's open to things in life. These are things of character. I have an anchor so that I can live my life instead of waiting for it to happen. He's the person I'm most excited about talking to every day. All of this transcends, *I want a hairy chest and a better sense of style and a person who loves dogs.*

25

Alexandra's Story — Mr. Right in Front of Me

I loved Alexandra's story because it shows that sometimes what we're looking for has been there all along. Here's Alexandra:

Believe it or not, my husband and I met through the guy I was dating at the time—they were roommates. John, my boyfriend, had let Kevin live with him temporarily while Kevin was going through a divorce. I was 33 and I had been dating John for more than two years and occasionally we'd all go out together. But I never thought of Kevin as anything other than John's roommate. He was absolutely not my type. He wasn't even on the radar. My type was athletic— Kevin was out of shape. He wasn't a go-getter. He wasn't as fun. Meanwhile, I thought John was Mr. Wonderful. John and I seemed to connect on that soul level. We had the same optimism about life, the same sense of humor. So I put up with the fact that John could be emotionally unavailable.

John was working so much that when I'd call, I'd end up talking to Kevin more and more. Kevin would make excuses for John throughout the relationship and, honestly, as much as I complained, I made excuses for John, too. He was my idea of Mr. Right, so I'd try to rationalize any behavior that didn't fit into my idea of Mr. Right.

Soon Kevin got his life back together and moved into his own place, but we'd become close friends by then. We'd talk on the phone about everything, the way I'd talk to a female friend. Even though we didn't have the same interests, we could take a conversation anywhere and run with it. I loved talking to Kevin every day, but I was "in love" with John.

John would always say he would be more available, but he was completely unreliable. The last straw with John came when he and I were supposed to have some couple time and he showed up with Kevin and said that he could hang out for a while, but then he had to go back to work. After he bailed, I was really mad, and Kevin was very sweet and understanding. He didn't make excuses for John that night. I'm sure it never occurred to John that Kevin was a threat, because Kevin wasn't charming like John. He was the "safe" best friend. And he was—I had no romantic interest in Kevin at all. He was the total guy friend.

He's Like a Brother

After that night, I broke up with John. We'd been together for three years at that point. I was crushed, but this relationship was going nowhere. John didn't want to break up, and begged me to get back together, so we did for a few weeks. But then I realized he was just giving lip service to what I wanted but wouldn't follow through. His actions weren't matching his words. John would always say whatever he needed to say to repair the relationship. I told him this wasn't working and, of course, he came back with the kinds of romantic lines I wanted to hear.

He'd say, "When we're older, I picture this," but he wouldn't give any commitment like, "I want to marry you, and spend my life with you." I didn't fall for it again. I was devastated, but I knew I had to break up with him. But here's what's crazy—*I still thought he was my soul mate*! I just thought that my soul mate didn't want to be with me. Now I realize that who I thought was my soul mate wasn't the right guy for me, but back then, I was so sad.

So I was feeling terrible, and Kevin and I had our daily check-ins. You know, "Hey, bud, what's up?" Kevin dragged me out with his friends to cheer me up. We'd go out dancing in a group. I was 34 at this point. He was dating again after his divorce. We'd both log on to eHarmony.com over the phone and help each other fill out our profiles. We'd click on people and ask each other, "Would he be a match? Would she?" It was fun. We hung out a lot. I always looked my worst around him. It never occurred to me to try to look good or treat this romantically. All our friends said we should date, but I said, that's like dating my brother and he said, that's like dating my sister.

CHASING THE WRONG IDEAL

Then one night, he had some people over, and after they left, we stayed up late talking and we ended up sort of cuddling. I remember being surprised and thinking, "This is very strange. But it also feels really good."

We talked about it, and we both thought there was a risk this could end badly, since we were such close friends. So we decided not to pursue it. But at the same time, I couldn't go back to our friendship—suddenly I was completely attracted to him! It was really hard for both of us to hang out with all that sexual tension now. So we said, "Let's see if there's anything to this."

It sounds so silly, but that's how we started dating, two years after we met and had no interest in each other. After all those nights out in groups of friends, or just hanging out as buddies, something sparked. We pursued that spark knowing that the core of our values matched, and it quickly became a flame.

The funny thing is, dating wasn't that different from our friendship except for the sex—which was great!—and that we started to open up a little more and share the more tender parts of ourselves. But basically, we'd been dating platonically for two years without even realizing it. In the old days, this would have been considered courtship, but because we didn't consider it dating, there was no pressure. We had just been ourselves. By being his friend for all that time, I knew how he dealt with other people. I saw him around his girlfriends. I helped him with what to wear. I knew what his insecurities were with other women and I knew his preferences. I could see through any veil he'd throw up. And it went both ways. We were who we were—there were no pretenses. And we fell in love with each other.

I think if I'd first known Kevin in a dating situation, I would have been critical of a lot of things—he's not this enough or that enough. But I wouldn't have gotten to the core of him, the part I fell in love with. Initially I didn't think of him as boyfriend material because he wasn't my physical type and he wasn't upbeat like the guys I'd dated. He put across those gruff airs and I'd think, "Ugh, here he goes again," but as I got to know him, I could see that he had a soft, tender inside that he was protecting.

I'm lucky that the friendship gave us the opportunity to see parts of each other we might not have discovered if we'd been dating and analyzing, "Am I going to marry this person?" I would have been comparing him to people like John, people who I thought were my type.

I was chasing that ideal. But finally I realized that what I thought was my ideal wasn't right for me.

THE RIGHT BALANCE OF EVERYTHING

Kevin and I have a very romantic relationship in the true sense of romance. Kevin does thoughtful things. He'll make dinner and do the laundry. He sold a car that was a financial burden because he knew it bothered me. He said, "It's our second anniversary coming up and I want to do the right thing about this." He even thanked me for helping him with it, even though he was going to miss the car! The friendship allowed us to establish a lot of respect for each other as individuals. It keeps the relationship interesting.

Kevin is the guy that John never was—the solid, stand-up guy who's there for you. In building our household, he's a full participant rather than a spectator. We share what's going on, what we're thinking, what we're going through. We can disagree and talk about why. We always go in with the attitude that we can overcome this. Kevin's very good at seeing where the other person is coming from. If we're both too upset, we'll say, "Let's address it at another time when we can both be calm." He has maturity without being patronizing and he's involved without being clingy. It's the right balance of everything.

As our marriage moves forward, so many of the things I wanted are coming to fruition one by one. Maybe because of a lack of unrealistic expectations, acceptance of each other, and mutual respect, all of those things I thought I'd have to do without in a partner are manifesting in the most amazing ways. Maybe I'm just lucky, but it makes me think of several stories of arranged marriages that end as true love. Our marriage is successful because it's built not on an unattainable fantasy of perfection, but out of the realization that love is created, not presented.

26

Hilary's Story—Finding What I Needed

Hilary *didn't need a dating coach to help her distinguish between wants and needs. She was smart enough to figure it out on her own. Here's Hilary:*

When I met Rob, I was in the process of breaking up with someone I'd been dating for over a year. My ex and I were both yoga people, and we had a lot in common. But the relationship was terrible. He wasn't nice to me. He put me down a lot. I finally got out of it.

I was 31, and I wanted to go back to school to become a physical therapist. I was taking pre-med classes, and Rob was in my physics lab. I thought he was cute, but there was no repartee, no "thing" between us. I didn't like his sideburns. I thought they made him look like he belonged to a certain type of group or clique—not part of my social circle. I flirted with other guys and there was banter. I like the talk and the banter. I didn't have that with Rob, but we were friendly in lab.

Then one day I was giving a dance performance and I handed my dance flyers out to people in class. Rob was visibly excited that I gave him the flyer. I thought, *Uh-oh, I don't want to give him false hope*. But out of all the people I asked to come see me in the concert and who said they were coming, he was the only one who showed up! It struck me that maybe I want somebody who shows up. After all the guys I'd been with who don't call when they say they will, Rob showed up. He was putting himself out there.

At the after-party, I got to know him a little bit better. I found out he was a pilot and I thought that was hot. I didn't find out his age until the end of the evening. He was only 26. He asked for my number and I said, "You probably need to know how old I am." I told him and he said, "That's bullshit. I don't care."

He called the next day and said, "I had a great time, and are you going to the review class?" I said I was and when he got there, I asked him to sit with me.

Maybe He'd Be Good for a Fling

I thought I could have a fling with him over winter vacation—if he shaved the sideburns. But the more I got to know him, the more attracted I was to his personality. He was extremely kind and gener-ous. I'd been missing that generosity of spirit in guys. I still didn't consider him boyfriend material, but I thought he was mature enough to handle a fling. All of my friends at this point were mar-ried with kids and I had nothing to do over the break. I hated being so alone. I had waved that single gal flag for many years, but now I was sick of it. I wasn't afraid of going to the movies or a bar alone, but I also needed some male attention.

So we hung out during my break, and Rob just started impress-ing me left and right. We had some group dates with friends and then we made out one night. He was a little overeager, so I was worried. I didn't want to lead him on. A few days later, it was New Year's Eve and my ex-boyfriend suddenly said he wanted to see me. Of course, I went. I knew he was bad news, but I was tempted because there was so much about him that I thought I wanted in a guy. Things that Rob didn't have.

The next time I saw Rob, though, it felt so nice to be with him again. Rob and I went ice skating, and when we were waiting in line for fries, he held my hand behind his back and there was something about it that felt so great.

DOUBTING MYSELF

But I didn't have butterflies. That nervous, excited energy and thoughts about the role you could potentially play in each other's lives—I had that with my totally inappropriate ex-boyfriend, but not with Rob. Early on, I told him I didn't like the sideburns and he got rid of them, but the chemistry thing was more about the overall vibe. He wasn't as cool as the guys I used to date.

Rob and I kept on dating mostly because I liked being with him so much. Every time I thought I should end it because he wasn't what I was looking for in a husband, it made me so sad to think about not being with him. So I was ambivalent about him for two years. I began to doubt my own intuition and instincts because other people had known that the yoga guy was a jerk and I had been wrong about him. What if I was wrong about Rob?

It didn't help that friends and even my own family thought Rob wasn't good enough for me. My sister thought he was too young and kind of boring. He was quiet and she thought he didn't have much to say. My mom said, "He's just kind of blah and you are such a force, Hilary," and that really got to me because those were my insecurities, too. So I started hiding him and not bringing him to family functions. Other people also said they pictured me with a very charismatic guy—I'm very outgoing and I always assumed I'd be with someone like me, too. Rob was quiet and slightly geeky. When we were alone, he satisfied my need for conversation and goofiness, but in groups, I would compare him to other people's boyfriends and think I should be with someone more like them. Then I'd go home and be so happy with Rob, and I'd remind myself that I'd dated those other kinds of guys and they weren't as this or that as Rob is.

There was a big disconnection between who I saw myself with and what I actually wanted.

He Talked About Race Cars

So I stayed in it, but I still thought, if something better comes along, I'll leave Rob. But every day he just impressed me so much. He cared about his friends, and he cared about my friends, and he showed this all the time by his nice gestures. I loved his values, but I never thought of him as my soul mate. I remember thinking that this guy could be a great life partner in terms of someone I could live with happily and have kids with. He's so compromising and such a good communicator and we have similar beliefs politically and artistically, and in terms of how we wanted to be in a house together. But we have completely different interests. I have no interest in cars and he's obsessed with repairing race cars. I'm a dancer who loves to be out dancing and he doesn't dance at all.

I felt bad that I wasn't that interested in his stories. He'd say, "Hey, hon, how was your day?" and he'd make comments and jokes as they related to my stories and my life. He seemed genuinely interested—or at least if he wasn't truly interested, he was a good listener. But it used to bother me when I would ask him about the car stuff and he'd go off on the technical stuff about a particular engine and I'd completely lose interest! I didn't think I could live with that forever.

I almost broke up with him two years into our relationship. I was getting my physical therapy degree and it was time to apply for internships. Rob wanted to go across the country to San Francisco because that's where his family is. I wasn't sure I wanted to make that move—it seemed like such a huge commitment. I thought if I was that unsure, we shouldn't be together. But then we were having breakfast on a Sunday morning and it felt so good to be with him, and he started cracking me up, and I tried to imagine breaking up, and I realized I couldn't imagine being without him.

RECALIBRATING THE BUTTERFLIES

I was 34 when we got married. At first I didn't feel like the words "soul mate," at least in the way I imagined them my whole life, applied to us. But now I feel like fundamentally we're soul mates because we intuitively get each other. I used to think, he's not an artist and I like artistic guys, but then I realized that he's actually creative, just in a different way. I thought I would have to be with someone classically artsy, but he has an artistic mind.

Now we talk a lot about work issues and family issues and the day-to-day stuff. Having different hobbies doesn't matter that much anymore. We're both focused on the future and things like the house and the kids.

I was worried about whether I was settling before I got engaged to Rob. I was sure I wanted him as my life partner, but I had to recalibrate what the butterflies are. I'd just started figuring out how incredibly great he is and I had a sense that this was the beginning of something really extraordinary and deep. He's very solid, and I knew that he would help me through everything I went through in life, and that I could trust him and count on him. And that's different from, "Oh my God, is he going to call me?"

Now that we're married, I feel so lucky to be with Rob. He's not everything I wanted on my checklist, but he's everything I need. Actually, maybe the more accurate way of describing it is that my marriage is not at all what I expected, but it's so what I *want*. I just needed to start wanting healthier things!

27

My Story—A Dating
Public Service Announcement

Okay, so you already know the ending of *my* story—sort of. When I said in the first chapter that this book wasn't my love story, that doesn't completely explain what happened. Actually, I ended up dating Sheldon2—for two months. I know, it doesn't sound like much, but considering that I started out nixing any guy who didn't instantly excite me, I was surprised by how connected I felt to Sheldon2 in such a short period of time. What I experienced wasn't, obviously, the deep love between people who've been together for years, but it was so much better than the crazy infatuation new couples often mistake for love.

What I felt instead was a contented calm that came from simply being in the same room together, even if he was working on his laptop and I was opening my mail. I looked forward to seeing him at the end of the day the way I look forward to vegging out on a comfortable old sofa. And I mean that in the most romantic way.

There was something wonderfully tranquil about being with Sheldon2.

With Sheldon2, there was no waiting by the phone. No wondering if he "liked" me. No pressure to be something I wasn't. One time I showed up in a sexy black dress to join him at a dinner with his important clients, and I hadn't realized that before I left home, my son had put soap handprints all over my backside. Sheldon2 thought it was hilarious, and he told me later that he loved it when I showed up like that, because it reminded him of the joy I get from my mischievous toddler.

The more time we spent together, the more there was the excitement, as the marriage researcher Gian Gonzaga had put it, of truly "getting each other." We didn't share some of each other's interests, but we shared the same sense of humor and could easily crack each other up. We had the same values. We had an eerily on-target mental shorthand. We had amazing physical chemistry, even if we probably weren't each other's ideal physical type. When I spoke to friends about my burgeoning relationship, I always used the word "mellow," or I'd mention the couch metaphor, and while my younger single friends had trouble understanding why this made me so happy ("He's like an old *couch*?!" they'd ask), my older married friends were delighted. They knew this had the potential to be real.

But reality also ended the relationship—the reality of dating when you're both old enough to have a lot more commitments and logistical issues to deal with. Since we each had kids but no exes to give us the night off, it got to the point that we felt uncomfortable leaving our sons with their respective babysitters as often as we wanted to see each other. Besides, we wanted to hang out with our kids *and* be together. We both reveled in domestic life.

To move forward, we would have had to meet each other's kid, but the more we talked about how to do that, the more Sheldon2 realized that his son wasn't ready. He had an 8-year-old who'd lost his mother a year before. When Sheldon2's friends told him he needed to "get out there" again, he wasn't expecting something serious to come around so quickly. To complicate things more, his parents had been urging him to move home to Chicago, where they lived, so that they could see their grandson and help him adjust to this new life. With no family in Los Angeles, and with siblings and nephews and nieces in Chicago, Sheldon2 knew it was the right thing to do for his son's sake.

So he moved two thousand miles away.

I won't say it wasn't a bummer. It was a huge one. I wanted my dating story to be over. But I'm glad I had that experience with Sheldon2 because I saw firsthand that I can be attracted to and happy with people I haven't looked at in the past. Sheldon2 wasn't the checklist guy, but he met my three "needs" and many of my wants. So many "wants," in fact, that the missing ones didn't matter. In the end, I had one important but simple "want": I wanted to be with him.

I even miss his bow ties.

But here's the kicker: I may have learned all this too late.

Wendy's New Suitors

After six months of scouring the city for a guy for me, Wendy, the local matchmaker, thought she'd finally found a couple of leads. She sent me an encouraging e-mail saying that she'd briefly met two potential fix-ups, and she'd be having more in-depth conversations with them later that week. One, she said, was 43 years old and never married, but he'd had serious relationships, was looking to get married, and was willing to date a 41-year-old. He was also handsome and intellectually engaging. The other, a 47-year-old divorced dad, was an involved parent and successful, but might not have the "mental grit" of the first guy.

I said, "Go for it. Either one. I'm open." And this time I meant it. I didn't ask for more information to microanalyze. I figured a first date with either couldn't hurt. Then a few days later, Wendy got back to me. It turned out that the 43-year-old was ambivalent about kids (which was why he was willing to date a 41-year-old; as Evan had said, if a guy is dying to be a dad, he generally makes it happen before age 40); and the "nice-looking, decent" divorced dad didn't seem to have, as Wendy put it, "that 'life of the mind' vitality I think is important here."

This wasn't me being picky. Or even Wendy being picky. It was her being realistic. A guy who's not highly educated but *is* intellectually curious can be a good match for me. Sheldon2 certainly was. But just as this divorced dad probably wasn't what I was looking for, it turns out that I wasn't what he was looking for, either. As Wendy got to know him better, she learned that he didn't go for intense intellectuals. So once again, it was back to the drawing board, and who knew how many months it would take before Wendy found another guy.

This, my friends, is what my dating life is like these days.

DRUNK DATING

I know, that's kind of a depressing thing to report. Everyone wants a happy ending, right? Everyone wants to be reassured that they can find someone great no matter how old they are. But here's the truth: A happy ending is always possible, but a happy ending for me is a lot less likely than—and will look a lot different from—a happy ending for someone ten years younger than me. The older you get, the more complicated dating becomes, and no amount of attitude adjustment can turn back the clock and change those realities.

I'm not trying to bum people out. I'm trying to help. It's kind of like those graphic anti–drunk driving public service announcements that show people crashing into poles and getting killed. If they just told you, "Don't drink and drive," you might think, "Yeah, I know, but I can have a couple of martinis, right?" It's not until you see people ending up brain-dead, lying in a coma in the hospital and surrounded by beeping monitors, that the message has an impact.

In the same way, if you don't see how easily people can end up alone by making the dating mistakes I did, you won't be dissuaded from making those same mistakes yourself. I had to show the reality of being single at my age because I used to be like the teenager who thinks she's invulnerable to drunk driving accidents—it's all in the abstract, something that happens to *other* people, but would never happen to me. It never occurred to me that I would become another dating casualty. I had to show, in grim detail, the accident that my dating life became so that you could make choices you won't look back on later and regret.

So consider this a dating public service announcement: If you recognized yourself in this book, I'm the ghost of what could happen to you if you don't broaden your idea of Mr. Right. I mean that nicely, because it's actually an *optimistic* message: If you're older like me, it'll be harder, but at least you'll have a better chance of finding a great guy if you change your approach. And if you're single in your twenties or thirties and wondering why, now you know not just why, but what to do to increase your chances of having a happy long-term marriage.

A Different Kind of Empowerment

My single friend Erica, who is 31, was skeptical when I asked her to read this book. She'd just gone through a breakup, and thought I was going to try to persuade her to "settle." I swore that it wasn't about settling for less than what's going to make her happy. I told her it was about learning how to value what's truly valuable.

She wasn't so sure, but after reading it, she said she was encouraged. "I felt like I could find the right person because he doesn't have to fit absolutely every one of my criteria, an idea which tends to induce panic," she said. "He doesn't have to fit the exact profile that I have envisioned for myself. I liked that sense of empowerment—that I could be happy and find love if I just adjusted my attitude, and not if I was just supremely lucky enough to be in the right place at the right time, which, again, induces panic."

Like Erica, I'm finding this more realistic way of dating kind of liberating. How reassuring it is to know that, in many ways, finding a good mate isn't just some random external event—it's based largely on our *own* choices and actions. The funny thing is, most of us aren't single because of how we look or what we weigh, our level of education or job description, or whether we asked the guy out first or waited three days to return his call. We're single because we have this underlying belief that we need to be completely in synch with our mates, and if we're not, we should find someone else.

And that makes it really hard to find *anyone.*

As my married friend Lynn put it, "Adjusting one's perspective actually makes the 'hunt' more interesting, manageable, entertaining, and less disappointing. When you adjust your standards—which doesn't mean you have to 'give a chance' to a guy who completely repulses you—you, well, give more guys a chance. You meet more people, and allow yourself to be entertained and surprised."

The silver lining for me is that while I wouldn't have chosen to be single and 41, my circumstance is forcing me to focus on what's important, so if I do meet someone, I'll likely end up in a better relationship. But how great would it have been to realize this a long time ago? I can't do much about that now—but maybe you can.

HEY, YOU—IN THE PINK SHIRT

Yes, you. The other day I sat in the audience of the movie *He's Just Not That into You* and watched in amazement as the twenty-somethings in the sold-out theater gasped, clapped, cheered, cried, and were literally propelled out of their seats when the guy who said he wasn't interested in marriage for the past seven years proposed to Jennifer Aniston's character, or when the slick guy played by Justin Long who said he wasn't into the sweet Ginnifer Goodwin character finally admitted that he'd fallen in love with her.

In a romantic speech, he told her that she was the exception to the rule—that when a guy seems uninterested, he almost always is, but in this case, the rule didn't apply. I'm guessing the women in the audience got so excited by these happy but wildly improbable endings because they also feel that the rules don't apply, that they're the exceptions. I used to be one of those women, even though I knew that, statistically speaking, it was unlikely. I wasn't the exception. You probably aren't, either.

So what I'm saying is, hey, *you*—yes, you. In the pink shirt. I'm talking to *you*. This isn't supposed to make you feel crummy. It's supposed to be eye-opening. Not thinking you're above it all makes you more self-aware, and self-awareness leads to better decisions. It puts you in a better position to get what you want. Denying it leaves you dating the way you always have, which so far hasn't worked out. If you're single, and not wanting to be, and you're reading this and thinking it's not about you—maybe it isn't. I'll give you that. But are you sure? Are you making smart, conscious decisions about the men you let into your life?

The good news is, if you want something different, it's available to you. It might take some time to change, but that's okay because how many years did it take you to develop these sabotaging attitudes in the first place? Ten years ago, nobody told me the things I learned in the course of writing this book—or, if they did, I didn't listen. You can't fault anyone for not telling you, but you can blame yourself for not listening.

You want to think that your ideal guy will magically land on your doorstep tomorrow? That's fine. You want to look at how you might get more reasonable about the way you date so that happiness comes by easier? That's fine, too.

Remember, the choice is yours. You have the information.

The rest is up to you.

Epilogue

Where They Are Now

Julia, who broke up with Greg because he wasn't "inspiring enough," later broke up with Adam, the charming surgeon, because he wasn't "supportive enough." It took dating Adam, she said, to realize that Greg was actually more inspiring in ways that mattered. They're now engaged.

"Please don't use our real names in the book," Julia said. "I don't want people to know what an idiot I was!"

Jessica, who regretted turning down Dave's proposal because she felt she was too young to get married, has tried to stop comparing every guy she dates to Dave. She also spends less time Googling him late at night.

"Dave is married, Dave has moved on, and if Dave could find the strong connection we had with someone else, I probably can, too," she said. "I just wish he wouldn't post pictures of his baby on Facebook. That's the one thing I still look at."

She recently joined Match.com.

Brooke, the graduate student in Boston, moved out of her boyfriend's apartment and has just started dating a guy who's the son of a family friend.

"When it comes to dating, I'm done using the word 'feminism,'" she told me. "With my new boyfriend, the important word is going to be 'marriage.'"

Kathy Moore, the matchmaker from Make Me A Match who told me to "save my pennies" for my love life, called me up eight months after our initial phone call and said that due to the economic recession, they were offering "all kinds of specials."

Coincidentally, I'd just gone on a blind date with a guy who'd hired Make Me A Match months earlier. He said they charged him *$450 for six dates* around the same time that Kathy had told me it wasn't worth her time to find me *three dates for $1,000.* Apparently, a 54-year-old divorced father of teenagers is an easier setup than a 41-year-old single mom with a 2-year-old.

Now Kathy was offering to reduce her price from $3,500 to $2,500. "It's a great deal!" she said.

I told her I still had more pennies to save.

Lisa recently got back together with Ryan, the boyfriend she'd dumped two years earlier because she didn't think he adored her enough. Last month, they ran into each other at a mutual friend's party, and despite having had other relationships in their time apart, both were still single.

"It turned out that he didn't find someone he loved as much as me," Lisa said. "Which was his point all along."

The woman who got insulted after I set her up on a blind date with a guy I described as being "just like her" is still single.

"It's frustrating," she told me, "because it's hard to meet people. I wake up, go to work, go to the gym, pick up some dinner, and go home. There's online dating, but the best way to meet people is through fix-ups, and people used to fix me up a lot, but nobody's fixed me up lately."

Hmm. I wonder why.

Annie, who said she'd learned from her first marriage what's important, but had trouble putting it into practice, never did go out on the setup with the corporate lawyer whose Facebook profile she found boring. Instead, she accidentally got pregnant by a slacker boyfriend who was neither "corporate" nor "boring." He instantly bailed, and now, at 35, she's a single mom.

Lauren was touched when her ex-boyfriend—the one she some-times found annoying even though he was "emotionally exactly what I wanted"—came over to comfort her when she got news that her mother's cancer had taken a turn for the worse. But as soon as he brought over an aromatherapy candle with a slightly blackened wick, Lauren lost all interest.

"It's the worst object to regift in the world," she said. "Nothing looks more previously used than a candle. It's funny because he can do something like that, and then text me to remind me to take care of myself, take long walks, and listen to my iPod. He genuinely cares. He's just a complete idiot about getting all the basic dating stuff straight. A moron, in fact."

She's still wondering if any of that matters.

ACKNOWLEDGMENTS

If dating requires a lot of moral support, so does writing a book about dating. My happily married agent, Liv Blumer, wisely hooked me up with the happily married Trena Keating at Dutton, who believed in this project from the moment she read the *Atlantic* article. Trena is that uncommon combination of very smart and very patient, and she always spent way too much time on the phone with me whenever I had a question, personal or professional. Then she left to become an agent, but continued to spend way too much time on the phone with me, for which I'm enormously grateful.

Meanwhile, as luck would have it, the happily married Carrie Thornton came on board as my new editor. With the efficiency of a surgeon and the empathy of a gal pal, Carrie read through the ridiculously disorganized mass of pages I'd typed out, made me turn them into a coherent first draft in the span of three weeks, and confessed that she could completely relate to my not wanting to date a guy who was 5'5". (I should mention that Carrie is 5'10", so there's still no excuse for me.) She also respected my "no bullet points, no worksheets, and no pink" philosophy, and in return, I promised never to use the phrase "cheesy relationship book" again.

The entire team at Dutton has been amazing. Brian Tart has been "on it" in the best possible way. Monica Benalcazar in the art department came up with a super-cool cover, bow tie and all. Lily Kosner expertly handled innumerable important tasks behind the scenes, juggling multiple balls in the air and never dropping a single one. And Amanda Walker and Liza Cassity wrote a pitch letter that still makes me laugh out loud.

While I was off talking to people about dating, going on actual dates, and trolling online dating sites, Aaron Kaczander carefully transcribed my interviews, while Susanna Stossel and Hilary McClellen provided me with top-notch research assistance. Andrea Siegel has a freakishly encyclopedic knowledge of pop culture, and her analysis of mass media was impressive and helpful.

The following people were kind of enough to take time out of their busy lives to read the manuscript and offer feedback: Daisy Beatty, Kathy Crutcher, Rachel Greenwald, Lynn Harris, Sarah Haufrecht, Rebekka Helford, Justine Isola, Hilary Liftin, Claire Lundberg, Eve Maremont, Wendy Miller, Scott Stossel, and Kyle Smith. For their insight, humor, and commiseration, I can't thank them enough.

Anat Baron did me the favor of telling me to write from my heart, no matter how unflatteringly I might come off; and reminded me that while hope might sell, the truth is life-changing. "People need to hear the truth," she told me late one night after I'd gone to that disastrous speed dating event.

I'm grateful to all of my friends and acquaintances, male and female, married and single, who allowed me to quote them in this book and who shared their experiences with remarkable honesty, no matter how mortifying or personal the information. Likewise to all the people I sought out for interviews and who took a leap of faith by revealing all to a complete stranger. I thank them for their candor and trust. It's not easy to tell a journalist the things that even your spouse or significant other doesn't know.

It couldn't have been easy for my mom and her friends to sit down with me and a tape recorder on the coffee table and talk about their marriages. I'm so glad I was able to include their thoughts and stories in this book.

I owe a lot to Evan Marc Katz for telling it like it is, even if it took me a while to hear it. As he put it: "I'm not going to tell you it's easy. I will, however, tell you that it's worth it."

Many experts in various fields gave me generous amounts of their time and wisdom: Paul Amato, Dan Ariely, Myles Berkowitz, Michael Broder, Lisa Clampitt, John Curtis, Paul Eastwick, Julie Ferman, Eli Finkel, Helen Fisher, Lina Fruzzetti, Gian Gonzaga, Rachel Greenwald, Scott Haltzman, Martie Haselton, Diane Holmberg, Ben Karney, Jayamala Madathil, Howard Markman, Steven Martin, Susan Page, Jody Podolsky, Edna Pollin, Helena Rosenberg, Barry Schwartz, Jeff Simpson, Marion Solomon, and Rabbi David Wolpe. I hope I did them justice in this book.

Bob Gumer helped me choose between more than "good enough" suitors for the movie adaptation by guiding me into the capable hands of Tobey Maguire and Polly Johnsen at Warner Brothers.

Several people at the *Atlantic*, past and present, have been tremendously supportive over the years, not to mention fun to kibitz with, particularly Toby Lester, Scott Stossel, Elizabeth Shelburne, and Kathy Crutcher. The super-talented Sage Stossel was generous enough to draw the cartoon for Part 1. And special thanks to Ben Schwartz for being brave enough to assign me the "Marry Him" piece in the first place.

I'd also like to express my gratitude to any friends who are still willing to set me up on a date after reading this book. I swear, I've changed.

Finally, the most important thanks go to my amazing son, Zachary Julian, who always understood when I posted a sign on my door that read, "Mommy's working." For this I owe him many hours of "playing construction workers." The greatest joy of my life, he has taught me more about what love really means than any expert ever could.